The Politics of Decline

The Politics of Decline

A Chronicle of New York's Descent and What You Can Do To Save Your State

Jay Gallagher

Whitston Publishing Company Inc.
Albany, New York
2005

Photograph Credits

Mark Vergari of *The Journal News* in White Plains, New York
Will Yurman, *Rochester Democrat and Chronicle*
Jamie Germano, *Rochester Democrat and Chronicle*
Keyla Cubi, *Rochester Democrat and Chronicle*
Aimee K. Wiles, *Rochester Democrat and Chronicle*
Michael Doherty, *Utica Observer Dispatch*
Trevor Kapralos, *Utica Observer Dispatch*
Tim Roske for *Gannett News Service*
Kayte Martens for *Gannett News Service*
Kenneth Dickerman for *Gannett News Service*
Kathy McLaughlin, *Poughkeepsie Journal*
Marilu Lopez Fretz, *Utica Observer Dispatch*

To Emily,
for loving me for all these years and giving me a happy life.

Table of Contents

Part 1: The Players

Part 2: The Problem

Part 3: Where the Money Goes

Part 4: What's Being Done

Part 5: Appendices

ACKNOWLEDGEMENTS

The two most precious commodities in the news business are time and space. This book happened because Henry Freeman, editor of *The Journal News* in Westchester, had the vision to devote unprecedented amounts of both to this project.

Then the other *Gannett* editors in New York backed him up and laid aside vast swaths of precious newshole real estate for the venture.

It also happened because Whitston publisher Mike Laddin had the vision to read a proposal about what was wrong with New York and decide it was something people would want to read a whole book about.

And for the 18 months I was out of the office (it was supposed to be a year, but it was a hard thing to give up) colleagues (and friends) Yancey Roy and Erika Rosenberg had to pick up the slack, which they did, admirably, and found plenty of time for suggestions and guidance on what I was doing. Cara Matthews, our newest colleague, also took it upon herself to read the entire manuscript and made many improvements.

A disadvantage of working in a bureau is that we have no staff photographers and sometimes we forget just how many words a picture is worth. *Journal News* photographer Mark Vergari, who shot the majority of the pictures in this book, reminds me of how a skilled shooter can multiply the impact of mere words.

And our set of interns during the period, Alexis Grant, Joe Manez, Diane Flagg and Jimmy Vielkind, were always more than willing to drop what they were doing and chase down some facts for me, do a chart and otherwise pitch in.

And finally to that Albany institution, the goo-goos (good-government advocates), Blair Horner, Barbara Bartoletti and Rachel Leon who, with a little help from newcomers to the fray (like Jeremy Creelan) were always fearless in calling them as they saw them, and who finally, maybe, after all these years, are starting to see some change.

FOREWORD

THE YEAR OF REFORM

☆ ☆ ☆

There were a lot of sore muscles among New York's 212 state senators and Assembly members on June 24, 2005, on a sunny day when the annual legislative session ended.

They were weary mostly from patting themselves, and each other, on the back.

Why?

First of all, there was this matter of sunshine. The New York State Legislature, dubbed the nation's "most dysfunctional" by a respected think tank in 2004, historically has been known as an institution that did most of its important work in the dark of night—with lawmakers so exhausted or confused or just fed up that they would vote for almost anything—and debate virtually nothing—just to end the pain. Merely ending the legislative session in daylight was considered something worth cheering.

Less than a year earlier, on August 11, 2004, they had wrapped up another dispirited session early in the morning, only a few weeks after their institution got the "dysfunctional" label hung on it by the Brennan Center for Justice, a respected research organization affiliated with New York University. They had just acted on a budget more than four months after the start of the fiscal year—the 20th consecutive year that they had failed in what many people see as their most elementary task: passing a budget on time.

But that seemed like a long time ago last June. Not only had the lawmakers passed a budget on time for the first time since 1984, but they had made some of the reforms that good-government groups (often derided as "goo-goos") had recommended for years:

> ➤ Require lobbyists trying to get state contracts to report their activities;
> ➤ Close the loophole that allowed state workers to escape sanctions for ethics violations by merely resigning;
> ➤ Increase oversight of public authorities like the Metropolitan Transportation Authority and the Thruway Authority that have operated largely in the shadows for decades;
> ➤ Take some steps to rein in the voracious $44.5 billion health-care program, Medicaid, that has threatened the fiscal stability of counties as well as the state for years.

Lawmakers even took some limited steps to open and clean up their own operations:

> ➤ Assembly members have to be in their seats to vote on all bills, and senators, important ones;
> ➤ The Assembly Rules Committee, a formerly phantom panel that was essentially a rubber stamp for the leader, had to start meeting in public;
> ➤ Both houses even agreed to start televising their sessions with a state version of C-Span.

Some parts of the budget were even debated openly with Gov. George Pataki and the legislative leaders meeting in public to try to work out their differences on how to spend the state's money.

To someone who doesn't follow state government closely, such steps sound more common-sense than revolutionary. But in the hidebound restrictive world of state government and politics they were important actions.

They were essentially forced on the powers that be at the Capitol by a disgruntled electorate who ousted a couple of incumbent lawmakers and threw major scares into others in the 2004 elections.

The reforms that were made fell far short of what most observers think is needed to really put the public back in charge of its state government.

"Most of the changes were just window dressing to try to show people they were responsive," said Barbara Bartoletti, long-time lobbyist for the state League of Women Voters.

More on that later.

But first a more fundamental question needs to be addressed: what difference does it make to the average New Yorker whether lawmakers are in their seats when they vote or lobbyists report whose arms they're trying to twist or whether the governor and lawmakers meet in public or behind closed doors to decide what to spend money on?

After all, most New Yorkers spend the bulk of their waking lives trying to make a living, going to school, caring for their families, with maybe some time out to watch "Desperate Housewives" and root for the Yankees or the Bills or having fun some other way.

What does Albany have to do with any of that?

And even for those people who find time to read a newspaper or watch TV news on a regular basis (a continually shrinking number), the latest news from Iraq and gasoline prices would seem to have a far more dramatic effect on their lives than any goings-on in the state Capitol. And local issues, like school taxes, potential plant closings and that new housing development all seem far more important than any statewide events.

While no one has put their lives on the line to protect the state they live in since the Civil War, in other ways how a state is governed has never been more important to its citizens.

Since Ronald Reagan started trying to cut down the influence of the federal government a generation ago, large chunks of federal power have devolved back to the states.

On issues ranging from welfare to health care to education to transportation, state capitols call most of the important shots.

And what has been happening in New York?

Basically, the Empire State has been slowly declining for the past half-century, losing much of its political and economic clout. Much of the blame, this book will argue, can be laid at the feet of the men and women we send to the Capitol to serve us.

All too often they have acted in their own self-interest and that of the thousands of lobbyists who spent $144 million last year trying to influence them and less for the general good.

What has been the effect?

The losses are most stark in economic terms:

> Higher taxes
> Fewer jobs
> More families split when young people leave the state to find economic opportunity elsewhere
> A declining standard of living compared to other parts of the nation.

Yet because the slide has been gradual, not only has there been little public uproar, but very little turnover among elected officials. Most incumbents are secure because few people are paying attention.

Gov. Mario Cuomo have let these cynical deals pass unchallenged as well.

They also stay in power by just not addressing some critical issues.

Bills that the leaders don't like don't make it to the floor of either house, and the committee system isn't set up to seriously consider ideas and build support for them. Almost all of the power remains concentrated with Silver and Bruno.

Why is this so important?

"Major improvements to accountability, like redistricting and campaign-finance reform, will never get passed unless committees can build public momentum and force a committee to vote, members are forced to vote up or down on the floor and conference committees are convened irrespective of whether the Assembly speaker and Senate majority leader approve of the bill," said Jeremy Creelan, author of the Brennan Center report.

"Until we have a legislative process that requires the Legislature and the governor to address tough issues—or else face voters who have the information and opportunity to hold them accountable on Election Day—we will not get real reform of our state government."

So did 2005 represent a start to that process or just "window dressing" designed to distract voters?

Certainly the key will be whether politicians think they have done enough or whether the public will demand more.

"The task of reform has barely begun," concluded a Rochester-based group called the Citizens for New York State Legislative Reform.

Jay Gallagher
Delmar, New York
August 2005

INTRODUCTION

HOW WE GOT HERE

Visitors to Albany are often confused when they try to find the state Capitol. They look for a dome—the signature feature of the U.S. Capitol and those of most states—but the sprawling, granite edifice looming on a hill over the Hudson River doesn't have one.

The original plans for the building, drawn up in 1876, called for the traditional Capitol topper, but by the time it was nearing completion—25 years later and $20 million over budget—it was so weighed down with additions put on by one of its six architects that it was too heavy to support a dome.

Anyone who has spent time in Albany knows that the building is an apt metaphor for the state government it houses.

As the Capitol building is missing a dome, the government also seems to be lacking the principle that should be its focus: a dedication to the prosperity and well being of its citizens.

The burden that the government imposes on the state is so large, often in the form of high taxes, costly requirements and irrational laws, that the government has lost its primary focus.

Just as the Capitol had multiple architects, government policies have been designed by different groups that are often pulling in different directions. All too often, the direction that wins out isn't the one that serves the interests of a majority of New Yorkers.

However, we can't deny either that both the building and the government have a certain majesty, partly because of the sheer size of both and partly because of their histories.

The Empire State, so named because it was such a bountiful supplier of wealth, had obvious geographic advantages that initially gave it a leg up on the rest of the colonies and states in the 18th and 19th centuries. It had a superb port: the 150-mile-long Hudson River estuary that connected the sea to its interior in the era when water was the most efficient means of transportation. A break in the Appalachian Mountain chain that the rest of the seaboard states lacked also gave New York access to the west via the Great Lakes.

Later, another natural advantage—the glorious falls on the Niagara River between lakes Ontario and Erie—would help generate in huge quantities the new wonder of electricity in the late 1800s.

While all these advantages were literally carved in stone, this didn't mean they were immutable. Human ingenuity was needed to capitalize on them. In the early years of American independence, New Yorkers showed remarkable skill in doing that.

Of all the founding fathers of our country, Manhattan resident Alexander Hamilton was the most important to the economy of New York. When he became the nation's first treasury secretary, New York City was already an important trading center. But he was responsible for embedding the banking and stock-market systems into the nation's fiber and having them centered in New York City—capital of the United States from 1789 to 1790. The financial industry is still far and away the state's greatest source of wealth.

In 1817, then-Gov. DeWitt Clinton persuaded the

Legislature to borrow $7 million to build a waterway from Albany to Buffalo. The 363-mile canal, then the longest in the world, opened eight years later. It was an expensive gamble, but it paid off handsomely. It cut the cost of shipping goods from Buffalo to New York by 90 percent. It made New York the preeminent commercial city in the country—a title it has yet to relinquish.

The canal was dug (almost totally by hand) largely by Irish immigrants, who made 80 cents a day for 10 hours of work. They and other immigrants, with Jews from Eastern Europe, Germans and Italians the largest groups, brought ambition, optimism and a capacity for hard work to New York that made them probably the state's greatest asset, just as the newest wave from other parts of the world adds so much to the dynamism and wealth of the state today.

They came and continued to come to the Empire State in such disproportionate numbers, partly because of the region's tradition of tolerance. This tradition is a product of New York's Dutch heritage, which traced its tolerant roots back to the Utrecht Constitution of 1579. That document said, "each person shall remain free, especially in his religion, and that no man shall be persecuted because or interrogated because of their religion."

This tradition of tolerance has helped New York City to be the most racially, ethnically and religiously diverse city in the world throughout most of its history.

More recently, even casual students of history know that, for the first half of the 20th Century, New York was not only the center of culture, finance, media and business in the United States, but also of politics and public policy.

Part of this was due to its sheer size.

In 1950, almost one out of 10 Americans were New Yorkers (14.8 million out of 150 million). It was by far the largest state. Not only did the Empire State have the most members of the House of Representatives (43 in 1950) of any state, it also had the most electoral votes in presidential races

(45). New York governors were almost automatically considered serious contenders for president.

More significantly, New York's state government was
the trend-setter for national policies and politics.

The state was the home of the Republican Party's progressive movement, led by Theodore Roosevelt, that tried to
cushion people from the harshest aspects of the Industrial
Revolution.

That trend accelerated after the Triangle Shirtwaist fire
tragedy in 1911, which killed more than 100 women trapped in
a Manhattan textile factory. After that disaster, the state
required employers to abide by safety regulations and pay a
minimum wage. Children under 14 were banned from the factory floor. Minimum education and health norms were put
into place. All of that happened first in New York.

Many programs of the New Deal, Franklin Roosevelt's
Depression-fighting policy that took some of the edge off the
nation's suffering in the 1930s, were bigger versions of ideas
that he'd tested as governor of New York. And many of those
he inherited from his one-time mentor and later political
enemy, Al Smith, another former New York governor.

Even after Roosevelt, New York was viewed as an inno-
vator. In a move that echoed Gov. Clinton's vision 130 years
earlier, Gov. Thomas E. Dewey in the 1940s championed building a cross-state express highway, the state Thruway, before
Dwight Eisenhower ever thought of the federal interstate highway system.

When the answer to society's problems was more government intervention, New York was out in front.

But around the middle of the last century, when other
industrialized states as well as the national government caught
up to New York in providing services to citizens, the Empire
State continued to pile on the public programs, and the taxes
that went along with them. The higher taxes and business
costs helped to knock New York off its perch as the nation's
most powerful and prosperous state.

Some of the decline was, of course, inevitable.

With the introduction of cheap air conditioning in the 1950s, thanks in part to the Syracuse-based Carrier Corp., the Northeast lost its climatic advantage over what has become known as the Sun Belt. Since people could not only survive but also be productive in places like Texas, Florida, California and Arizona 12 months a year, it was only natural the population would spread out.

Businesses were attracted to places with people willing to work for lower wages than in New York, and governments in the Sun Belt had relatively lax regulations, low taxes and a hostility to labor unions. Those states became magnets for immigrants, both from other countries and within the United States—especially from New York.

Other factors were at work as well.

Few realized it at the time, but when the St. Lawrence Seaway opened in 1959, Buffalo lost its unique geographic edge—the eastern terminus of water-borne shipments of commodities like iron ore and grain from the Great Lakes region. This advantage had made Buffalo a natural location for steel-making, grain processing and other industries.

The seaway allowed ships to sail all the way from northern Minnesota to the Atlantic Ocean and points beyond (and later, down the Mississippi to the Gulf of Mexico) without stopping at a lake port.

In 2005, Buffalo is still the state's second-biggest city with about 300,000 people (although three Long Island towns now have more people), but was once twice as big, and would now have trouble surviving without huge state subsidies. The total value of property in Amherst, its largest suburb, now exceeds the value of Buffalo properties.

But some of the wounds to New York were self-inflicted, especially moves that raised taxes.

The tipping point was reached during the 15-year tenure of Gov. Nelson Rockefeller, from 1959 to 1973, when the state dramatically raised taxes to pay for a new state university, low-income housing and especially for health care for the poor.

In 1967, the state joined the federal Medicaid program, which requires a match of dollars with state and local funds. The program has had the biggest fiscal wallop in New York because the feds pay the minimum share, which was 50 percent (other states get as much as 80 percent) and because New York jumped in with both feet.

The program costs $44.5 billion in New York in 2005—far more than any other state.

Governors and lawmakers since the Rockefeller era have cut tax rates (until a temporary hike was imposed in 2003 on sales and income taxes that were rescinded in 2005), but the damage was already done. Over the last 40 years, New York has had the lowest rate of job growth of any state.

Even within the Northeast, New York's poor record stands out. Since 1965, according to federal Bureau of Labor Statistics figures, the number of jobs here has grown by only about 30 percent, the lowest figure of any state, or just a little more than a quarter of the rate of the nation as a whole.

Massachusetts and New Jersey have experienced a growth in jobs more than twice as fast. Even fellow rust-belt state Pennsylvania outpaced the Empire State.

During the national recession that started in March 2001 and ended in 2003, the state lost 265,000 jobs, or 3.1 percent of the total. That compares to a loss of 2 percent of jobs nationally. The New York losses include 107,000 manufacturing jobs, a decline of almost 15 percent.

Largely because of the manufacturing and Wall Street slumps, the median wage in the state (with the same number above and below) slipped by almost a percentage point in the first half of 2003 to $14.18 per hour. Since the end of the recession, the New York City area and the Hudson Valley have prospered, but most of upstate has missed the recovery.

The early years of the economic decline were met with mostly denial by political leaders.

Despite the deep economic slowdown in the early 1970s, leaders in New York City continued to spend like the boom would never end. The state had to rescue it from bankruptcy in 1975, even as bankers started to doubt the state's own creditworthiness.

But then, the main culprits in the state's fiscal problems were public authorities—quasi-governmental organizations like the Port Authority, Metropolitan Transportation Authority and Thruway Authority, which are controlled by public officials but are legally separate. One of them, the Urban Development Corp., set up by Rockefeller to build low-cost housing, found itself unable to pay its bills and depended on taxpayers to bail it out.

In 2005, as for most of the last 30 years, politicians are probing the authorities and demanding more accountability and other changes.

So for reasons both inevitable and avoidable, New York has evolved from the nation's most populous, powerful and progressive state a half-century ago to an economic laggard of diminished influence and importance.

It now has 29 members of the House of Representatives, down from 43 two generations ago, because its share of the country's population has plummeted to about 6.5 percent (19 million out of about 295 million). California passed New York to become the most populous state in 1960 and Texas became the second-largest state in the mid-1990s. Florida is expected to pass the Empire State to become number three within a decade.

Between 2000 and 2004, the state population grew by 1.3 percent, a bit less than one-third the national increase. If that trend continues, New York will likely lose two more seats in Congress after the 2010 census.

The diminished importance of New York has made it easier for Washington to treat the state less than fairly. For example, in the next-to-last round of military-base closings, both of the upstate Air Force bases (in Rome and Plattsburgh)

were closed. New York also ranks near the bottom annually in
how much money the state gets back from Washington compared to what its citizens pay in federal taxes.

While it is still one of the richest states in the union
(with an annual gross state product in excess of $800 billion, it
represents a 10th of the nation's economy, even with only 6.5
percent of its population) New York has an income disparity
that rivals that of Mississippi and rates of child poverty, infant
mortality and teenage pregnancy that belie its history and reputation.

Behind these dry-sounding statistics are millions of
personal dramas:

> Families split because the children can't
find rewarding work near where they
grew up. New York lost more people
between 21 and 34 in the '90s than any
other state, according to the Census
Bureau;
> Those who are left behind aren't doing as
well as their fellow Americans for the
most part.   The average income of
upstate slipped in the 1990s to 11 percent
below the national average, according
the Census Bureau;
> Retail activity in downtowns all over
upstate is dying, with plywood re-
placing window displays on many
streets;
> For those in areas that are prospering,
like much of the Hudson Valley and
Long Island, the tax burden, especially
property taxes, is helping to drive the
costs of home ownership beyond the
reach of young families.

It's not surprising that old industries that supported
great swaths of the state are dying out—that has been the cycle

of capitalism for centuries and is happening all over the Northeast and Midwest.

What sets New York apart is that it has been slower to reinvent itself than other states. Despite the fact that New York is the home to the original computer company, IBM, most of the dramatic growth in the information-technology industry that transformed areas like the Silicon Valley of California, the Research Triangle in North Carolina, Austin, Texas and the Route 128 region of Massachusetts has bypassed the Empire State. It remains to be seen whether the state's investment of hundreds of millions of dollars in high-tech university-based "centers of excellence" will get New York back in the game.

While New York could count more than its share of path-breaking entrepreneurs earlier in the last century (George Eastman of Kodak, Thomas Watson of IBM, Joseph Wilson of Xerox, among others) the current generation of ground-breaking inventors and entrepreneurs like Steve Jobs and Bill Gates are doing business elsewhere.

Many large firms don't even give New York a look in deciding where to expand. In the summer of 2005, Toyota announced a new assembly plant for its RAV-4 compact SUV in Ontario, Canada—a more expensive place to do business than New York. The Intel Corp. disclosed plans to build a new $3 million computer-chip factory near Phoenix, Arizona, disregarding New York's multi-hundred million-dollar investment to attract just such a plant.

It's not that the raw material isn't here.

Curiously, the Rochester region generates more patents per capita than any place in the country. Just 60 miles away, the Buffalo region is near the top of the nation in the number of engineering-school graduates per capita. Yet this wondrous mix of ideas and practical know-how have failed to mate to form large numbers of new enterprises.

The state also has an unrivaled network of private colleges and universities (as well as an extensive public system) that have spawned new businesses. But again, there have been

no great discoveries here in recent decades or enough of a concentration of marketable new technology to make a region
prosperous.   (An exception is Tom Golisano, founder of
arguably the most successful new upstate company in the past
generation, Rochester-based Paychex, which provides payroll
and personnel services to companies around the country.)

2004 was a good year for the national economy,
although some think the prosperity might be temporary since
the federal-government deficits and war spending that helped
to fuel it might not be sustainable.

The New York City region grew in 2004, as the nation
came out of a recession, along with the Hudson Valley and
Long Island. But most of upstate continued to struggle, especially Rochester, Buffalo and the Southern Tier.

In 2002, the Eastman Kodak Co., which employed
61,000 people in Monroe County in the early 1980s, announced
that it was stopping the production of single-use cameras in
Rochester. As a result of pressures to cut costs, the photo giant,
which now has about 18,000 workers in the Rochester region,
moved production to Monterrey, Mexico and Szeunan, China.
About 500 jobs were axed.

Kodak claimed it was moving the jobs outside the
United States to better compete in this important market with
Fuji. According to the company, labor and other costs would
be far lower outside the United States.

However, Kodak neglected to mention one important
detail: Fuji makes its single-use cameras in the United States—
in South Carolina. Costs there are comparable to overseas—
and far cheaper than in its native Japan, Fuji officials said.

For decades, business leaders have been saying that the
disparity in costs between doing business in New York and the
rest of the country have been strangling the state's economy,
especially the manufacturing base that had been the foundation of upstate New York's prosperity for generations and the
chief ladder up to the middle class for immigrants in New York
City.

Not only are taxes the highest in the country, but other costs of doing business, like health and liability insurance, workers'-compensation payments and utility bills also near the top of the list.

Kodak is only one of hundreds of companies that made the cost calculation and decided it couldn't afford to expand in New York. That, of course, has happened to other Northeast and Midwest states as well. But it has afflicted New York more than anywhere else, and the Empire State has been slower to identify the problem and move to correct it.

None of this has escaped the attention, of course, of politicians that New Yorkers send to Albany.

"The days of wine and roses are over," then-Gov. Hugh Carey famously declared in his first State of the State address in 1975. He fought to cut spending and taxes during his eight years in office, but was only partly successful.

Mario Cuomo succeeded him in 1983, just as the economy was turning up. He and lawmakers continued to cut tax rates as tax receipts bulged. He looked like a hero until the late 1980s and early 1990s when another recession hit, and the state's still-high costs contributed to its suffering more than any other state. That downturn arrived a year earlier in New York compared to the rest of the country and stayed a year longer and bit deeper than elsewhere.

While the state accounted for only 7 percent of the jobs in the country, the loss of more than 500,000 jobs was one of every four axed in all 50 during that recession.

The economic malaise (as well as high crime and Cuomo's opposition to the death penalty) were the major reasons Republican George Pataki ousted him in 1994, despite the fact that the state had 1.2 million more voters enrolled as Democrats than as Republicans.

It seemed that New Yorkers had decided that they were paying too high an economic price for New York's expensive web of public services.

At the same time that Republicans took control of both

houses of Congress for the first time in 40 years, the GOP in
New York also appeared to be in ascendancy, with an avowed
champion of smaller government in the governor's mansion.
And initially, Pataki delivered. For the first time in decades,
the state government spent less money in fiscal year 1995-1996
than the year before.

Income and business taxes were slashed, and the state
made a dent in controlling school property taxes.

It wasn't that Pataki was a magician. He was fortunate
that his arrival at the Capitol coincided with national welfare
reform and a flattening out of medical inflation. Those trends
were among the major reasons he was able to control spending.
The state also got a windfall worth billions when the federal
government changed the welfare system, which had paid the
states for a portion of benefits for the number of recipients they
had, into a flat grant. As the rolls dropped precipitously, the
state continued to collect far more from Washington than it had
to turn over to the people still getting government assistance.

Crime had also peaked and began to fall at a faster rate
in New York than the rest of the country. In a development
that seemed impossible two decades earlier, New York City
became the safest major city in America.

For a while in the 1990s, it looked like the political system in New York had, albeit tardily, reacted to the problem of
the state's sliding economy and put into power leaders who
would make the necessary corrections.

But after the first two years of Pataki's term, the old
patterns reemerged. Hungry to maximize his re-election
prospects for 1998 and looking at dismal poll numbers, Pataki
acquiesced to big hikes in state spending for education and
medical care. He won a huge re-election victory in 1998.

For the next few years, the unprecedented boom on
Wall Street allowed him, like Cuomo a decade earlier, to continue to cut tax rates while raising spending at the same time.
(The state gets almost half of its personal-income-tax revenue
from the wealthiest 5 percent of the population, a majority of

whose incomes are tied to Wall Street. It also benefited hugely from taxes on capital gains when the market was going strong.)

When the high-tech bubble burst in 2000, the state seemed to face a choice of scaling back spending or raising taxes. The problem was immensely complicated by the September 11, 2001 terrorist attacks on Manhattan's World Trade Center, which not only killed almost 2,800 people but also cost the state 100,000 jobs and billions in tax revenues.

Still, facing another election in 2002, Pataki and legislative leaders increased spending, drained reserve funds, borrowed more cash and approved a dramatic expansion in gambling as a new source of state revenue rather than cutting spending. The betting was that the recession would be brief.

The political calculation was correct—Pataki won a third term handily over the Democratic comptroller, H. Carl McCall, who presented no credible fiscal alternative. Almost all legislative incumbents won another term.

But the fiscal gamble failed.

The recession turned out to be longer and deeper than they had hoped. The next year, lawmakers raised income and sales taxes (over Pataki's veto) and borrowed money to meet operating expenses—the same practice that led to the near-bankruptcy of New York City 30 years ago.

So once again New York found itself ranking near the top in undesirable categories, like tax burden and debt load, and near the bottom in things like credit-worthiness and creation of new jobs.

Why have other states, faced with similar circumstances, manage to adjust better than New York? At least part of the answer lies at the state Capitol, where too often the interests of well connected and powerful individuals and groups, ranging from labor unions to lawyers to corporations, have triumphed, proving to be detrimental to the state as a whole.

New York isn't unique in having people looking for special breaks from government.

But elsewhere, such interests are better balanced by the

pressures of doing what's best for the entire state. That balance may be restored if the crisis continues to deepen in the depressed part of the state.

It remains to be seen whether some procedural changes made by the Legislature in early 2005 will result in more reasonable tax and spending policies.

Democratic Attorney General Eliot Spitzer, who developed a national reputation for prosecuting brokerage houses, accounting firms and banks that were cheating clients, and insurance companies for fixing premiums, has made reform of the Capitol the early theme of his campaign for governor in the 2006 election.

In July 2005, Pataki announced he wouldn't seek a fourth four-year-term. Originally elected as a reformer, he has now become in the eyes of many the face of the status quo. There was no other Republican candidate likely to give Spitzer much of a race. Former Massachusetts Gov. William Weld is one of the best known Republicans interested in running.

High taxes, sluggish economic growth and economic and political dysfunction will be among the key issues that potential candidates running for governor must address.

Certainly these questions should be asked of the candidates: if the Empire State is truly a democracy, why aren't more decisions made that benefit a majority of the people, and what has to change in order for that to happen? If other states can reinvent themselves and develop new businesses that provide good-paying jobs, why can't New York do the same?

This book is an attempt to help frame that debate.

Top:
New York's
domeless Capitol

Left:
The Capitol's
"million-dollar
staircase," built back
when a million
dollars was a lot of
money

(Photos by Mark Vergari)

Left:
Lobbyists at work in
the Senate Chamber

Bottom:
Reporters crowd
around the entrance
to "Fort Pataki" on
the Capitol's second
floor

(Photos by Mark Vergari)

Part 1

☆ The Players ☆

CHAPTER 1

GEORGE PATAKI

☆ ☆ ☆

On a sunny Monday afternoon in October of 2002, Gov. George Pataki faced a group of reporters on the Empire State Plaza that adjoins the state Capitol after he spoke at a ceremonial event.

Pataki, who was seeking a third four-year term as governor, was asked whether he had ever written letters on behalf of friends of relatives seeking jobs.

Such letters were a campaign issue because his Democratic opponent, H. Carl McCall, had been criticized for writing one for his daughter. Over the previous weekend, Pataki had said he couldn't remember writing such letters.

His response sounded a little like the Abbott & Costello' "Who's on First?" routine.

"I talked about that over the course of the weekend, and I'm not going to talk about it today," Pataki said that Monday.

"I didn't hear the answer. What was it?" said the reporter who asked the question, Frederic Dicker of *The New York Post*.

"That was the answer," Pataki said.

"What was it?" Dicker asked.

"That was the answer," the governor said.

"You're not going to say if you ever wrote such letters?" Dicker asked.

"I talked about it over the weekend," Pataki repeated. "I'm not going to talk about it."

"But I wasn't there," Dicker persisted. "Couldn't you please tell me now? Why not tell me?"

"That, that's my answer," the governor said.

"O.K., well, if there are such letters would you make them public? Carl McCall says he's going to make his letters, all of them, public," Dicker said.

"I talked about it over the weekend and I'm not going to talk about it again," the governor said.

A Pataki press aide, Suzanne Morris, then cut off questions and scolded reporters for badgering the governor. Pataki started walking the hundred yards or so back to the Capitol, with the pack of reporters trailing. He didn't tell them anything on the subject either.

Later in the day, Pataki's press office issued a statement saying the governor had never written such a letter.

As Pataki, 60, the nation's longest serving governor, said himself late in 2004, it's still too early to talk about his legacy as New York's 53rd chief executive, even as he mulls a run for president.

But one thing is clear after more than a decade in office: Pataki at almost every turn has limited the amount of information flowing to the public about its government. His moves in this area range from being frequently unavailable for interviews to not answering questions directly. He even cited, at one point, Richard Nixon's use of "executive privilege" during the Watergate scandal as a reason for trying to withhold state documents from the public.

He and his aides said early in 2005 that he planned to change—to set aside time to talk to reporters to not only answer their questions but to help them understand what he was thinking. So far, the follow-through has been uneven, although the outright hostility that used to greet even routine questions to Pataki's press office is gone since a new top press aide took over late in 2004.

Certainly such a stance would be a dramatic change from his first decade in office.

In that period, even when the subject was mundane, he often was, apparently out of habit, evasive.

For example, before the 2000 World Series between the Yankees and the Mets, he was asked about which New York team he planned to root for. The Mets had already won the National League title, and the Yankees were playing the Seattle Mariners for the right to play the Mets for the title.

"Right now, I am clearly out on a limb, rooting for the Yankees to beat the Mariners," he said.

"But if it's the Yanks-Mets, which one do you want to win?"

"I will root for the New York team in the World Series," he said, allowing that he was a "rabid Yankee fan" as a kid growing up in Peekskill. A few days later, long after all other significant New York politicians had taken their stands, he finally said he wanted the Yankees to win in seven games (they won in five).

His reticence to speak—or to take positions on controversial issues—is more than a character quirk or nuisance for reporters. Some see it as a basic flaw in his style of leadership that has contributed to the state's decline.

"Even though Teddy Roosevelt is supposed to be his hero, I doubt there is any governor in history who has used the bully pulpit less than George Pataki," said E. J. McMahon, a former state deputy tax commissioner and deputy SUNY chancellor who now follows state government for the Manhattan Institute. "Bully pulpit" was Roosevelt's phrase for the position his role as governor (and later president) and access to the media offered him to try to sway public opinion.

Reformers think Albany would be a far different place

now if Pataki had used the "bully pulpit" to push for change, although Pataki contends he has been a leader on reform issues. Others think he could have made a stronger case that state spending and borrowing needed to be held down, that Medicaid needed to be restrained and that state-imposed rules on local governments and businesses should be changed.

They also fault him for presiding over an administration with more than its share of scandals and not moving more forcefully to change the political culture that fostered them.

Pataki, for his part, thinks that he has led well enough so that the state is a far different place from when he took over as governor in 1995.

"There are so many different areas of this state that are dramatically different from where they were 10 years ago, and I'm proud of all of them," he said.

It's not as if New Yorkers didn't know what they were getting when Pataki was first elected.

If they wanted an orator, they would have elected Mario Cuomo to a fourth term. They preferred the plain-spoken, little-known state senator who was also a former Assembly member and Peekskill mayor.

But they would end up knowing less about Pataki than most candidates for governor. Early in his campaign in 1994, Pataki and his supporters decided that he would "turn side-ways," as the then-Republican state chairman, William Powers, later put it.

In other words, he would expose his views and plans as little as possible and make the campaign about Cuomo as much as he could.

Pataki then proceeded to cut back on interviews, kept details of his plans for governing mostly to himself except to push for a death penalty and cut taxes. Remarkably, he and Cuomo didn't engage in any debates. (There is no public financing of campaigns for state office, and therefore no lure in races for governor comparable to what exists in presidential campaigns.) Cuomo insisted that minor-party candidates be included and Pataki insisted on only a one-on-one. So none were held.

In the weekend before the election, when many papers ran grids so voters could easily compare the candidates' position on issues, Pataki's column was blank—his campaign didn't respond to questionnaires and ignored follow-up calls to try to get the information.

The enforcer of the campaign was Zenia Mucha, a former top aide to Alfonse D'Amato, then a U.S. senator and Pataki's political mentor.

She was asked during one campaign trip to Buffalo that year whether she intended to be the governor's press secretary if Pataki won. She said probably not, because she was more interested in politics than policy.

But she did go on to become first communications director and then senior policy adviser to Pataki, with the power and forceful personality to make department commissioners quake to hear she was calling for them. She left to become a spokeswoman for the Disney Co. in 2001.

The first days of the administration showed it would be the same as that of the campaign.

The Pataki era was kicked off with a lavish inaugural celebration paid for largely with donations from firms that had business with the state. It took a lawsuit from Assembly Democrats before the source of the donations was disclosed.

Almost immediately, Pataki closed off the second floor of the Capitol, where his offices are located, from the public. A state trooper was installed to make sure that no one without official business, or people on formal tours of the Capitol, were allowed in—even though the hallways contained the portraits of former governors and had been a regular stop for tourists. Elevators near Pataki's office no longer stopped on the second floor.

Reporters quickly dubbed the area "Fort Pataki" more than six years before the terrorist attacks on the World Trade Center made such precautions seem less unreasonable.

Not long after Pataki took office, Mucha convened a meeting of the state government's scores of public-information officers—the people who work in state agencies who answer questions and track down information for reporters and other members of the public—and made clear to them their job was to promote the governor and his agenda, not to be accommodating to reporters.

Early on, Pataki held press conferences in the former Court of Appeals chambers on the second floor of the Capitol that Cuomo used for that purpose. But that soon proved unworkable.

Unlike Cuomo, who would stay until every question was answered, Pataki would leave while hands were still in the air. That would lead to a scrum of reporters and TV camera operators chasing him down the hall back to Fort Pataki, trying to get more information.

He later shifted the rare question-and-answer sessions to a room inside the fort, adjacent to his office. Then he just needed to take a few steps to get behind a door that was off-limits.

It also allowed his staff to control who could get in to the press conferences. Sometimes they allowed in the League of Women Voters' lobbyist, Barbara Bartoletti, and sometimes they didn't. Bartoletti suspected the decision was based on how critical she had been of the administration in public.

"Open government to this administration is a joke. Why do you think it's called Fort Pataki?" she said. "Sometimes it's like pulling teeth to get into a press conference."

The tone was set, and it has softened only slightly over the years with the departure of Mucha and her equally aggressive successor, Michael McKeon, who now, like several former Pataki aides, is a lobbyist. Reporters have gotten used to their queries being answered with formal statements, or with a refusal to answer any questions.

Occasionally, reporters got a glimpse from the inside that gave them another perspective on the administration.

In September of 1995, a small group of Capitol reporters accompanied Pataki, his wife, Libby, their son Teddy, his mother Margaret, Mucha, state trooper Daniel Wiese and a few other top aides on a 10-day tour of Hungary and Italy. It was billed as an economic development trip, but it also gave Pataki a chance to visit relatives (his father was Hungarian and his mother of Italian and Irish heritage) and revel in the adulation of the locals, some of whom seemed to think (mistakenly) that he was coming with an open wallet.

Pataki was ebullient and charming, sometimes leading staff and reporters on late-night excursions to bars. Mucha demonstrated to reporters why Pataki (and now Disney Co. executives) leaned on her so much.

When a Hungarian waiter tried to overcharge a group of reporters for lunch, she swiftly intervened, and the tab was halved. She didn't speak the language, but her tone, volume and body language got the point across. When another reporter complained, mostly jokingly, that he didn't have time to grab a pastry at a picnic held in Pataki's honor (Hungary is justifiably famous for its pastries), she swiped one from a stunned-looking elderly woman, telling her in English she could go get another one, and presented it to the reporter.

When an American free-lance reporter living in Budapest expressed an interest in meeting the handsome, single (and English-speaking) mayor of Budapest, Mucha whispered in Pataki's ear, and the introduction was made.

For some reporters, it was the last time Mucha was on their side, but they understood better why she was so valued by Pataki.

The bad news about that excursion didn't come out until about two years later. Reporters on the trip, whose companies paid their expenses, asked who was paying for the Pataki party. Pataki said the Hungarian-American Chamber of Commerce was picking up the tab.

This sounded reasonable, but in 1997, when others looked into that organization, it turned out to have been funded mostly by Philip Morris, the tobacco company that at the time was fighting efforts in the Legislature to restrict smoking in public places in New York. Pataki said he saw nothing wrong with the arrangement, but it seemed like a clear conflict.

Reporters turned up other unsavory deals as well, some of them related to Pataki's prodigious fund-raising (about $70 million for his three gubernatorial campaigns).

In 1997, a Long Island construction company, Silverite, landed a $97 million contract from the Pataki-controlled Metropolitan Transportation Authority to repair the Queens-Midtown Tunnel after first being rejected as unqualified. The firm's president, Angelo Silveri, other Silverite officials and related firms gave Pataki and the Republican Party more than $200,000 in donations between 1994 and 1998. Pataki said there was no connection between the donations and the contract.

In 2002, top officials of the State University Construction Fund, which is also controlled by the governor, were fired after they improperly awarded a no-bid architectural contract to a Pataki neighbor and relative by marriage. Pataki wasn't implicated.

In 2003, the *Village Voice*, a weekly New York City newspaper, reported that Wiese, the former state trooper and Pataki bodyguard who had become head of security for the state Power Authority, which Pataki controls, refused to answer questions before a federal grand jury. The panel was probing the alleged sale of paroles in 1997 for donations to Pataki's re-election campaign.

Wiese involved himself in an investigation of reports that Pataki fund-raisers were promising potential donors that relatives would be paroled if they made large campaign contributions, the paper reported. Then when called before the grand jury to testify, Wiese invoked the Fifth Amendment against self-incrimination so he wouldn't have to answer questions, the *Voice* and other papers reported.

Three parole officials were convicted of perjury in the case and a fund-raiser was convicted of obstruction of justice. Pataki wasn't implicated.

This has led to questions about whether Wiese, 51, a long-time Pataki friend and neighbor making $160,000 as security chief for the Power Authority and $60,000 a year from a state pension from his time with the State Police, should lose his job.

The state constitution requires that public officers who invoke the Fifth Amendment when asked about something they did in their official duties be dismissed and not allowed to hold a public job for five years.

But the Power Authority has responded that courts have ruled that government workers can't be punished for invoking their Fifth-Amendment rights, and that since the grand jury records are sealed, authority officials have no knowledge he did it anyway.

When the *Voice* story first ran, Pataki tried to downplay it.

"I'm not going to comment on those things," he said, terming questions about them "ridiculous."

Then he called Wiese a "very, very professional person."

Then a Pataki spokeswoman accused Assemblyman Richard Brodsky, D-Greenburgh, Westchester County, of "playing politics" by asking the Power Authority to look at whether Wiese should be fired.

Pataki did nothing to indicate he was interested in finding the answer to the important question here: was Wiese, one of the state's key law-enforcement officials, trying to block a federal investigation into the alleged parole-selling scheme?

On the other hand, he claims to be very interested in cleaning up the way state government is run and giving citizens more of a say in decisions.

According to his press office, Pataki has "championed a comprehensive series of bold reforms to help empower New Yorkers, enhance the openness and effectiveness of government and to improve the way Albany conducts business."

His spokesman cited his support of an initiative and referendum that would allow citizens to bypass the Legislature by putting proposed laws on the ballot and his proposal to overhaul campaign-finance and election laws.

But the Capitol's best known good-government lobbyist pointed out that none of those things have become law—in large measure, he said, because Pataki didn't aggressively push them.

"From where we sit, the governor has been the single biggest obstacle to reform," said the lobbyist, Blair Horner of the New York Public Interest Research Group, an offshoot of an organization founded by consumer activist Ralph Nader. Horner has been a thorn in the side of Albany officials for two decades.

"Despite the rhetoric, when there were real efforts to change things in Albany, he either did nothing or deliberately undermined reform," Horner said of Pataki.

He gave these examples:

> In 1999, in the wake of the scandal involving Philip Morris giving lawmakers and state officials illegal gifts to try to kill anti-smoking legislation, the Senate was ready to pass a measure limiting gifts and requiring disclosure of lobbying for state contracts. But Pataki and Assembly Speaker Sheldon Silver killed it;

> While Pataki introduced a campaign-finance reform proposal on the last day of the 1999 legislative session (when it was too late for it to be enacted that year), he did nothing to promote it;

➤ He did introduce an initiative-and-referendum plan (the vehicle used by voters
in California and Massachusetts to limit
tax hikes) in 1995, but didn't talk about it
again until 2002. In that election year, he
was seeking the nomination of the
Independence Party, which had made
initiative and referendum one of its top
priorities.

"We met with the governor's staff in 1996 and said we'd
support it," Horner recalled. "They didn't do anything. They
just went to sleep."

➤ In 2003 and 2004, he blocked another
attempt to require reporting of lobbying
activity for state contracts by introduc-
ing a competing bill that was too limited
to be effective.

Horner and other good-government lobbyists also say
that Pataki missed a golden opportunity to force lawmakers
into meaningful reform when he signed a bill in 2002 setting
up new legislative districts based on the 2000 census. The
majorities in both houses had drawn the new lines to maximize
their advantages, but it couldn't take effect without the governor's signature.

"That's when he had the most leverage to force
changes," Horner said. "He didn't do it. . . . His overall record
has been excessive secrecy, bare-knuckled political hardball
and torpedoing political reform proposed talks when the
reform might be coming to a head. He's been governor status
quo."

And right at the end of 2004, he almost appeared to be
"Governor Retro," when his lawyers cited the "executive privilege" doctrine Nixon made in 1973 during the Watergate scandal to try to keep records out of public view.

Pataki wanted to block the public release of about 600 pages of memos and e-mails between his office and the state Thruway Authority. The information concerned efforts to deal with the public fallout over a decision to award development rights along the state Barge Canal for only $30,000 to a favored developer. The contract was later voided, with Comptroller Alan Hevesi and Attorney General Eliot Spitzer, both Democrats, issuing scathing reports about the favoritism that led to the award.

The information Pataki wanted to block was ordered released by state Supreme Court Judge Joseph Cannizaro. He issued this stinging rebuke in his decision: "We are the people's government, made for the people, by the people and answerable to the people," he wrote. "Consequently, inasmuch as government is the people's business, it necessarily follows that its operations should be at all times open to the public view. Openness, accountability and transparency are as essential to honest government administration as freedom of speech is to representative government."

Pataki can also point to several positive trends since he has been governor.

When asked about accomplishments he's most proud of, he replied, "We're the safest large state in America."

Indeed, violent crime in 2004 was down 52 percent since its peak in the early 1990s, with the drop in New York City almost double the national rate.

The welfare caseload is also down—by a million people, or almost two-thirds, from when he took over.

The prison population has also shrunk; from a peak of about 72,000 in 1999 to about 62,000 in August 2005. New York and Massachusetts are the only two states to have fewer state-prison inmates in 2004 than in 1995.

The state has also acquired title or development rights to 785,000 acres of environmentally sensitive land—an area about the size of Rhode Island.

The responsibility for the land acquisitions is clear-cut—it was a Pataki initiative—but the reasons for the other positive trends are murkier.

For example, McMahon thinks credit for the drop in crime goes more to New York City Mayor Rudolph Giuliani than Pataki, since almost all of the drop was recorded in the city. But he said state measures like lengthening prison sentences for violent crimes played some role.

Pataki has also shown he can fight with the Legislature—and win. In 1996, he forced through changes in the state workers' compensation law that have cut costs for businesses, and in 1998 also got reluctant lawmakers to approve setting up as many as 100 charter schools in the state and have the state enter into a cartel-like arrangement designed to boost the price farmers get for milk.

His big carrot in that fight: a 38 percent raise for lawmakers as well as himself. But he has had no comparable successes since.

Probably the most contentious issue of Pataki's record is fiscal policy. He came into office vowing to put an end to the state's failure to adopt a budget by the start of the fiscal year. But he failed until this year. The state has also continued to borrow money so that it has the second-highest debt of any state (behind California).

State tax rates have been cut, but in many areas local taxes have risen, at least in part because of rules set down by the state. New Yorkers are still the highest taxed people in the country, if you count both state and local taxes, just as they were when Pataki was elected.

In defense of his fiscal record, Pataki's press office pointed out that he's proposed a constitutional amendment to require a two-thirds majority vote of both houses of the Legislature to enact tax increases. He's also signed into law what he called "the most sweeping debt-reform legislation ever enacted in state history." And he's proposed a measure to make on-time budgets more likely.

But these are at best timid steps, McMahon said.

"That's pretty empty stuff," he said. He pointed out that the Legislature in 2003 raised the sales and income taxes and had far more than the two-thirds votes Pataki wants to require.

The debt reform is the "most sweeping" in history because it's the only one, McMahon said. But it is so weak that it was not tough enough to stop the Legislature from converting about $1 billion in debt that New York City incurred in the 1970s into 30-year bonds in 2004—a move fiscal analysts said was irresponsible and that Pataki opposed. That means that taxpayers in 2030 will still be paying for costs like police and teacher salaries that were incurred almost 60 years earlier.

Perhaps more disturbingly, the state is now about in the same place fiscally that it was when Pataki took office—facing potential deficits, with big unfunded obligations looming.

"It's all awful," said state Comptroller Alan Hevesi, a Democrat, about the state's fiscal prospects. He cited a court order for billions more for New York City schools, billions needed for transit upkeep and expansion, and a shortfall in medical services as among the big bills coming due.

"The political culture doesn't object to shenanigans like spending more money than you take in," he said. "There is no long term in our political decision-making."

Changing things, he said, will take a "culture change. . . . We're going to get to a point where austerity has to come to the state."

McMahon thinks the answer might be a cap on spending, a move other states have tried. But he doesn't think Pataki is the one to embrace it.

"He has not been a guy to push the envelope," McMahon said. "He is not an audacious figure."

Pataki, for his part, acknowledged the state was in for a rough financial time in 2005.

"There are significant pressures," he said. "Yes, there are very real fiscal challenges in the upcoming year," but he said the state has overcome bigger problems. An unexpected surge in state tax revenue in 2005 helped ease the state's short-term fiscal problems.

It would be out of character for Pataki to mount the "bully pulpit" to push for spending controls that might ease the state's fiscal woes. Indeed, sometimes it seems that he is so loathe to give out more information than is required that he even allows potentially damaging questions to remain hanging.

For example, in November 2003, Pataki and his wife took a trip to St. Barts, an exclusive resort island in the Caribbean. His reaction to questions raised by the excursion shows his reluctance to disclose more than required by law, even if it means that some people's confidence in the integrity of their government is at issue.

Their host on the trip, who also provided private-jet transportation, was Earle Mack. Mack is a longtime Pataki friend, millionaire real-estate developer and major campaign contributor who has a business relationship with the state.

After a reporter came across a record of the trip, Pataki was asked why he wouldn't make public a cancelled check or other record indicating that he followed state law and reimbursed Mack for the cost of the flight. State law, adopted to try to prevent the perception that government is for sale, bans state officials including Pataki from taking gifts worth more than $75 from people who have business before the state.

Pataki's answer was, essentially, that he doesn't have to.

"We have followed the procedures that have always been followed," he told reporters at a Capitol news conference. "In fact we've gone beyond them. In the past if I had said 'we paid for it, we gave a check, that was acceptable. . . .' Now the Ethics Commission has seen the check."

The question arose about making the check public because the Associated Press filed a freedom-of-information request to Pataki's office in December of 2003 asking for all documents related to reimbursements made for trips in

2003. Pataki's office responded that it had no such public documents.

In December of 2003, state Ethics Commission executive director Karl Sleight said in a statement that he had seen a check from Pataki and other documents showing he had made the necessary reimbursements. So he said any further probe of the trip was unnecessary.

But commission officials say that they're prohibited by law from disclosing any of the records to support their conclusions.

Three of the five members of the commission are appointed by the governor. The commission has never issued a ruling critical of either governor who has ruled since it has been in existence, Pataki or Mario Cuomo.

Mack, the Patakis' host for their vacation, is a director of the Mack-Cali Realty Corp. That company is helping to develop a $1.3 billion complex of sports, entertainment and retail stores in the Meadowlands area of northern New Jersey.

The Port Authority of New York and New Jersey, which Pataki and New Jersey acting Gov. Richard Codney control, has approved a rail link that could benefit that project. A Pataki spokeswoman told the Associated Press that Mack has not lobbied Pataki about that project.

Mack is also on the board of the New York Racing Association, which has a state franchise to operate Saratoga, Belmont and Aqueduct race tracks. The organization made a plea agreement with federal prosecutors in December to shake up its management in exchange for avoiding criminal prosecution. NYRA had been indicted in 2003 for allowing employees to engage in tax fraud.

Mack-Cali has also gotten more than $1 million in state business, and has contributed at least $75,000 to political campaigns in recent years, including almost $24,000 to Pataki and $30,000 to the Republican State Committee, records show.

In other words, New Yorkers have reason to be interested when their governor accepts hospitality from a man in a position such as Mack's, and they understandably want to be sure that the governor doesn't take gifts designed to influence him when taxpayer concerns should be his priority.

But Pataki wouldn't budge.

"I'm not going to be in a position where I have to show all my actual checks for every single trip I've taken," he told reporters. "I think that's ridiculous."

But what about just trips you take with someone doing business with the state, a reporter persisted.

"Next subject," chimed in Pataki's then-communications chief, Lisa Dewald Stoll.

The governor answers reporters' questions at the
door to Fort Pataki
(Photo by Mark Vergari)

Gov. George Pataki in his office
(Photo by Tim Roske)

CHAPTER 2

THE LEGISLATURE

The New York Legislature convenes in two grand rooms on the third floor of the Capitol.

The 150-member, Democrat-controlled Assembly meets in a recently restored chamber with red granite columns and carved sandstone pilasters. Down the hall, the 62 senators (35 of them Republicans) ponder bills while reclining in red leather chairs and surrounded by walls of gold leaf and embossed Spanish leather. Bring back spittoons and elaborate facial hair and it could pass for a scene out of the 19th Century.

The men and women in the seats seem as impressive as the surroundings at first blush—most speak forcefully when they rise to orate, often in strong, modulated voices, on topics that sound important. They address each other formally, offer amendments and vote on bills. The presiding officer slams the gavel to keep order at appropriate moments.

But if one watches a little closer over a period of time, some other trends emerge: a majority of the chairs are often empty; bills that come to the floor are almost always approved; the political minorities are almost always on the losing side of a vote on a contentious issue; and those who are not speaking often aren't attentive to what is being said.

Then you notice that the number of votes announced always seems to exceed the actual men and women sitting in the chambers.

Eventually, it becomes clear that despite the impressive surroundings and trappings of popular government, the New York Legislature is in many ways a Potemkin democracy. Pull back the façade and a different reality emerges.

Issues are discussed and decided elsewhere, usually behind closed doors. The public debates and votes usually are merely pro-forma confirmations of what has already been determined. That means while the public's chances to influence issues are minimized, those with special access to powerful people call the shots more in Albany than in most other capitals.

Indeed, New York has the "most dysfunctional" Legislature in America, a report released in the summer of 2004 from New York University's Brennan Center for Justice concluded. The report found:

> ➢ The legislative chambers often are mostly empty of lawmakers as bills are voted on. Only in New York and Arkansas can lawmakers routinely vote while not being in their seats. If they check in at the beginning of the day, they're automatically recorded as voting with their party leaders on every issue;
> ➢ Amendments to bills on the floor always lose. None of 308 major bills passed from 1997 to 2001 were amended on the floor, according to the report;
> ➢ When bills are voted on, they virtually always pass (4,365 bills voted on, 4,365 passed in the Assembly from 1997-2001, 7,109 out of 7,109 in the Senate);
> ➢ And they're passed quickly (fewer than 5 percent of the major bills passed in that

period were debated, the third-lowest
proportion in the country);
➤ Few senators attend committee meetings. Sometimes only two lawmakers
show up out of maybe a dozen or more
members. (The New York Senate is one
of only three legislative chambers in the
country that allows proxy voting so the
members don't have to appear.);
➤ Committee hearings, where issues can
be thoroughly aired and proposals at
least theoretically refined are almost
never held. (The Senate had a hearing
on one bill out of 152 major bills adopted
from 1997-2001, and the Assembly one
out of 202.)

The lack of hearings is a critical flaw, one expert on the
Legislature said.

"Committees are where you really develop policy," said
former Democratic Senate legislative counsel, Eric Lane, now a
professor at Hofstra University Law School on Long Island.
But to do that, committees need to hold hearings and issue
reports—two events that rarely happen here—and have chairs
who can hire their own staffs, he said. The staffs now are hired
by, and report to, the legislative leaders.

Albany is "a crude representation of democracy," said
Lane.

But that doesn't mean lawmakers were idle. They
introduced far more bills than any other state (16,892 in 2002,
almost twice as many as runner-up Illinois). But they passed
the lowest proportion of any legislature (4.4 percent).

Such dysfunction doesn't come cheap. The budget for
the Assembly and Senate last year was just over $200.5 million,
the third-highest in the country. Included in that total was
$1.66 million for the reapportionment task force, which
redraws legislative and congressional districts after each federal census.

Even though the next count won't be held until 2010, keeping up with the latest technology to help draw gerrymandered districts to assure that Republicans keep control of the Senate and the Democrats the Assembly is apparently a never-ending job.

Albany insiders know that when Blair Horner of the New York Public Interest Research Group, an organization affiliated with Ralph Nader, and E. J. McMahon of the Manhattan Institute, a business-supported right-leaning think tank, agree on something, they can't be dismissed as just partisan whiners. They were among a group of experts who unloaded on the Legislature when the Brennan Center report came out.

"Albany is a mess. These (legislative) rules are just a reflection of that mess," Horner said.

"The report deconstructs the cynical charade known as the New York State Legislative process," said McMahon, who represents an organization where Nader would be about as welcome as Michael Moore on Rush Limbaugh's radio show. "This report is trying to blow up a big mutual-protection racket."

Other critics piled on too.

"Most New Yorkers are represented by people with no say," said Evan Davis, former counsel to Gov. Mario Cuomo. "They vote on bills they have had no opportunity to read, let alone study."

The report "systematically documents the non-democratic nature of the legislative process in New York," said Gerald Benjamin, a SUNY New Paltz dean and academia's leading expert on New York State government. It also "demonstrates through rigorous comparison with other states that New York's failures are sometimes unique and always atypical."

The condition of democracy in the Legislature and the report brought out some contrasting reactions, based not on party or ideology but on whether someone is on the inside or the outside of the legislative process.

"It's hard to believe anyone could read this report and not think reform is necessary," said Jo Brill of the Citizens' Budget Commission, a Manhattan-based fiscal-watchdog group.

Maybe not so hard.

"I think it's nonsense—total nonsense," said the Legislature's top Republican, Sen. Joseph Bruno, who lives on a horse farm in the Troy suburb of Brunswick. He said power needed to be concentrated in one person's hands (in this case, his) for the Senate to operate efficiently and compete with the Assembly and governor, who in New York has more power than the chief executive of most other states.

"Nothing happens here in Albany in the Assembly without the input of rank-and-file members," protested the top Democrat, Assembly Speaker Sheldon Silver of Manhattan said. He pointed out that since his power comes from the other Democrats, he has to do what they want him to do.

The leaders relented on the report at least to some degree early in 2005 and adopted some of the reforms the Brennan Center recommended. Most visibly, lawmakers now have to be in their seats for most votes. But none significantly reduced the power each leader has to keep rank-and-file members in line.

It is the power of the Assembly speaker and Senate majority leader that sets the New York Legislature apart from its peers. Long after other states dispersed power formerly held by its leaders among committee chairs, rank-and-file members and even voters (through initiative-and-referendum procedures, most famously in California and Massachusetts), Silver, Bruno and their New York predecessors have fought fiercely—and successfully—to protect theirs.

They are, in some ways, an odd couple.

Silver, a 61-year-old lawyer from the Lower East Side of Manhattan, is a savvy political infighter with a perpetual funereal mien and close-to-the-vest style.

He was first elected to the state Assembly in 1976. Only

the late Republican Oswald Heck of Schenectady, who was speaker for 22 years, had a longer tenure as speaker than Silver.

Bruno is a voluble, sharp-dressing 76-year-old million-aire former telephone-company executive whose energy seems to defy his age. Neither an artificial hip, a bout with prostate cancer in 2003 nor a torn artery in his stomach appears to have slowed him down much.

Only fellow Republicans Walter Mahoney of Buffalo (11 years) and Warren Anderson of Binghamton (16 years) have served longer than Bruno as Senate majority leader in the past 100 years.

He has political dexterity that has surprised those who figured he was over his head when he seized his current job more than a decade ago. And he's disappointed others who thought he would be a more reliable conservative voice at the Capitol.

Although they're from different political parties and represent radically different constituencies, both Silver and Bruno hold similar levers of power that makes crossing them a dangerous proposition. They control:

> The pay of lawmakers, through deciding who gets extra pay for "leadership" (which often consist of nothing more demanding than announcing the time of meetings) and committee-chair duties;
> What bills get to the floor;
> How much money lawmakers get for staff, offices and other expenses;
> How much individual lawmakers get for "pork-barrel" spending in their own districts for projects like fire trucks, Little League fields, soccer uniforms and other items sure to redound to their political benefit;
> Huge campaign war chests, which can

be directed (or withheld) from lawmakers in tight races. Or they can be used to
unseat minority lawmakers whom they
don't like;
➢ The boundaries of individual Senate and
Assembly districts, through their control
of the redistricting process.

"I know some members would stand up on issues, but
they don't want to take a salary cut," Assemblyman Thomas
Barraga, a Suffolk County Republican, told a group of business
leaders in 2004, talking about the bluntest instrument the leaders wield. The base salary is $79,500. Extra pay for "leader-
ship" posts and committee positions range from $9,000 to
$41,500 a year. Every senator and more than two-thirds of the
Assembly members get some extra pay.

The reason the system has stayed in place so long here
is that it works for the lawmakers. Incumbent legislators seeking another term almost always win.

But if it works for those on the inside, it is far less clear
that it works in the best interests of everyone else.

In a state where residents already pay the highest combined state and local taxes of anyone in the country, lawmakers regularly add onto whatever the governor proposes spending. They voted in 2003 to raise state income and sales tax rates
by a quarter of one percent over Gov. George Pataki's veto.

Part of the reason for this increase in taxes is that the
most frequent solution to deciding where to spend money is to,
essentially, spend more money everywhere.

Want to spend more than $1 billion expanding New
York City's Javits Convention Center? Then spend $350 mil-
lion as well on (unspecified) upstate projects, to be paid for
with borrowed money. Want to add school aid for schools in
poor districts? Make sure everyone else's goes up too.

And with its chronic partisan division (the Democrats
have controlled the Assembly since 1975 and Republicans the

Senate every year but one since 1938) gridlock is frequently the order of the day.

A budget wasn't passed by the start of the fiscal year from 1984 to 2004, by far the longest streak in the nation. A court decision requiring that more money be spent on New York City schools has been ignored. Reform proposals to make lobbyists trying to get state contracts report their activities wouldn't pass until 2005.

The lobbying issue, in fact, was at the center of a moment that is the favorite example of legislative dysfunction for one long-time good government lobbyist.

In the early-morning hours on June 20, 2003, Barbara Bartoletti of the state League of Women Voters and her allies thought the Legislature, under pressure following a number of scandals (including the disclosure that former Sen. Alfonse D'Amato was paid $500,000 to make a phone call to an official of the Metropolitan Transportation Authority on behalf of a client seeking a contract) was poised to pass a bill requiring reporting of such lobbying activities. It had already passed the Assembly and seemed set to go in the Senate as well.

But at 2:30 a.m., a new lobbying bill appeared on the Senate floor—one that not only didn't match the Assembly version (bills have to be exactly the same in the two houses or them to become law) but would have actually weakened the existing law. She said it was clearly meant to scuttle the whole idea of reform while at the same time providing senators with the political cover of having voted for a "reform" bill.

"That was about as cynical a move as I've seen the Legislature make," she said.

She and others suspect that the bill was scuttled at the behest of Pataki, who although he has backed a competing lobbying bill, is not seen by advocates as a strong supporter.

Pataki, along with Bruno and Silver, are the oft-cited "three men in a room" who essentially decide which bills get approved. This trio has survived intact longer than any such threesome in state history.

They hold almost all the cards, because in order to become a law, all bills have to be passed by the Assembly (Silver) and Senate (Bruno) and then signed by the governor.

It's not quite that simple, of course, since Bruno and Silver both have to persuade their members to go along. But with so many ways to enforce discipline, it is rare that the two men don't get what they want.

As with any triangle, the relations among this trio are complicated. The key dynamic among the three is that Silver and Pataki don't like each other. They usually manage to disguise it, but sometimes their animosity breaks through to their public comments.

In June of 2003, when asked about a Pataki remark on a dispute they were having over how to increase state support for New York City schools, Silver said, "There's no presumption that he ever tells you the truth."

Pataki responded that the problem had been created by Silver. He said the state's most powerful Democrat is "like the guy who killed his parents claiming he was an orphan." Pataki had made a slightly more subtle thrust at Silver the previous week, saying that the Assembly he controls "can only do one thing at a time, and I'm not sure they can do that."

Pataki sometimes doesn't invite Silver to public events at the World Trade Center site—in the speaker's district—and Silver never seems to pass up an opportunity to take a swipe at what he sees as Pataki's lack of leadership.

Bruno has a foot in each camp. He is like Pataki a Republican and like Silver a legislative leader. At his best, he can manipulate his position to get the better of both of them.

In 2003, for example, he joined forces with Silver to override Pataki's vetoes of spending measures and tax increases that his members wanted. It seemed that the two legislative leaders could do what they pleased without regard to what the governor wanted.

But later in the year, Bruno switched sides and with Pataki forced through an extension of New York City rent-control laws that Silver and the Democrats wanted to change.

At his worst, critics say, Bruno doesn't offer enough of a contrast to Democrats—indeed, in recent years the Republicans have approved bills banning smoking in bars and guaranteeing civil rights for homosexuals—all anathema to social conservatives—as well as continuing to run up state spending and taxes and overriding Pataki's veto of a rise in the state minimum wage.

"The time has come to take the position that we're not going to tolerate it anymore," state Conservative Party chairman Michael Long said in 2004 before deciding to withhold his party's endorsement from some GOP senators seeking reelection. "They may be our friends—they are our friends—but we just cannot continue to watch people vote on the liberal side of the aisle and think there's no consequence for it," he said.

But for his part, Bruno said, "We haven't moved—the people have moved." In other words, he thinks the only way for the GOP to hold onto the Senate is to move to the left.

A key question at the Capitol is how long Bruno and the Republicans can maintain their hold on the Senate in light of the Democrats' widening enrollment edge statewide (5.5 million Democrats to 3.2 million Republicans). They lost three seats in the 2004 elections to narrow their majority to 35-27.

While Bruno has more trouble staying in step with the conservative wing of his party, Silver has a bigger challenge trying to keep his huge (105 members, to only 45 Republicans) Democratic Assembly conference in line.

In 2000, a group of Democrats, angered by what they saw as Silver's imperious leadership style, tried to oust him and replace him with the majority leader, Michael Bragman of Syracuse.

But the "Bragmanistas," as the dissident group was called, made the fatal mistake of announcing several days in advance their intention to try to topple Silver. Silver used the intervening time to twist enough arms to reduce the rebels to a core of just 25 members. The coup failed.

Then Silver flexed his muscles. Bragman was stripped of his staff and majority-leader status and didn't run for re-election. Silver promised to pay more attention to members in the wake of the challenge, and some say he has.

He has remained a cautious and sometimes maddening leader. For example, when asked to explain in 2004 where the money should come from to pay for billions more in school aid ordered by the courts for New York City, he compared the budget issue to shopping at a supermarket.

He said the extra money for schools is just one more item to be dropped into the state's shopping cart, and that how to pay for it could be determined at the checkout counter.

Both leaders have also had to contend with recent scandals involving legislators and a staff member ranging from bribery to theft to sexual misconduct.

"Any father who would let his daughter be an intern in the state Legislature should have his head examined," former Albany County District Attorney Paul Clyne said in the spring of 2004, in the wake of an allegation that an Assembly member had forced a 19-year-old intern to have sex with him. She later said the sex was consensual. But earlier Silver's top lawyer, Michael Boxley, was forced to quit after pleading guilty to a sexual-misconduct charge involving a young legislative aide.

In 2003, former Democratic Assemblywoman Gloria Davis of the Bronx was forced to resign her seat after admitting she took a bribe to try to steer a state contract. And in 2004 another Democrat, Roger Green of Brooklyn, quit after admitting he asked for and got thousands of dollars from taxpayers to pay for his commute to Albany—even though he was getting free rides with a company seeking a state contract.

Although he pleaded guilty to a misdemeanor and quit his post earlier in the year, Green ran to regain his seat in November 2004—and won.

In the Senate, Republican Guy Velella of the Bronx pleaded guilty last year to a bribery-related charge and gave up his seat before going to prison.

"As a state senator, I made phone calls and met with government officials to help clients who paid fees in excess of $10,000 to a law firm other than mine in which I was not a partner but my father was," Velella admitted before a judge in Manhattan.

"I made these phone calls with the understanding that my efforts on behalf of these people could assist them in obtaining business from these government agencies," he continued. "I knew that making these calls under such circumstances was wrong."

After a raft of scandals in the 1980s, the Legislature created an Ethics Committee. But it has never referred any cases for prosecution nor criticized the actions of any lawmaker.

Despite the problems, individual lawmakers generally remain popular with their constituents.

A Quinnipiac University poll in 2004 found that voters overwhelmingly (51-29 percent) disapprove of the way the Legislature is performing. Two-thirds of those polled said state government is broken and needs to be fixed.

But those same voters give a thumbs up to the way their own senators (58 percent approve, 25 percent disapprove) and Assembly members (54-24) are conducting themselves.

Why the disconnect?

"Rocks thrown at these guys bounce off a dome called 'the Legislature,'" former Gov. Mario Cuomo said. "They aren't held individually responsible."

"It has a lot to do with their guys being featured in mailings that come into their houses, and with them showing up at what seems like every senior-citizens' center, every children's group, every dinner," said Bartoletti, the League of Women Voters lobbyist. "They do the retail (political) thing very well."

Is the Legislature's poor performance the fault of the leaders? Voters questioned by Quinnipiac were split about evenly on whether to blame Bruno and Silver. But significant minorities (30 percent Silver, 40 percent Bruno) said they didn't know enough about either man to respond. (That figure may have gone down in the summer of 2005 when Silver and Bruno killed a plan for a new football stadium on the West Side of Manhattan—a project Pataki and Mayor Michael Bloomberg wanted.)

Bruno makes the case that no matter what you think of the way the Senate operates now, it is an improvement over when he took over in 1995.

When asked to provide a list of his major accomplishments since he took over, the top was that he has the Senate operating mostly on time (instead of hours late, as used to be the norm), and has cut down on late-night and all-night sessions.

He and Silver also started having rank-and-file members meet in public in conference committees (a staple of Congress and well as most other state legislatures) to forge compromises on a limited number of issues like school-budget voting and highway speed limits.

The leaders have also started the practice of publishing legislative spending reports twice a year, so the public can keep track of trips, staff salaries and other expenses, made more information available to the public and putting Senate sessions live on the Internet. Assembly sessions are televised on cable TV in the Albany area.

They have also held the legislative budget relatively flat for the past few years, at about $200 million, while other state spending has been going up. Bruno said this was accomplished by cutting staff, newsletters and offices.

Still, the Legislature, tarred with late budgets, scandals and gridlock, is not well thought of by a majority of New Yorkers.

"There is a disconnect between the legislator you know and this place called Albany," said Quinnipiac pollster Maurice Carroll, a former long-time New York political reporter. "People aren't paying attention."

"They may come to rue that inattention," he said.

"Wait until this school funding thing pops," he said, referring to the court order to pay more to New York City schools. "Somebody is going to have to come up with billions in school aid for this."

Then the reaction will likely be, he said, "Holy smokes. Look at what they just did."

One thing that has changed little in the last few years is the status of minority-party legislators. Since their votes are seldom needed to pass bills Silver and Bruno favor, they have sharply limited power, especially in the Assembly, where the GOP has only 45 of the 150 seats. But Senate Democrats are also essentially irrelevant on most issues as well. An exception was a bill passed in 2005 allowing emergency contraception pills to be sold over the counter. Only 10 Republicans—and 25 Democrats— voted for it, while a majority of Republicans said no. But Pataki then vetoed it.

There also isn't the cautioning factor of majorities worried about how minorities are treated, as there is in Congress and most other states, since they could end up on the losing end after the next election. Those power flips don't happen in Albany.

There are broadly speaking three ways that lawmakers deal with being a minority. One is to be mostly quiet, work behind the scenes and hope to influence issues indirectly. Another is to do little and just collect a paycheck. A third is to be vocal about problems, forcefully debate bills even though it is almost always a futile exercise.

Richard Dollinger, who represented a portion of Monroe County from 1993 to 2002, fell into the third category.

Here is what happened to him.

While packing up his office near the Capitol in late 2002 after deciding not to seek a sixth two-year term, Dollinger, a 53-year-old lawyer and former newspaper reporter, came across a chattering-teeth toy.

He placed it on a box cover and watched it scurry along, opening and closing.

"Maybe that's the most fitting memento of my career," he said, self-mockingly.

Since arriving in the Legislature a decade earlier, Democrat Dollinger arguably uttered the most words on the floor of the Senate of any of his colleagues.

Many were loud. Some were said in anger. Few were for bills that the Legislature passed.

How loud?

While debating a gun-control bill with Velella, the since-disgraced Bronx Republican, they both got so loud that the senator presiding over the session, Randy Kuhl, R-Hammondsport, Steuben County (now a member of Congress) slammed down his gavel hard enough to break it into pieces, which went sailing away from the podium.

"That's the only thing that got us to quiet down," Dollinger recalled.

How angry?

During a Senate Health Committee meeting in 1995, Dollinger attempted to question then-state Health Commissioner Dr. Barbara DeBuono about a $28,000 payment she received even before taking her job. The money came from Pataki's inaugural committee, which, Dollinger pointed out to DeBuono, was funded in large part by tobacco and drug companies.

The Republican committee chairman, Kemp Hannon of Nassau County, ruled him out of order, as Dollinger loudly protested. Finally, he got up and left. "For that performance, Senator Dollinger deserves a good spanking," Hannon said.

How futile?

Like the other Democrats in the Republican-controlled Senate, Dollinger got few bills enacted with his name on them. In fact, some obviously routine measures, like allowing a town he represents, Brighton, to set up a trash-collection district, were vetoed by Pataki.

"That was a rude awakening to the harmful effects of partisan politics when it's aimed at a legislator," said Brighton town Supervisor Sandra Frankel, a Dollinger ally, who pointed out that such routine local matters are almost never vetoed.

Dollinger also was a champion of rules changes to increase the power of individual legislators, changes that have gone nowhere, and also pushed hard in 1997 for voters to approve a constitutional convention. That idea got less than 40 percent of the vote in a referendum.

In addition, he was one of the Legislature's most outspoken opponents of casino gambling. Lawmakers approved the creation of six new casinos in 2001.

Dollinger did all this in a sometimes lecturing style that did little to sugar-coat his message. Still boyish-looking if jowly, Dollinger was a formidable figure on the floor, and has a strong voice that easily filled the Senate chamber.

Some Republicans found his style exasperating, and they retaliated.

Dollinger once sponsored what seemed like a political no-brainer: a bill to rename four state office buildings after four famous New York women: abolitionist Harriet Tubman, suffragette Susan B. Anthony, settlement-house founder Mother Cabrini and former first lady Eleanor Roosevelt. But the Republicans wouldn't allow a vote on it.

"The Republicans rejected it out of pure malice," Dollinger said. "It was too good an idea for them to accept and condone a Democrat having."

But a GOP spokesman said the Senate's "Women of Distinction" program has already honored those women.

"There are better ways to honor these women than to just name buildings after them," said spokesman Mark Hansen. He added that the state office building in Poughkeepsie is already named after Roosevelt.

Dollinger became such a target for the Republicans in part because he so openly took them on.

In 1995, he protested a delay in the Senate adopting limits on assault weapons in the wake of a multiple murder of children in New York City by putting a sign on his desk that read "Day 1." He explained that was the number of days the Senate was "holding the state hostage" by not passing the bill.

Kuhl, then the presiding senator, ordered the sergeant-at-arms to remove the sign, while Dollinger complained that his First-Amendment rights were being violated.

Then Dollinger started to wear a smaller sign on his lapel. He finally gave up at day 100.

Later, he guzzled milk on the floor to show his support of dairy farmers—but also his opposition to the creation of a cartel that he said would drive up milk prices that Republicans supported.

Despite his conflicts with Republicans, Dollinger left on good terms with many of them.

"He would have made a great judge," said Velella, the former Bronx lawmaker who got into the heated exchange with Dollinger that led to Kuhl breaking the gavel. Dollinger lost an election for a Monroe County Court judgeship in 2002.

"I have a lot of respect for the guy," Velella said. "He's one of the brighter people we've had around."

But Pataki never warmed to him after Dollinger sued the governor to get him to make public the records of who contributed to his 1994 inaugural committee. The suit was dismissed in state Supreme Court.

"Richard who?" asked Pataki spokesman Joseph Conway, when asked if Pataki had anything to say about Dollinger's exit.

Nor were Dollinger's relations always smooth with fellow Democrats.

At a Senate Finance Committee meeting in 2002, he was trying to question the head of the state Human Rights Division about the agency's backlog of cases. Two Democratic senators, one of whom admitted to being a friend of the commissioner,

Evonne Jennings Tolbert, joined with Republicans to cut him off.

"I'm disappointed we can't have a legitimate debate about the future of an agency when 8,000 people have been waiting a decade for justice," Dollinger said then. "They won't even allow the questions to be asked. It's outrageous."

In 2001, Dollinger was the Senate Democrats' representative on the panel that drew new legislative district lines to conform to the 2000 census results. Democrats had high hopes that population gains in Democrat-dominated New York City and losses in Republican strongholds upstate would give them a chance to take the majority even though Republicans have through the years skillfully gerrymandered districts to hold onto their seats.

The Democrats were again outfoxed in 2001 by Republicans, who held dozens of hearings that Dollinger sat in on regarding various plans to redraw the existing 61 districts. Then at the last minute they laid out one with 62 districts (the constitution doesn't call for a fixed number of seats in the chamber). It gave most of the Republican incumbents new districts even more immune to challenges than they were before. At the same time, they changed Dollinger's district enough so that it was attractive for Joseph Robach, a popular veteran assemblyman who was planning to switch from Democrat to Republican because of an ongoing feud with Silver, to challenge Dollinger (Robach had been a "Bragmanista").

"I wanted competitive districts, but all I got was one—mine," Dollinger joked ruefully.

He decided to quit rather than fight for the seat against what he saw as an overwhelming financial advantage to Robach, who was elected by a huge majority in 2002 over political newcomer Harry Bronson and easily won a second term in 2004.

"I think its safe to say that I'm done," Dollinger said when asked if he might run for public office again. He said he's glad to pass the torch to other reform-minded lawmakers.

"I think it takes new members with new ideas and new initiatives to make it happen."

Even within the constraints of a strong-leader system, individual lawmakers in the majority parties can influence legislation, although in the end it's the leaders who call the shots.

In 1996, two lawmakers decided they wanted the state to crack down on bootleg cigarettes and to work together to get a bill passed to do that. They also decided to let a reporter sit in on normally private meetings—the forum for virtually all serious discussion at the Capitol—in exchange for a pledge not to write anything about it until the issue was decided.

Here is the story of their bill, which illuminates how the Albany system works.

The dining room of the Mansion Hill Inn Restaurant may not qualify as a classic smoke-filled room, but it was where the two lawmakers had their first conversation about the issue while they were puffing on cigars one cold February evening.

The process ended, as is so often the case, in the middle of the night in the middle of the summer, with bleary-eyed lawmakers paying scant attention to what they were voting on, unanimously adopting the measure.

In between, in a process officials say was not unusual, the original plan was drastically overhauled, leading the Senate sponsor to charge he had been double-crossed and the Assembly sponsor to complain that the legislative staff has too much power.

The path of the bill also illustrates the power of lobbyists, the behind-closed-doors style of negotiating that characterizes most talks, the overwhelming power of legislative leaders to shape decisions and other characteristics of the Albany system of lawmaking.

It also shows how the often-disparate interests of New

York City and upstate, as well as Republicans and Democrats, are resolved, how concerns of citizens are translated into action and how the persistence of individual lawmakers pushing a bill can make a difference.

The bill was one of 5,152 introduced in the Legislature in 1996, and one of 811 to pass both houses. In 2005, a total of 14,926 bills were introduced in the Senate in the Assembly. Only 882 passed both houses.

The problem of untaxed cigarettes being sold was brought to the attention early that year of two lawmakers, Sen. Thomas W. Libous, R-Binghamton, and Assemblyman Jeffrey Klein, D-Bronx, by constituents who were being hurt by it.

Libous, 51, married to a nurse and the father of two sons, was then a four-term senator and former Binghamton City Council member. He has been re-elected five times since and is considered a contender to become majority leader when Bruno retires.

His constituents include Joseph and Thomas Mirabito, who ran a string of convenience stores.

"They've been telling me for a long time that they have to compete against stores that sell untaxed cigarettes," Libous said. The Mirabitos complained to Libous that some competitors buy their cigarettes on Indian reservations, where the state's $7-a-carton tax isn't levied because state law doesn't cover them. Then they're resold to retailers at a substantial discount.

Klein, 44, a lifelong Bronx resident, has the same problem on a far bigger scale in his north-central Bronx district, where Italian homeowners, Jewish shopkeepers and Hispanic merchants give the area more stability than many upstaters think of when the Bronx comes to mind. (Klein was elected to the Senate in 2004, taking Velella's former seat after five terms in the Assembly.)

One summer day, five of six stores Klein visited with a reporter sold him cigarettes without the stamps showing the state and city tax had been paid. Most came from Virginia, where the per-carton tax is only 25 cents. Interstate 95, the main north-south road between New York and Virginia, is known as "Tobacco Road," Klein said.

"There are illegal cigarettes being sold all over the place here," said Klein, a former trial lawyer and Congressional aide.

A Democrat from the Assembly and Republican from the Senate interested in the same issue is vital for any idea to become law, because the majorities in both houses have to approve any bill.

The two had never met until February 1, 1996 when former Assemblyman Jay Dinga, R-Chenango Bridge, then like Klein a freshman assemblyman and like Libous a Broome County Republican, got them together outside the Assembly chambers.

"We knew right away we were on the same wavelength on this issue," Klein said.

The interest of both men was heightened when a news report appeared a week later, in which the state Tax Department estimated the state was losing $80 million a year in revenue.

Then a couple of weeks after that, Libous, a former smoker who still likes cigars, and Klein, another cigar smoker, ran into each other at the Mansion Hill Inn, a restaurant near the Capitol that has a monthly cigar night.

"We smoked cigars together and talked about it some more," Libous recalled.

On March 5th, Libous filed his bill. It called for tougher criminal and financial penalties for retailers who sell cigarettes without tax stamps, licensing of retailers and a 15-day suspension of that license for any retailer caught selling cigarettes to anyone under 21.

When it appeared on March 6th on a list of newly filed bills, it nearly spoiled the day of Constance Barrella. She was a lobbyist for convenience stores and former deputy commissioner of the state Department of Environmental Conservation. She's also the sister-in-law of Michael Finnegan, Pataki's for-

mer counsel. Finnegan is also a neighbor and close friend of
the governor who now works for the Wall Street firm J. P.
Morgan.

What caught Barella's attention was the provision calling for a 15-day suspension for selling to minors.

"That's way too harsh," she said. She also was struck by
the $1,500 cost for the stores to get a license to sell cigarettes.

She immediately faxed a message to the 20 members of
her executive committee of the 3,500-member state
Convenience Store Association, telling them to write or call
Libous to say they didn't like the bill.

She also called Libous's office to ask for a meeting to
discuss the bill, which took place on March 18th. Other lobbyists concerned about the issue—Michael Rosen of the Food
Merchants Association and Brian Meara, who represented the
cigarette wholesalers—also attended.

"They asked good questions," Libous said, adding he
agreed that the $1,500 licensing fee seemed excessive.

Later that week, Klein held a hearing in lower
Manhattan in preparation to introduce his version of the
bill.

Presiding was Assemblyman Herman D. "Denny"
Farrell, chairman of the Ways and Means Committee, then
Manhattan Democratic chairman and now also state
Democratic chairman. His presence was a sign to Klein that
Silver was interested in the issue.

He was especially heartened to hear Deputy State Tax
Commissioner Robert Shepherd say that the cigarette tax eva-
sion was costing taxpayers $82.5 million a year.

About two weeks later, on April 11th, Klein introduced
his bill in the Assembly. It was similar to Libous's, but didn't
include stiffer criminal penalties. It also included a 1-800 telephone line to call with reports of bootleg sales.

"I think hitting them in the pocketbook is the way to
go," Klein said. "We're not going to prosecute anyone in Bronx
County for selling bootleg cigarettes."

Before long, a snag developed. On April 15th, Libous got a memo from state Deputy Tax Commissioner Steven Teitelbaum, pointing to problems in trying to license all 22,859 retail cigarette outlets.

"If retailers were required to be licensed, and subject to the same pre-licensing screening which wholesale dealers are subject to, the department's registration units would be overwhelmed by the additional volume of required tax compliance and background checks," Teitelbaum said.

The Pataki administration, it seemed, was not on the same wavelength as Libous.

On April 23rd, Klein and Libous met in Libous's office with the lobbyists Barrella and Rosen, members of Libous's staff and two officials of the Senate Finance Committee, Leroy VanRiper and Mary Teetsel.

VanRiper was a key deputy of Abraham Lackman, the former New York City budget director who was then the Senate's top staff financial official and now a lobbyist for private colleges.

With the legal deadline for adopting a state budget already 23 days behind them, VanRiper and Assembly staffers had been meeting with Pataki's Budget Division officials, trying to sell them on the Libous bill as a way to raise as much as $82 million.

"Budget says we're losing $82 million a year, but they won't say how much we can recover," VanRiper told the lawmakers. "It's like fighting the marshmallow guy," since administration officials refused to be specific.

Libous and Klein decided to have VanRiper keep the issue open as part of budget negotiations.

Three weeks later, on May 14th, as the budget deadlock dragged on, the same group got back together without the lobbyists present. This time, Klein brought with him Laura Anglin, a tax expert from the Assembly's Ways and Means Committee, the equivalent of the Senate Finance Committee.

"There's a concern with the underage smoking piece," said the Libous aide Robert Nielsen.

"Let's take it out and put it in a separate bill," Libous said. "The crux of what we want to do here is collect this tax and raise some revenue."

"That's what's holding this up," Klein agreed.

Thus the provision most objectionable to Barrella's and Rosen's clients was out.

But there was still not much headway being made with the state Tax and Finance Department, Anglin and Teetsel, the legislative staffers, reported to the lawmakers.

Meanwhile, the administration had virtually finished work on its own version of the bill. To keep wholesalers happy, it included provisions to require wholesalers to obtain bonds to prove they had at least $25,000 in assets. That was designed to keep out fly-by-night operators who get a license from the state but then also sell bootleg cigarettes to retailers.

"We wanted something tougher," Libous said. "But this was something."

It also didn't have the licensing provision that Barrella and Rosen opposed; instead it would make retailers provide more information on their annual application for registration to sell cigarettes, which costs only $100.

But at this point, Libous and Klein were unaware that the administration had a plan ready to go.

It wasn't shared with them because the "big boys," as Pataki, Bruno and Silver are called, were squabbling over other budget issues, administration officials said.

Libous later described his style of trying to get a bill adopted as "to keep hammering away."

"Frequently, when you think there's a master plan, you pull back the curtain and it's the Wizard of Oz, meaning things aren't nearly as organized as one would suppose," said Nielsen, his top aide.

On May 22nd, the legislative leaders announced what

they called a "framework" for a budget agreement that included $20 million in revenue from the Libous-Klein bill.

This agreement virtually assured that their bill would be adopted in some form, because the leaders were counting on the revenue.

But Pataki didn't buy this package.

"Budget is stalling," Teetsel reported at the next meeting on the cigarette bill, on May 30th. Budget officials wouldn't tell VanRiper and Teetsel, or Steve Plydle, VanRiper's equivalent on the Assembly Ways and Means Committee, how much they thought the measure would raise.

That meeting on May 30th also had a new player: Marty Rosenberg, who worked for the Assembly Codes Committee. He raised a number of concerns about the criminal penalties. These concerns would later prove to be a major sticking point.

With Bruno promising to send the Senate home for the summer by June 14th, budget or no budget, Libous knew he was running out of time.

It wasn't until June 10th, when the leaders were again on good terms and making progress on the overall budget, that Libous got a copy of Pataki's proposed bill. Libous noticed immediately it excluded increased criminal penalties for selling bootleg cigarettes.

"It's a bit odd to have something like this just pop out," Nielsen said. "The most charitable explanation is they were too busy to call us and talk about it." The administration seemed determined just to go its own way and ignore the lawmakers' bills.

On June 14th, the day the Senate was scheduled to leave town for the summer, Libous's bill still hadn't shown up on a Senate calendar. But he talked that day to Lackman, who had great influence over what financial bills were considered, and was told that it would be brought up later that day.

However, Ronald Stafford, the Senate Finance Committee chair, told him he had a "problem" with the bill.

Libous went to Stafford's ornate office on the fifth floor

of the Capitol, where Stafford told him that some cigarette wholesalers in his district thought the bill would hurt their business.

"They didn't understand the bill. I just had to explain that it would probably help them, since it would drive their illegal competitors out of business," Libous said.

The Senate Rules Committee, which gives perfunctory review to measures Bruno wants to pass, adopted the bill with no debate around 7 p.m. Ninety minutes later, it passed the full Senate unanimously without debate.

Now it was up to the Assembly, which unlike the Senate was back in town the following week.

"We've agreed on all the amendments. It's all set to go," Klein said on June 19th. "I've been dealing with Fred Jacobs (then Silver's chief counsel). He kept telling me it was moving, but then I found out on my own it wasn't. . . . It just seemed like incompetence."

He was sure it would be approved by the Ways and Means Committee—a strong signal it would pass the whole Assembly—the next day or following week.

The next day, Klein found out his bill had been changed—it was no longer the same as Libous's.

"The staff around here has too much power," he said. "Fred (Jacobs) knows I've worked hard on this bill."

That night, the bill was considered by the Ways and Means Committee as the Assembly was trying to get its business done to leave town for the summer.

"I think we've got 70-something bills here," said Farrell, the committee chairman.

"We'll give them due consideration," joked Assemblyman Robin Schimminger, D-Kenmore.

"I misspoke," Farrell said. "We have 120."

"An act to amend the tax law. (Any) Negative votes. Bill reported," Farrell said without pausing for breath a few moments later as Klein's bill passed.

"Silver's people did a double-cross," Libous said when

he found out what happened. "They don't want to do the penalties. They think it's too harsh."

And since the Senate was coming back to the Capitol to do only budget bills, it seemed the Klein-Libous bill was dead, since the two houses had passed versions that were different.

But both Klein and Libous were still confident there would be an effort made to step up enforcement because the state needed the money.

On the night of June 25th, 86 days after the start of the fiscal year, Silver, Pataki and Bruno met behind closed doors in Pataki's second-floor Capitol office to try to reach a final agreement on how much revenue was available to spend.

They struck a bargain that the cigarette enforcement would be stepped up, and that it would raise an extra $10 million, with another $1.23 million in new revenue being used to hire new enforcement agents.

"We had talked about it at virtually every meeting," Silver said later. "There was never a disagreement about whether we should do it. There was disagreement over how much it would raise."

"After that (June 25th) meeting, the discussions changed from whether we're going to do it to how are we going to do it," VanRiper said.

Such a small matter could have been handled as a few lines in the overall budget bill, which runs hundreds of pages and is known as "the big ugly." But Silver and Bruno decided this would be a separate law.

"Jeff Klein had done a lot of work on the bill. I like to encourage younger members to be creative. It's important to show members creativity is rewarded," Silver said.

A new bill was drafted, largely the same as the one the governor's staff had written, and passed without debate in both houses, at about 10:30 p.m. on July 12th by the Senate and at about 2 a.m. the next morning by the Assembly.

It was one of 178 bills that were passed over two days

and overnight by the Assembly, which met for 30 hours straight before adjourning for the summer at 10:15 a.m.

The new law increases financial penalties for selling untaxed cigarettes, including the possibility that retailers could lose their licenses to sell lottery tickets and beer—two big profit items. The measure also added new requirements for wholesalers and the promise of stepped-up enforcement.

But not included in the bill were steps to curb underage smoking requirements for licensing of stores that sell cigarettes or increased criminal penalties for violating the law.

Klein and administration officials were generally pleased with the outcome, while Libous wasn't.

"Believe me, it's less than a compromise. It's not the bill I passed. It's not the bill I wanted," he said.

Postscript:

The measure, signed into law by Gov. George Pataki, largely solved the problem of bootleg cigarettes coming in from other states, Klein said in 2005.

"Threatening to take away the stores' beer and lottery licenses really did the trick," he said.

But then the problem arose in a new form: bootleggers reselling cigarettes purchased from Indian reservations, where by federal law they can't be taxed.

Klein sponsored another bill to fight that by banning private carriers like Federal Express and United Postal Service from delivering them.

But the bootleggers merely switched to the United States Postal Service, which can't be regulated by the states.

"What we really need now is federal legislation," Klein said.

And how did the legislative process change between 1996 and 2005?

"It's worse now," Klein said. "Back in those days, I

could do more negotiating on my own. Now it's more leader-
ship-driven than ever."

Bruno answers reporters' questions
(Photo by Mark Vergari)

Silver ponders an answer

The Assembly Chamber

(Photos by Mark Vergari)

Libous in his Binghamton office
(Courtesy of Sen. Thomas Libous)

Dollinger debating on the Senate Floor
(Courtesy of *Democrat and Chronicle*)

Sen. Jeff Klein
(Courtesy of Sen. Jeff Klein)

Part 2

☆ **The Problem** ☆

CHAPTER 3

UPSTATE JOBS:
"I NEED SOMETHING BETTER"

☆　☆　☆

On the morning of August 14th of 2003, a bubbly middle-aged woman walked into the conference room in a shuttered IBM plant outside of Binghamton, where about 20 unemployed people, mostly men in their 50s, had been comparing notes about their largely futile searches for jobs.

The woman, Myra West of the state Labor Department, had good news and bad news. One of their number, an aviation engineer, had just accepted a job with the Sikorsky Aircraft Corp. in Connecticut. But since his family wasn't willing to move, he would see them only on weekends.

"It'll be tough being away from home all week, but he'll look more attractive to his wife on weekends," she suggested brightly.

Some of the men in the room, in a former IBM plant in the Binghamton suburb of Glendale that now houses state Labor Department offices, smiled ruefully. They would take good news any way they could get it.

"We're all in the same boat. We're all sinking," one of them, Mike McManus, 59, of the Binghamton suburb of Endwell, said later. He did defense-related contract work for

30 years before being laid off more than 18 months earlier. His daughter left the area to take a public-relations job near Asheville, North Carolina two years earlier, and he said his son, who manages a local arts-and-crafts store, is thinking of following her.

"We're dead," said Ronald Regon, 57, of Binghamton, the shrinking Southern Tier city that is the epicenter of the statewide drop in manufacturing jobs. He had been out of work for 18 months after being laid off by the aerospace firm Lockheed Martin, where he worked as a designer. He left the area in the 1970s for a job in California, but family ties drew him back to Broome County in 1978. "The politicians are doing things as usual, even as the state goes down the tubes," he complained.

The Binghamton region has lost half of its manufacturing jobs in the last decade, and almost 10 percent just from 2002 to 2003.

Other areas of the state have been hit hard as well. Rochester, for example, long the most affluent region in the state north of Westchester County, lost 6,300 jobs in the year that ended on October 31, 2004, even as the state overall eked out a slight gain. Its flagship employer, Eastman Kodak Co., which two decades ago employed almost 61,000 people in the region, announced layoffs last year that will reduce the Rochester workforce to between 18,000 and 19,000 people.

Jobs that provide services like health care and fast food have replaced some of the Kodak losses, but younger workers are finding it's hard to live on their own—much less have a career—on the money they pay. Total wages dropped by 1.6 percent in the Rochester region from 2001-2002, according to a study done by the Fiscal Policy Institute, a labor-backed think tank.

"I want to make enough to live on," said Renee Lygas, a 25-year-old single woman living in East Rochester who had been making about $15,000 a year working at the front desk of local hotels for the past four years, and said she sometimes needs help from family members to pay for groceries. "But there doesn't seem to be anything around."

She is part of a generation that is fleeing the state in record numbers. Between 1995 and 2000, New York lost 150,000 people ages 25 and 34—the biggest drop in that age group of any state.

Like several other people interviewed, Lygas said she wanted to stay in the region because she has family and friends there. But those ties were fraying.

Her 54-year-old father, a longtime toolmaker for the Xerox Corp. in Webster, was laid off in 2002 and moved to Florida. And one of her best friends recently moved to Baltimore where her husband finally landed a job after being laid off 18 months earlier by Kodak.

"Looking in the paper today, there was nothing for what I'm working for, she said one day last summer. "You can clean somewhere, or get a part-time job. That's not doable for me."

In 2004, she moved to Texas to take a better paying job.

If New York is a frustrating place to look for a job, it can be even more frustrating for those trying to create them.

Roger Hannay, whose family has run a company that makes reels for hoses just south of Albany for almost 70 years, isn't ready to pull out. But sometimes he is tempted.

"If we were doing a 50-state search for a place to locate a business, New York wouldn't be near the top of the list," he said. "But we're staying here because we like it here and because of tradition. But you could build a strong economic case that we should leave."

The failure to rein in the cost of prescription drugs Medicaid purchases in 2003 wasn't the only, or even the most important recent failure of Pataki and the Legislature to stop the rising cost of government and the flight of business.

For Hannay, the biggest failure of lawmakers was their decision not to change lawsuit rules to give them protection against having to pay what they consider unfair awards.

He and other business leaders wanted the state to limit the time a suit can be brought for damages caused by their products. They also don't want a firm to have to pay the full cost of a settlement when it is only partly responsible.

"All of our pleas fell on deaf ears," he said.

Beyond the $2.8 billion in tax hikes voted in 2003, business and local government leaders said they were also disappointed that Pataki and lawmakers:

> Borrowed $4.2 billion to close the budget gap in the 2003-2004 budget year, ensuring that gap would remain in future years. The cash, borrowed from the payments the state is due over the next 17 years from tobacco companies in settlement of a lawsuit, was used to pay for on-going expenses—the practice that led to New York City's near-bankruptcy 30 years ago;

> Failed to enact any of the steps that local governments said were needed to help control taxes. Those include getting rid of a law that makes governments award four separate contracts for big public-works projects and another that gives a state panel the final say over the salaries of local police and firefighters. Another would have limited the payments of lawsuits by local governments in a procedure similar to one that limits awards against the state;

> Voted, over Pataki's veto, to take over $2.5 billion in New York City debt incurred in the 1970s and have it picked up by state taxpayers, at a cost of about $2.6 billion in additional interest over 30 years;

> Failed to enact limits in the length of

time injured workers can collect benefits—a provision unique to New York
that helps to account for workers'-com-
pensation insurance rates being out of
line with the rest of the country, even
though weekly benefits that are paid to
injured workers are below average;
> Left intact the "Scaffold Law" that makes
employers liable for all injuries incurred
by a fall on a work site—even if the person injured was drunk, under the influence of drugs or even trying to steal
property;
> Didn't change the "vicarious-liability"
statue, a law unique to New York that
makes car-leasing companies liable for
claims against their customers.   (That
law was eventually overturned by the
U.S. Congress.)

These results were particularly discouraging to business leaders because the state was in such bad condition that
some significant changes seemed inevitable. The collapse of
the dot-com economic bubble, the fallout from the 9-11 attacks
and the huge potential deficit seemed to bring things to a head.

Yet even the confluence of momentous events couldn't
shake the cement in Albany's political foundation.

"If ever there was an opportunity for the governor and
the Legislature to slice into the fat in state government, the
budget deficit was it," said James Roche, formerly president of
the Mohawk Valley Chamber of Commerce. "In my view they
blew it."

"It's amazing how incredibly resistant to change Albany
is," said Mark Alesse, head of the New York chapter of the
National Federation of Independent Businesses, a lobbying
group for small businesses. "Nine-eleven didn't change the
way we do business, the recession didn't change the way we

do business and the enormous deficit didn't either."

So lawmakers did nothing to change the most obvious cause in the state's overall poor economic performance over the last several decades, making it tougher for those in Binghamton and Rochester and elsewhere to start new careers.

"We're a high-cost state," said Rae Rosen, an economist with the Federal Reserve Bank of New York. "Right across the board we tend to be the highest or among the highest for wages, utilities and taxes. So it's difficult to either to get companies to replace here or grow new companies past a certain point."

Some of the costs that are out of line:

> Taxes: Average state and local taxes were the highest of any state in 2002, 31 percent above the national norm, according to a survey done by Economy.com, an economic-research firm. New York City is the nation's most expensive place to do business, with costs almost 32 percent above the national average;
> Unemployment insurance: The most costly and complicated system in the country, according to the Tax Foundation;
> Auto insurance: An average cost of $1,015 per car, second highest in the country, behind New Jersey;
> Workers'-compensation costs: third-highest per case in 2002, even though weekly benefits paid to injured workers are among the lowest;
> Electricity: second-highest at 11.6 cents per kilowatt hour, behind only Hawaii;
> Health-insurance premiums: third highest, at $8,227 a year.

With such costs, one might expect New York to be the most expensive place in the country to do business. But the Economy.com survey ranked it only the ninth most expensive.

But it turns out that's not such good news. The state owes its relatively healthy ranking in that category to the cost of labor—ranked 28th among the states. That means, as the Business Council's Robert Ward pointed out, that the wages and salaries New Yorkers are paid don't stack up well with the rest of the country.

The hopes of those who thought the state might be forced to rein-in state spending because of its dire financial circumstances were dashed in January 2001. That's when Pataki, again looking to shore up his re-election prospects, made a late-night back-room deal with the politically powerful health-care union, Local 1199 of the Service Employees International Union, that set aside about $1.8 billion for raises for its members over three years.

Although few can begrudge health-care workers more money, the flimsiness of the state plan to pay for it (depending on hikes in the cigarette tax and some one-time revenues at a time when finances were already stretched perilously thin) made it seem like a bad deal for taxpayers. Plus the funds were to be spent "off-budget," meaning they wouldn't be subject to normal fiscal controls, like a review by the comptroller.

The health-care bill, in typical Albany fashion, passed at 12:30 a.m. on January 16th of that year. The bill pages were still warm to the touch when lawmakers gave their approval, so recently had the bill emerged from the printing press. No hearings had been held, no committees had considered it and virtually no lawmakers had even read it.

When asked at the time why the bill was jammed through with no chance for public input, Pataki said he was interested in results, not headlines. (He said late in 2004 that he wants the program to become part of the regular budget process and it was included in the 2005-2006 budget.)

While that deal was clearly Pataki's doing, the higher

sales and income taxes enacted by the Legislature in 2003 were passed over the governor's vetoes. But legislative leaders pointed out that those hikes headed off steep increases in local property taxes and a deep cut in aid to local schools (about 70 percent of the money in the state budget goes to localities, mostly for education and health care) that would have taken effect had Pataki's budget plan been adopted.

"An educated workforce is one of the key things for a healthy economy," Silver said, in attempting to defend the tax hikes in economic terms. "It makes (the state) more hospitable for businesses."

A survey done by Economy.com showed that the state had been making progress in getting costs of doing business more in line with the rest of the country before those tax hikes. A decade ago the overall costs were 3rd highest among states, but had dropped to 7th highest by 2003. This drop was helped by labor costs that were only the 11th highest in the country. But now some fear that more recent actions will reverse that progress.

Meanwhile, the overall high costs make the state vulnerable to other states picking off New York companies, one economic-development official said.

"It's common knowledge in economic-development circles that New York is at or near the top of the list for other states to cherry-pick," said Roche, formerly of the Mohawk Valley chamber, who until about a year ago worked in Minnesota trying to lure firms there.

The business leaders think that the political clout of lawyers and the health-care workers' union largely account for the Legislature's failure to act on issues like making it harder to sue employers and trimming Medicaid spending.

"It's those that pay that get to play," said Alesse, the small business lobbyist who doesn't pass out much in campaign donations.

"It gives the appearance that they have turned the process over to special interests," said Daniel Walsh, head of the state's largest business lobby, the state Business Council, referring to the state's political leaders. "That's the disturbing thing to those who view the body politic from afar."

The state Trial Lawyers' Association spent more than $1.4 million in 2003 trying to influence state government in 2003 through lobbying expenses and campaign donations, according to a report from the New York Public Interest Research Group, a watchdog organization. That ranked fifth highest of any group behind three unions and the state Medical Society.

The health-care-workers' union that the business leaders decry, Local 1199 of the Service Employees International Union, ranked seventh, spending $1.276 million.

Walsh's group, the Business Council, ranked 11th, spending just over $783,000 on lobbying and campaign donations last year.

But that report overstates the financial power of the trial lawyers, since there are numerous groups on the other side of the issue, said Chris Goeken of the state Trial Lawyers' Association.

And Jennifer Cunningham of the 237,000-member Local 1199 said the spending her union advocates makes the state's health-care system stronger, which is an asset to the state's economy.

"Since the health-care industry is such a fundamental underpinning of the economy as well as a service that people need, it is highly irresponsible for the state to consider dismantling its health-care infrastructure to balance its books," she said.

One reason for the success of the trial lawyers and the health-care union at the Capitol is they're normally trying to prevent bills from passing, rather than pushing for any new measures.

"It's easier to play defense than offense," said NYPIRG's Blair Horner. "To play defense all you have to do is get one of the three major entities to agree with you (the governor,

Assembly or Senate), and you win," since any of the three can block passage of any bill. All three have to agree before anything new can be adopted.

While the pharmaceutical companies were successfully playing defense in getting the bill squashed that would have reduced the profits on Medicaid sales in New York, Nate Wright, a 40-year-old food-preparation worker at St. Luke's Hospital in Utica, was trying to play offense—to advance to a job that pays enough for him to support his five children.

He made $13.50 an hour before being laid off two years ago from the Utica Boiler Co. He makes $7.50 an hour now.

"I'm definitely trying to get something that pays more," he said, with words that could be echoed by thousands of New Yorkers. "I need something better."

Job Creation in New York

New York lags behind the nation as a whole in its rate of job creation. Downstate is New York City, Long Island and Westchester, Rockland and Putnam counties.

	Sept. 2004	Sept. 2003	Percent change	2003	1990	Percent change
Total jobs (in millions)						
NYS	8,444	8,388	0.7	8,400	8,212	2.3
Upstate	3,111	3,105	0.2	3,097	2,995	3.4
Downstate	5,333	5,283	0.9	5,307	5,217	1.7
U.S.	131,939	130,135	1.4	129,931	109,487	18.7
Private sector (in millions)						
NYS	7,006	6,942	0.9	6,918	6,739	2.7
Upstate	2,496	2,486	0.4	2,461	2,391	2.6
Downstate	4,510	4,456	1.2	4,457	4,348	2.8
U.S.	110,467	108,820	1.5	108,356	91,072	19.0
Manufacturing (in thousands)						
NYS	595.5	611.6	-2.6	614.6	983.1	-37.5
Upstate	357.9	365.4	-2.1	367.6	528.9	-30.5
Downstate	237.6	246.2	-3.4	247.0	454.2	-45.6
U.S.	14,453.0	14,441.0	0.1	14,525.0	17,695.0	-17.9

Source: Federal Bureau of Labor Statistics

Ron Regon checks for job openings online

Mike McManus talks about job prospects

(Photos by Mark Vergari)

Renee Lygas has moved from Rochester to Texas
(Photo by Will Yurman)

Nate Wright is looking for something better
(Photo by Trevor Kapralos)

CHAPTER 4

WHY THEY'RE LEAVING:
KODAK-FUJI

For 20 years, Patricia Archetko of Rochester worked for the Eastman Kodak Co., long the economic anchor of the Rochester region. But when the film giant decided to make single-use cameras in Mexico and China instead of Rochester in the summer of 2003, she found herself out of work.

"I'm 50, on my own, and my health insurance is about to run out," said Archetko, who used to make about $600 a week from Kodak. "They took my job. China took my job away from me, and I'm an American."

But while Kodak found it too expensive to keep making the cameras in New York, resulting in the loss of about 500 jobs, its bitter rival, Fuji Film, Inc., is still making them in the small South Carolina city of Greenwood, a former textile center not far from the Georgia border that is trying to remake itself as a high-tech manufacturing mecca.

Although global economic forces, rather than New York business policy, have shaped Kodak's decision, the jarring comparison between the Kodak and Fuji single use camera factories illustrates what has been happening in New York for decades. The state is losing manufacturing jobs at a more drastic rate than anywhere else in the country.

That trend has led to hardship for thousands of New Yorkers like Archetko, who have seen their economic security suddenly dashed.

Meanwhile, the Fuji plant is providing steady paychecks for people in South Carolina.

Todd Dalton, 38, is a Greenwood native who used to work at a textile factory. When it closed five years ago, he was hired as a supervisor in the Fuji camera plant, one of eight in the Japanese firm's complex on the outskirts of town.

"It worked out well for me that the job opened up just as my old plant was closing," Dalton said one day while taking a break at the plant. "It allowed me to stay in my home town and still make a good living," said Dalton, who is married and has one child.

Kodak officials insist that their decision to ship the 500 jobs overseas had little to do with the cost of doing business in New York. But the company's top manufacturing official also said that the state's climate is not as good as that in other states where the company does business, and that New York regulations can present a problem.

In South Carolina, meanwhile, the state goes to extraordinary lengths to lure and keep manufacturers—even, in the case of Fuji, spending about $1 million in taxpayer money to send hundreds of workers back to Japan for six weeks of training. The state picks up the tab for air fare, hotels and all other expenses.

"It seems like a lot of money going out the door, but payback is well paying stable jobs," said Fuji spokesman Craig White. New York has no comparable program.

It's not just Fuji that sends its workers overseas at the expense of South Carolina taxpayers for training. Michelin, BMW, Bosch and other foreign-based firms do the same thing.

"That's a big asset, and it's been a significant selling point for us trying to attract foreign companies," said South Carolina Commerce Department spokeswoman Clare Morris.

The Palmetto State spends about $6.5 million a year on a 43-year-old program designed to offer trained employees to a company when it first opens for operation. It has trained almost 200,000 workers for nearly 1,600 firms since it was launched by then-Gov. Ernest Hollings in 1961, who retired in 2003 after six terms in the U.S. Senate.

"Both South Carolina and North Carolina have very good reputations for having a community-college system that is focused on the needs of business and industry and are good at providing good, solid technical training," said Ray Uhalde of the Center for Workforce Development, a national organization that studies job-training programs. "New York's program has been improving, but its reputation isn't nearly as good."

Most job training programs around the country are funded by the federal government and are designed to help workers find jobs. The budget for the programs this year in New York is $162 million, with most of that going to help workers find jobs. But more unusual are ones built on the South Carolina model, which is helping businesses find workers.

"As a general matter, the Southern states have had a longer history of connecting work development and job development," said Jack Mills of Jobs for the Future, a 20-year-old nonprofit group that is trying to improve technical education. "North Carolina and South Carolina especially have seen workforce development and connected it to their economic-development strategy. . . . People are seeing this is a major competitive factor. Companies are making decisions on that basis."

The South has moved more aggressively on job training for its workers mostly because it had to, economic development officials said.

"This was the last part of the country to move from an extraction (mining) and agricultural economy to industrial," Uhalde said. The big concern of companies initially interested

in moving South to take advantage of the lower costs and lack
of unions was the skill of the workers.

One of those companies was General Electric, which
decided to move its gas-turbine-manufacturing business from
Schenectady to Greenville, South Carolina in 1967. The company got a five-year exemption from all property taxes—and a
promise that the state would provide a trained workforce.

"I don't believe there is anybody putting the focus or
emphasis on technical training the way we do," said Thomas
Barton, president of Greenville Technical College and part of
the group that lured GE south. "The basic philosophy is industry is the very backbone of what we're doing. Whatever we do
there will come back to us in spades."

"We do all the screening and basically hire the people
for them," Barton said of companies that move to the
Greenville area, the industrial center of the state that is about
50 miles north of the Fuji plants in Greenwood. "Whatever
they want, they get."

South Carolina isn't unique in paying for overseas
training for workers. Uhalde cited Kvaener Philadelphia
Shipyard Co. workers being sent to Sweden at taxpayer
expense—but it still is unusual and hasn't been done in New
York.

However, New York has embarked in recent years on
programs designed to be more useful to employers, spokes-
men for the state Labor Department and the state-run Empire
State Development Corp. said.

In 2000 the Legislature approved spending $34 million
over three years on a program known as STRAP designed to
help firms train workers. The most popular program run by
the Labor Department is called Building Skills in New York
State. It provides grants of up to $100,000 for companies for
training, said spokesman Robert Lillpopp. About 200 contracts
totaling $11 million have been awarded, mostly to small busi-
nesses.

The state also spent $5 million in taxpayer money to

train 1,000 workers for the new IBM computer chip-fabrication plant in Dutchess County, said Empire State Development Corp. spokesman Alex Dudley.

But business leaders say that generally the state-funded programs are not easy for them to use and are not as effective as they need to be.

"None of our members have mentioned to us that these programs are particularly useful," said Margaret Mayo of the state Business Council, the largest business lobbying group in the state. "The things I found relatively easily did not have any information about how a company can apply for this money."

The programs are "not as accessible as the employer community would have wanted them to be," said Brian McMahon of the New York State Economic Development Council, a group that promotes economic growth. "The application process turned out to be bureaucratic. It took longer than it should have—several months, instead of several weeks."

A report published in December 2003 by a Manhattan-based think tank criticized the state's job-training system as "utterly fragmented."

The think tank, the Center for an Urban Future, counted $1.3 billion in state and federal money spent on job training distributed through 59 different funding streams and administered by more than 200 agencies in New York.

"Right now there isn't anything that could be accurately described as a 'system,'" said John Twomey, who helped write the report.

Lillpopp, the Labor Department spokesman, called the report "dead wrong."

"No other state is doing more to provide job training to those who need it than New York is doing," he said.

Beyond training, South Carolina officials go to (by New York standards) extraordinary lengths to attract and keep foreign businesses.

In the fall of 2003, South Carolina Gov. Mark Sanford

joined several of his colleagues from the Southeast on a trip to meet business and government leaders in Japan and China. He came back with a commitment from one Japanese company, Suminoe, to open a plant to make seat covers in South Carolina that will create 130 jobs. He also announced a $70 million deal between the Chinese Rail Ministry and Harsco, a South Carolina rail-track company. The governors make the trip every odd-numbered year, with the Asian officials coming to the Southeast in the even years. Gov. George Pataki led a first-ever New York recruiting trip to Asia in the fall of 2005.

New York also has its own Japanese investment to brag about: $300 million that Tokyo Electron has pledged to spend on nanotechnology research in Albany. And an Israeli aviation company plans to move its aircraft-maintenance and repair facility from Miami to the former Rome Air Force base in Oneida County that will create about 500 jobs. Other foreign companies have also invested in the state.

But South Carolina has attracted more companies from overseas, relative to its size, than any other state. The 65 Japanese firms in the state have invested $5 billion in the state and employ 19,000 people, according to the South Carolina Department of Commerce. Overall there has been $18 billion in foreign investment.

"It's not just tax incentives, it's the human issue that bonds Japan to the South," said Yuji Kishimoto, a professor of architecture at South Carolina's Clemson University, who lived in the Boston area for a decade before moving south 24 years ago.

"It just feels more hospitable here," he said. "It's a slower pace, more welcoming people."

This hospitable climate gives South Carolina an edge in trying to hold onto and attract manufacturing jobs, which were plummeting nationally before leveling off recently. They're being fiercely sought because they pay more than service-sector jobs, like retail-sales positions and telemarketers.

Manufacturing jobs have been the backbone of the

upstate New York economy—and the main way into the middle class in New York City for immigrants—for most of the last century.

They're so desirable because they're relatively well paying and usually bring in money from outside the state. New York manufacturing workers made an average of $54,541 in 2000, compared to $38,317 for service workers, according to the state Labor Department.

But New York has been losing the fight for manufacturing jobs for decades.

The state lost almost 625,000 of them between 1975 and 2002, according to the federal Bureau of Labor Statistics. That's a drop of almost 44 percent, or five times the national rate.

The November 2003 announcement that the Everlast sporting-goods factory in the Bronx was closing, eliminating 100 jobs, made a splash because its boxing gloves and other supplies are world-famous. But, as Robert Ward of the state Business Council pointed out, the loss was nothing new in terms of the state's economy.

During the five years that ended in September 2003, Ward noted that the state lost an average of 100 manufacturing jobs a day—a drop from 798,300 to 615,400, according to the U.S. Bureau of Labor Statistics. The figure was down to just under 595,000 in October of 2004, according to the statistics bureau. In the year that ended that month, the state lost 2.7 percent of its manufacturing jobs even as they were growing slightly (0.3 percent) in the country as a whole.

South Carolina, which has seen most of its once-dominant textile industry move out of the country, also lost manufacturing jobs between 1975 and 2002. But the drop of 15 percent was just one-third the rate of the New York loss. Recently, as the textile flight has accelerated, the rate of loss has matched New York's.

An advantage that Fuji and other South Carolina firms have over New York is lower taxes. New Yorkers pay 12.3 cents of every dollar they earn in state and local taxes, compared to 10 cents in South Carolina, according to Economy.com, an economic consulting firm. That places New York second in the firm's ranking among states. South Carolina is 30th.

On Economy.com's "cost of doing business index," South Carolina ranked 29th, almost five percent below the national average, while New York was 8th, 8.5 percent above the norm. Besides taxes, the ranking considers the costs of labor and energy.

No employer in the state has shed more manufacturing jobs than Kodak. In 1981, the company had more than 60,000 workers in the Rochester area. It has announced plans to trim that to between 18,000 and 19,000. Its revenues have plummeted from just over $20 billion in 1992 to about $12.8 billion annually now. (The company has shed some chemical and consumer-products businesses in the last 11 years.)

"We just aren't going to need as many people working in the company in Rochester in the future as we have today," Kodak CEO Daniel Carp told the Rochester Democrat and Chronicle editorial board in the fall of 2003 after the company announced it was shifting its emphasis from its traditional film business to the already crowded field of digital photography.

The film business has been slipping for two decades, as people have shifted to the digital camera, which use a computer chip rather than film to capture images. Those images can be much more easily and cheaply manipulated before being printed and bypasses film, the product that has sustained Kodak for more than a century.

An exception to the slide of the film business has been the growth of single-use cameras. Consumers have been enthusiastic about buying an inexpensive camera already loaded with film and then returning it to a photofinisher with the film still in it. They get back prints and the camera goes back to Kodak, Fuji or other manufacturers to be recycled.

About 400 million of them were sold last year, with Fuji and Kodak the biggest suppliers.

But prices Kodak and Fuji can charge for the cameras began to plummet in the face of intense competition in the late 1990s.

"The (profit) margins are getting crushed," said Charles Brown, Kodak's head of global manufacturing. He said while five years ago the cameras sold for $10, but now sometimes retail for as little as $3 as cut-rate manufacturers move into the field.

Starting in 2001, the managers and workers did their best to cut costs to keep the Rochester operation, located at a plant on Lee Road in Kodak Park, competitive.

"We were pressed to produce more and more with fewer people," recalled Carmen Zoccali, 27, who worked in the plant for eight years before it closed. "It was hard, but we thought we were making progress."

But to Brown and other Kodak managers, the economics were stark: labor costs are about one-tenth in China, and one-quarter in Mexico, of what they are in New York. And while labor accounts for only 20 to 30 percent of the cost of the camera (materials and distribution are the rest), moving the manufacturing to China would make the cameras more profitable.

Brown said that while global conditions were the major factors in the decision to axe the Rochester jobs, business conditions in New York are far from ideal.

"We get tied up in the court system," he said. "We have a problem with frivolous class-action lawsuits in New York."

He cited a need for more "sensible environmental regulations," a reduction in paperwork and filing requirements and lower taxes to improve the business climate and help lure good workers to the state and keep them here.

Kodak has been fined millions of dollars by state and federal agencies for spills, toxic emissions and other environmental problems at Kodak Park in the past decade. Five families are suing the company for $75 million, claiming that emissions from Kodak facilities contributed to their children developing cancer.

Brown noted that emissions at Kodak Park have been cut by nearly 80 percent since 1987 and that the company has taken many voluntary steps to clean the environment.

"We believe our environmental record is a strong one," he said.

Fuji has not been cited for any environmental problems since it opened its doors in South Carolina in 1988, according to a state Environmental Conservation spokesman.

Brown also said business conditions have improved since Pataki took office in 1995.

In an interview, Pataki recalled that he talked to then-Kodak CEO George Fisher shortly after the governor was elected in 1994 about why the company built a new plant in Colorado rather than Rochester in the early 1990s.

"Yes, it's the economic structure of the state," Pataki recalled Fisher telling him, "and it's also regulatory. Colorado has very high environmental standards, as does New York. But we can get the plant done in six months in Colorado, and here it would have taken, if we were lucky, two and a half years. And in the market, we couldn't wait that long." (Fisher, now retired, declined to be interviewed.)

In contrast, Kodak was able to put up a new $200 million film-base manufacturing facility at Kodak Park in less than a year in 1996-1997, according to company spokesman Christopher Veronda, largely because state permitting processes had been streamlined.

But the state's more business-friendly environment didn't affect Kodak's plan to close the Lee Road plant in the summer of 2003.

The decision may have looked logical from the managers' perspective, but it still shocked Mike Flanagan, 40, who had put in 14 years with the company and figured he would retire from Kodak.

"I was with the company all these years, never called in sick, then they call us and say we're closing up shop," said Flanagan, who is single and lives in Greece just a few blocks from Kodak Park, the sprawling Kodak manufacturing facility. He made about $40,000 a year before losing his job.

"I'm a good worker. They won't fire me," Flanagan said he told himself.

Flanagan wants to become a financial planner (using the $5,000 educational grant Kodak gave him as part of his severance package). But he suffered a setback when he was in a motorcycle accident. Still, he's determined to eventually work for himself.

"I don't want to work for a company again," he said. I want to rely on a job I can do myself and not worry about a boss."

"If (downsizing) hits you personally, you don't really care much about the high-level vision of things," Carp, the Kodak boss, acknowledged. "You care about you personally. So, we'll continue to have to deal with that in the way we always have, which is, offer people transition training where we can" and give generous severance packages to those who are let go.

Flanagan and other laid-off workers got 60 days' pay, plus two week's salary for every year of service, or a total of 38 weeks in Flanagan's case. They also got paid medical benefits through the end of 2003, and the educational benefits were also available.

Nobody is talking about severance packages at the 500-acre Fuji complex in South Carolina (about one-fifth the size of Rochester's Kodak Park) where in 2003 the photo company announced a $100 million expansion to increase production of new x-ray film.

It brings the total investment by Fuji at the site to $1.4 billion since ground was first broken in 1988.

About $130 million of that was for Fuji's single-use camera plant, which opened in 1995. Neither Kodak nor Fuji will say how many cameras those plants produced annually. But one Wall Street analyst who follows the industry, Ulysses Yannas of Buckman, Buckman and Reid, estimated Fuji makes about 30 million of them a year in Greenwood and Kodak made about 25 million in Rochester.

One reason nobody is talking about layoffs at the Fuji single-use camera plant is there are so few people there in the first place.

While about 500 people were needed to keep Kodak's plant in Rochester operating around the clock seven days a week, the head count at the Fuji plant, which also never closes, is about 170.

A visit to the plant shows why: it seems almost deserted.

"No human hands touch these cameras from the time the plastic is molded until they're wrapped and packed for shipment," said White, the Fuji spokesman.

("We prefer to invest in people rather than machines," Kodak's Brown said, when asked why Kodak didn't go the heavy-automation route.)

Those touring the Fuji plant have to be careful to avoid miniature-train-like devices that shuttle parts from bins to machines and from one machine to another. What starts out as raw plastic (most of it retrieved from cameras that have been returned for recycling) and pre-made parts like the flash moves from one line to another in the 150,000 sq. ft. plant until they're ready to be shipped.

There are 35 or so "associates" in strategic points in the plant around the clock, mostly monitoring the machines, repairing them and making sure they're supplied with raw materials and parts. They make between $27,000 and $32,000 a year—good salaries by local standards.

One of them is Kyle Neal, 35, an 11-year Fuji veteran who inspects the flash attachments that Fuji buys to put on the cameras. He also repairs machines.

Like most of the other Fuji workers, Neal works an

unusual two-week schedule: three 12-hour days, 7:30 a.m. to 7:30 p.m., then two off; two 12-hour nights, 7:30 p.m. to 7:30 a.m., then three off; two days on, two days off. Then the reverse of days and nights for the next two weeks.

Neal, who is married and has two children, 9 and almost 4, said he gets by on five hours of sleep.

"The only bad part is working nights and being away from my family," he said. On the other hand, Neal says that "If I want to take off for a few days, I can" since he has several days off in a row frequently.

"It's a long day," said Donna Brooks, 34, another Fuji worker, who has a 14-year-old daughter and a 10-year-old son. She keeps tabs on the machines that mold plastic.

But the schedule allows her to do some volunteer work at her children's school.

"Is the work demanding? Yes," said Peter Arnoti, head of the Greenwood Alliance, an economic-development group, and the key figure in luring Fuji to the area. "It's not all hunky-dory. It's not a punch-in, punch-out work environment."

Allison McAlaster, 28, a mother of two children, 12 and 8, and a Fuji plastic-molding technician, would agree with that.

"I came from working in a doctor's office, so the night shift was really rough on me in the beginning," she said.

But she has a steady paycheck, good benefits and grandparents who watch her kids while she's at work.

"I feel very lucky," she said.

Kodak bilingual symbol

Kodak Park in Rochester

(Photos by Jamie Germano)

Kodak's headquarters, a downtown Rochester landmark
(Photo by Will Yurman)

Kelya Cubi stacks Kodak single-use cameras at a Kodak Park plant
(Photo by Aimee K. Wiles)

The Fuji single-use-camera factory in Greenwood

The Fuji Greenwood complex

(Photos by Mark Vergari)

Peter Arnoti in downtown Greenwood

Donna Brooks, a molding technician at the Fuji plant,
helps daughter, Dayla, 14;
also at the table is her son, Kelvis Louden, 10
(Photos by Mark Vergari)

<u>Top:</u>
Tod Dalton supervises
production of Fuji
one-time-use cameras

<u>Left:</u>
Yuji Kishimoto, Clemson
professor, "It's not just the
tax incentives, it's the
human issue that bonds
Japan to the South. It just
feels more hospitable
here."

(Photos by Mark Vergari)

Part 3

☆ **Where the Money Goes** ☆

CHAPTER 5

THE MONEY PIT:
MEDICAID

☆ ☆ ☆

When she turned 100 in 2002, Gladys DeWitt felt well enough to get up and dance. She enjoyed her birthday cake as people made a fuss around her and a newspaper photographer snapped her picture.

But she couldn't have what she really wanted for her birthday.

"I wanted to go home," she recalled in 2004, lying in her bed in the van Rensselaer Nursing Home just a few miles from the state Capitol.

But like most of the 360 other residents of the county-run facility, she had no home to go back to. It had been sold long before when she could no longer take care of herself.

Now, she depends on Medicaid, the taxpayer-supported health-care-insurance program, to pay for her care.

While she is well cared for, she is not happy to be where she is. Nor are taxpayers happy to be footing the bill.

Every day she has been at the home, a little more than two years, Medicaid has paid the home $159.85, or more than $58,345 a year. In 2003 alone, nursing homes in New York got $7.4 billion in Medicaid funds to care for about 88,000 residents—about 78 percent of all people who live in nursing homes.

Exploding Medicaid costs are a problem everywhere in the country, but it is most severe in New York, which spends far more than any other state, about $44.5 billion.

"Medicaid is the biggest reason our taxes are the highest in the country," said Robert Ward of the state Business Council.

Only in 2005, under pressure from counties, the federal government and the media, has the state begun to take steps that have the potential to at least slow its growth.

"When you look at the Medicaid system, you realize pretty quickly that what we have is a system that is designed to make payments," said Sen. Raymond Meier, an Oneida County senator and former county executive who was the co-chair of a Senate task force set up to look at how to control costs.

Maybe most discouragingly, the system may be losing billions to fraud.

A Brooklyn dentist billed Medicaid for 991 procedures she claimed to have performed in one day. Van services give rides to people who can walk. Students who might not even need it are enrolled in speech therapy classes. One doctor prescribed $11.5 million worth of drugs, ostensibly for AIDS patients, which were then diverted to body builders.

These were some of the horror stories disclosed by *The New York Times* series in July 2005, which also said that some officials think fraud could be taking between 10 percent and 40 percent of the money spent on Medicaid.

State Health Department officials grumbled, mostly to themselves, that much of what *The Times* wrote about, including the alleged abuses by the Brooklyn dentist Dr. Dolly Rosen, was already known to them and that they were going to be prosecuted anyway. But they also understood there was no way to win a public relations battle taking the position that fraud allegations are overblown.

Shortly after those disclosures, Pataki appointed a relatively low-level official, Kimberly O'Connor, 36, a lawyer who was working in the state's Department of Criminal Justice Services as Medicaid inspector general. She is also a former Schenectady County assistant district attorney, and a former assistant counsel in Pataki's office.

"Those individuals who commit Medicaid fraud will be investigated and brought to justice," she said when she was appointed in August 2005.

But some doubt how much influence she can have, since she comes to the job with no background in Medicaid and no money for new investigators. She'll also likely be out of the job at the end of 2006 when Pataki leaves office.

Lawmakers also voted in 2005, after years of resistance, to limit the choice of drugs Medicaid patients can have for common ailments, like arthritis or ulcers—a step most private insurers took years ago.

It was still unclear, however, whether a potential loophole written into the law that gives doctors the final say over the choice of drugs will significantly erode the savings, which some officials think could top $100 million a year.

"There's no overnight cure for out-of-control local Medicaid costs," Sen. George Winner, R-Elmira, reminded his constituents when detailing Medicaid changes made by lawmakers in 2005. But he said at least the state is on course to rein in costs.

Democrats point out that Pataki's active encouragement of expanding the Medicaid rolls is a major reason for the current crisis, and that only three years ago he signed a deal with an influential union that added billions to health-care costs.

Still, the biggest expense in Medicaid is paying for long-term care—for people like DeWitt, a former seamstress who loved to swim and ice-skate in her hometown of Troy until just a few years ago.

Three levels of government split the cost of her care:

Washington pays almost $31,000 a year, the state almost $22,000 and Rensselaer County about $5,000 through Medicaid.

The price tag for the 3.7 million New Yorkers (one in every five residents) covered by Medicaid is helping to balloon the federal deficit and widen the state budget gap. But it is being felt most acutely at the county level, where spiraling Medicaid costs are driving double-digit property-tax hikes and sales-tax increases.

"Medicaid is killing us," said Rensselaer County Social Services Commissioner John Beaudoin, sounding like county officials all over the state. Like many counties, Rensselaer, which has about 154,000 residents, spent every nickel collected in property taxes in 2003, about $31.5 million, on Medicaid.

Many counties enacted either big hikes in sales-tax rates or big property-tax hikes in 2003, which has led some county executives into the unlikely role of revolutionaries.

One wanted to start his own Medicaid program. Another threatened to work to defeat incumbent state legislators unless changes were made. The head of the counties' lobbying group wanted the state to freeze the counties' Medicaid bills. That idea, with modifications, was eventually adopted.

They found themselves in that role because they were in probably the most uncomfortable place in New York politics: the intersection between Medicaid and property taxes.

"The greatest job-killing tax is the property tax," said Republican Chemung County Executive Thomas Santulli, who wants to scrap Medicaid altogether and develop a new health-care plan for poor people in his county of about 90,000 people centered around Elmira near the Pennsylvania border.

"People have connected the dots," he said. "They understand that Medicaid is the reason their property taxes are going up."

Santulli's county raised property taxes by 14 percent

last year and the sales tax by a percentage point to keep pace with the growth of Medicaid. Virtually all of the $21 million the county raised in property taxes was spent on Medicaid he said, leaving sales tax receipts to pay for most other county services.

The local share of Medicaid costs in New York has exploded in the last few years, going from $4.35 billion in 2001 to $6.3 billion in 2004. That's a rise of one-third in just three years.

Nassau County Executive Thomas Suozzi, a Democrat, thinks that the counties' problem is political as much as fiscal. He said since county officials pose no threat to state lawmakers (the way health-care unions and provider do) they feel no compunction about voting for extra benefits that add to the counties' expenses.

"Albany is a horrible, rotten, terrible, broken system," he told a group of government reform advocates in the fall of 2003. "The problem is these guys are not threatened." He vowed to make them pay in last fall's elections. Two of the candidates he backed won.

Suozzi said his county faces a $90 million budget gap caused by the state in 2004: $50 million in increased Medicaid bills, $20 million in higher health insurance premiums for its workers and $50 million more in contributions to the state public-employee pension system.

New York is one of only a handful of states that require localities to pick up any of the costs of Medicaid. That was done in part because New York City gets about two-thirds of all Medicaid dollars upstate and suburban lawmakers were wary of shipping so much money from other parts of the state into the five boroughs when the program started in the 1960s.

That's still true today.

If the state were to assume the entire non-federal share of Medicaid now, as the county executives want, taxpayers outside New York City would have to contribute $1.9 billion more through their state taxes to Medicaid programs within the city than they would save on their local taxes by having local Medicaid costs removed from them, according to an analysis by the state Business Council.

This is one instance when it seems that the interests of county executives, who are sick of trying to explain why they're raising taxes and want the state to take the Medicaid burden off their hands, and upstate taxpayers who would pay even more in total taxes if that happened, diverge.

But if the state took over the whole non-federal share of the program, overall costs might come down because Pataki and lawmakers would be more careful about how the money is spent, the head of the state Association of Counties said. And limiting the counties' payments would be a first step.

"The counties are more determined than ever," Robert Gregory, former executive director of the state Association of Counties said in 2004. "We need a cap."

The counties now pay 10 percent of the long-term care expenses and 25 percent of most other Medicaid programs. While the growth of the long-term care expenses has moderated, the programs the counties pay a quarter of have been shooting up.

They're programs like prescription drugs, managed care and reimbursements for physicians, said the association's fiscal expert, Kenneth Crannell.

He added that while the state has been able to save money by shifting the cost of mental health and mental retardation patients off of the state general expense ledger to Medicaid, counties have to pick up part of that expense.

"We're our own worst enemy" in terms of driving up Medicaid costs, he said.

Although most counties have seen big jumps in their property tax levies, that hasn't translated into dramatic increases in most property tax bills. County taxes account for an average of just under 20 percent of a total tax bill. School taxes take the biggest bite, and city, town and village taxes also account for a significant share.

A cap is what they got. Pataki and lawmakers agreed that the increase in the local share would be no more than 3.5 percent starting in 2006, and 3 percent in 2008 and later years.

To pay for at least part of the extra state share—because the costs of Medicaid are almost sure to rise faster than 3 percent a year—the state is counting on savings to be identified by a commission Pataki established in 2005 to decide which hopsitals and nursing homes should be closed.

Extra beds, experts agree, are a major factor in driving unnecessary spending, with potentially tens of thousands of beds to be declared surplus. But getting health care officials to agree on which ones to close has stymied earlier attempts.

The trick to this commission is that Pataki and the Legislature have to accept or reject the whole list the commission presents—like federal military base-closing commissions.

This will likely kick up a political firestorm that Pataki will avoid. The final recommendations are to get accepted or rejected by the end of 2006—just as he is leaving office.

While others are talking about making relatively modest changes in the program or simply rearranging how it's paid for, Santulli wanted to do something far more dramatic.

He planned to set up a committee of doctors, nurses, pharmacists, Medicaid recipients and others to figure out how to fix it. He wanted to have a plan ready by August of 2004 to run for two years and serve as a test to see if the changes they recommended could be implemented statewide. But the idea stalled when the state failed to issue the needed approval.

Suozzi's rebellion had mixed results in the 2004 elections. One of his Assembly candidates in Nassau County, Chuck Lavine, did topple a Democratic incumbent, David Sidikman, in a primary.

It's not just county budgets that Medicaid has been devouring. The state portion of the Medicaid tab is expected to approach $14 billion this year—a total nearing the amount of money the state spent on education. For decades education has been the biggest state expense.

Even the federal government, facing record budget deficits, is looking for ways to slow the growth of the $280 billion program.

The spending in New York dwarfs that of any other state. Twelve percent of all Medicaid dollars in the country are spent in New York, even though we have only about 6.5 percent of the nation's population.

Making the problem worse is the fact that the federal government pays only 50 percent of New York's share. Mississippi, in contrast, has 80 percent of its Medicaid funding paid for by Washington.

State officials say the formula Washington uses to pass out Medicaid funds, which uses average wealth as a key criterion, should be thrown out. They point out that, although New York has more rich people than most other states, we also have an above-average proportion of poor people (about 16 percent compared to the national average of about 13 percent).

"It would be political malpractice to let the federal government off the hook," said James Tallon, the former Assembly majority leader from Binghamton who is now president of the United Hospital Fund, a Manhattan-based group that analyzes health care.

But so far the feds haven't budged.

Further clouding the future of Medicaid and all health care in general is that in 2011, the first of 76 million members of the baby-boom generation will turn 65 and put unprecedented stresses on the system.

"The debate now is: how is the baby-boom generation going to pay for the expensive years of its health care?" Tallon said.

☆

For now, many elderly people and their heirs are doing what they can to see that taxpayers keep picking up the tab. And a small army of lawyers is doing what they can to help.

"No way around it, nursing homes are a huge expense," estate-planning lawyer Phillip Tribble told about a dozen people sitting in a nondescript Holiday Inn meeting room just off a Thruway exit in Kingston, a small Hudson Valley city, one afternoon last winter.

"One of the ways to pay for it is out of your own pocket," he told the group, most around retirement age. "But there are other options."

And it's the "other options" that the people wanted to know about at this seminar, one of a regular series that Tribble's law firm and scores of others hold across the state.

Tribble is an "elder-law attorney," someone well versed in the details of the state's Medicaid law. What he was selling that day, as thousands of other lawyers are every day in the state, are legal ways for people to hold onto their assets, while still meeting the legal definition of poor, which they have to do to qualify to have taxpayers pay for their nursing-home care.

The financial stakes are huge, both for the individuals and for taxpayers.

The per-day cost of nursing-home care ranged from $192 in the Buffalo region to $306 a day on Long Island in 2002, according to the state Partnership for Long Term Care. That translates into annual rates of $70,000 to more than $111,500.

But relatively few people—less than 15 percent of the 110,000 nursing-home residents in the state—pay for it themselves. For more than three-quarters of the residents, taxpayers, through the Medicaid program, pay the bill.

That translates into a whopping $7.4 billion a year.

"By default, Medicaid has become the main insurer of long-term care in this country," said Carol Raphael, president of the Visiting Nurse Service of New York, the largest provider of home care in the country. "That was not the intention when it was created in 1965."

A nursing-home resident on Medicaid can have only $3,950 in assets and $50 a month in income to qualify. The resident's spouse who is still living in the community can have $2,319 in monthly income and between $74,820 and $92,760 in assets, plus a house and a car.

But there are legal ways around those limits.

For instance, there is a technique called "spousal refusal," where someone headed to a nursing home can transfer all of his or her assets to a spouse—who can then refuse to pay for the wife or husband's care, making him or her "poor" under the Medicaid definition.

"You just sign a piece of paper. Even if they have $1 million," Audrey Toussaint, another elder-law attorney, said on a radio show in Albany.

Or here's another tip that Tribble gave to his audience. Say you gave your son $800,000 35 months ago. If you applied for Medicaid today, you would have to disclose that gift, since the law requires you to report all financial transactions within the last 36 months. That would make you ineligible for Medicaid for more than the next five years.

But if you wait just two more months, it would be beyond the so-called "look-back period," and you wouldn't have to disclose it. You'd be eligible for taxpayer support immediately.

"They never see the $800,000 gift," Tribble said.

Some see moves like this as a taxpayer ripoff.

"It's absurd. It's a taxpayer subsidy of private inheritance," said Carl Young, president of the New York Association of Homes and Services for the Aging, a lobbying group for nursing homes. Many of the group's members are nursing-home owners strapped because while the number of private-paying residents is shrinking, the Medicaid payments they get fall short of meeting the cost of care.

Young himself is facing a potential problem trying to arrange care for his mother.

"We could have her deed over to me and my brother

her house, and then she'd be eligible for Medicaid sooner," he said.

But then he added, "I do that, I'm the biggest hypocrite in Albany, and that's saying something."

A group looking at the Medicaid system last year for Pataki found a couple of instances of rich people using loopholes to transfer the cost of care of their spouses to taxpayers.

In Nassau County, according to a report issued by the group, a man wanted to donate $1 million to a university to have a bench named in his memory. He refused to pay for the care of his wife in a nursing home so he would have the cash to make the donation.

In another case cited in the report, the wife of a New Jersey man who was injured while on a business trip in Suffolk County had his assets transferred to her. She then refused to pay for his care, most of which was provided in Rockland County. New York got stuck for the $800,000 tab. If he had been hospitalized in his home state, his wife's assets, under New Jersey law, would have been counted in determining whether he was eligible for Medicaid.

Pataki has proposed closing what he calls loopholes that allow for such situations. If they are closed, "people with financial means will not be eligible for Medicaid, except under very limited exceptions authorized under federal law," according to the Medicaid-study group.

But there's another way to look at it.

"Take money away from the woman who's left (at) home? I think that's unbelievable," said Michael Burgess, executive director of the New York Statewide Senior Action Council. He said that impoverishing the spouse outside the nursing home would just make two people dependent on taxpayers instead of one.

There are no recent figures on how many nursing-home residents shelter assets or much money is involved. Young said studies in other states show that the numbers are probably substantial.

But Howard Krooks, chairman of the Elder Law section of the state Bar Association, which opposes tightening the eligibility rules, pointed to a 1993 study done by the federal General Accounting Office that estimated only one in 10 nursing-home residents transferred assets.

He also defended the rule that allows spouses to keep their assets while Medicaid pays for the care of an ailing partner.

"It prevents the healthy spouse from being pauperized," he said. "If they had to spend all of their assets (on their sick spouse) then most likely they would become a public charge."

Although some wealthy people do manage to keep hundreds of thousands of dollars for themselves or their heirs, most trying to shelter some of their assets are of far more modest means, Krooks said.

"This really is a middle-class issue," he said. "Most of my clients have $200,000 to $300,000 in assets."

All sides agree with the Pataki task force's idea that steps need to be taken to encourage people to buy long-term-care insurance. The state Long Term Care Partnership offers policies that protect assets, but so far has sold only about 40,000 policies, too few to have much of an impact. Tax breaks or other incentives are needed, advocates say.

"If we don't change, there aren't going to be enough taxpayers to keep the system viable," Young said. "You can't sustain a system that gets 70 percent of its money from government. That's a train wreck."

Meanwhile, people continue to consult lawyers on how to take advantage of the current system. Those at Tribble's seminar learned that his firm will prepare a Medicaid application for them for $4,700, and set up an asset-protection trust for another $3,100.

☆

Despite the huge Medicaid expense, the state hasn't done enough to see that the money is well spent, critics say.

"I always thought we had a bad Medicaid policy, but I discovered we have no policy," said Meier, the Oneida County senator and Medicaid expert. "That's the problem. There's no coherent set of principles and policies that guide the system."

Meier, who wrestled with Medicaid as a county executive before being elected to the Senate, added, "We decide a whole bunch of people are going to be eligible, we decide they can access a whole bunch of services," he said. "So we set up a system that provides those services. But no one asks questions about who's using services or why there are more hospitalizations in one county as opposed to another."

It's no mystery where the money is going.

New York spends by far the most in the country on nursing homes and other kinds of long-term care, like home visits from nurses. It also spends the most on hospitals, in part because New York City is the doctor-training capital of the world.

Almost 10 percent of New Yorkers over 65 are either in nursing homes or getting services at home, according to an analysis done by the Center for Governmental Research, a Rochester-based think tank. That's more than double the rate for the other large states the center used as points of comparison.

But those costs have been going up relatively slowly in the past several years, as new services have diverted thousands of seniors away from the homes.

What has led to the current crisis is a huge runup in the overall number of recipients, which exploded from 2.7 million four years ago to more than 4 million now. In addition, like other states, New York has had to deal with a rapid escalation of prescription-drug costs.

The number of people on Medicaid has been going up so rapidly in part because of decisions made by people like

Lisa Sivers, a 32-year-old mother of three who lives in Binghamton.

She makes between $15,000 and $20,000 a year driving a bus for a preschool program while her 48-year-old husband stays home to care for their three boys, aged 8, 9 and 12.

Her employer offers health insurance, but she would have to pay about $40 every two weeks to get that coverage.

"That may not sound like a lot, but we have five people to feed," she said.

So instead about five and a half years ago, she signed up for Family Health Plus, a new Medicaid program available to so-called "working-poor" families like hers. Unlike the regular Medicaid program, there is no limit on assets, like a house and car, that recipients can have.

The income limit for the normal Medicaid program for a family of five is less than $12,000 a year, but for Family Health Plus, the limit for that size family is just under $29,000.

She said the program has been important for her family. Recently her husband, who has diabetes, had a stent installed to open an artery, and he also needed to get new eyeglasses.

"It's been a lifesaver," she said.

But the program has helped to put serious holes in the budgets of counties, which have had to pay 25 percent of the cost. But starting in October 2005, the state was scheduled to pick up the local share. The state pays its share with the proceeds of a 55-cent-a-pack hike in the cigarette tax enacted in 1999.

"The state is providing an enormous incentive for employers to point people to Family Health Plus," said E. J. McMahon of the Manhattan Institute.

Family Health Plus has enrolled about 325,000 members, spurred in part by an aggressive TV-advertising campaign featuring Pataki. New York City advertised a plan called Health Stat to get people signed up that the state also helps to pay for. It cost more than $2 billion last year.

The thinking behind that program and other taxpayer-backed plans, like Child Health Plus, which insures children whose families have incomes too high for Medicaid, is that providing them with insurance will in the long run save money and improve lives by reducing serious illnesses and also cutting down on the charity cases that hospitals have to treat.

But, as McMahon pointed out, there's no evidence yet that has happened, and in the meantime taxpayers are footing the bill.

Pataki's former top health adviser acknowledged that Family Health Plus has grown significantly and its costs have to be reined in.

"That is why the Governor proposed changes to the program to reduce its cost and make it more like the type of insurance most working families have," said the former aide, Robert Hinckley, who now works for a health-maintenance organization.

The Legislature went along with some of Pataki's plans to reduce some Family Health Plus benefits, as well as closing eligibility loopholes and capping marketing costs. But lawmakers watered them down so they will save only about $49 million, according to the Center for Governmental Research.

The center also noted that, more ominously, while the Legislature agreed to shift around some funding for Medicaid from the counties to the state, there was still little commitment to actually holding costs down.

The recent surge in enrollment sparked by Family Health Plus added costs on top of a system that already was by far the most extensive and expensive in the United States.

Why New York spends so much more than any place else, especially California, can be traced to the origin of the program, a key Great Society initiative of President Lyndon Johnson passed by Congress in 1965.

It was a ground-breaking piece of legislation designed to have the federal and state governments share in the cost of making top-quality health care available to poor people. Medicaid was the lesser publicized half of Johnson's health-care plan, which also included Medicare, the health-insurance plan for people over 65, regardless of income.

"You've got to remember who were the governors then," Tallon said. "Ronald Reagan (of California) and Nelson Rockefeller (of New York)," the leaders of the conservative and liberal wings of the Republican Party at the time.

"Reagan's attitude was 'we're not going to take a nickel, we're not going to spend a nickel,'" Tallon recalled. "Rocky's was 'we're going to take every dollar from Washington that we can, and spend what we need to get it.'"

Almost from day one, New York, which already had an extensive system of publicly financed health care, was the most aggressive state in designing programs that Medicaid would help pay for, even if it cost a dollar from state and local tax-payers for every "free" greenback coming from Washington.

"The problem with that approach is after a while it's like shopping at too many sales," Meier said. "You still go broke. . . . We've become addicted to Medicaid."

From the beginning, New York has offered more serv-ices to more people than most states, now ranging from smok-ing cessation to Viagra, while at the same time being more aggressive than most in figuring out how to get every possible nickel out of Washington. (Viagra was available even to con-victed sex offenders through Medicaid until May of 2005, when an audit by State Comptroller Alan Hevesi found 198 offenders were getting the drug and Pataki issued an executive order banning it.)

For example, the state used to pay for its extensive mental health and mental retardation treatment system out of state tax dollars. But now $7.2 billion of it is paid for by

Medicaid—which means Washington foots more than half the bill.

"Most states don't have the capacity or the ideology or the inclination to maximize federal aid the way New York does," said John Rodat, a health-care consultant, former state Budget Division official and Medicaid expert.

But that mindset clashed almost from the beginning with concerns about how to pay the half of the costs that Washington requires states to pay. Almost no one envisioned Medicaid growing as big as it has.

"I asked what the price tag was going to be. It was a rule of the Senate you could get the cost of any item coming up for a vote," recalled former Sen. William T. Smith, R-Big Flats, Chemung County, who was the only vote against the program that Rockefeller pushed through the Legislature on April 29, 1966.

Smith, who served in the Senate from 1963 to 1986, held the bill up until the administration came up with a cost estimate: $66 million, which turned out to be $36 million below the cost the first year.

Smith said he voted against it because he feared the costs could get out of control.

"It didn't take too many brains to figure it would be a big one," he said. "If they had told the truth, they might not have passed. . . . I wish they could figure a way to control it. But I don't think they can."

In his first State of the State message in 1995, Pataki said, "the Medicaid system has grown far beyond its original intent as a provider of care for the needy. Its costs have become staggering and the quality of care it provides leaves much to be desired. . . . Today, New York's Medicaid system costs three times as much per recipient and often delivers a quality of care inferior to the programs run by other states. We can do better and we must."

When he made that speech 11 years ago, the cost of the program was $23.5 billion—compared to $44.5 billion this year.

That's not to say he hasn't had success in reining in costs. Between 1997 and 2000, when the state's economy was booming, welfare rolls were shrinking and managed-care plans were squeezing hospitals for lower rates, the number of Medicaid recipients actually fell, from more than 2.9 million to 2.73 million, and the cost went up a not unmanageable rate of about 4 percent a year.

But then the economy turned down, the World Trade Center was destroyed by terrorists, hospitals and doctors started to demand higher payments from HMOs, the cost of prescription drugs started to take off—and the state as well as New York City started to actively push people to enroll. Costs jumped from $32.5 billion to $42.1 billion in just three years.

When the state was facing a potential budget gap of more than $11 billion three years ago, Pataki proposed $1.3 billion in health-care cuts that would have led to the loss of 38,000 health-care jobs. In response, health-care unions as well as hospital and nursing-home executives led a throng of 25,000 people to the Capitol, where they marched and chanted against the cuts in a snowstorm.

The Legislature rejected most of the reductions Pataki proposed, in a prime example of why the politics of the state make it so hard to control Medicaid spending.

The demonstration on that snowy day was led by Dennis Rivera, president of one of the most politically powerful unions in the state, the 250,000-member Local 1199 of the Service Employees International Union, who uses a huge political war chest and the energy of his members to push government leaders for more government spending on health care.

"There is no effective opposition to him," said McMahon, referring to Rivera.

Part of what makes Rivera such a powerful political figure—and Medicaid such an important issue for him—are two key facts: Medicaid accounts for about one-third of all health-care spending in the state; and the 1.17 million-worker health-care industry, where employment grew by 1.7 percent last year, is one of the few areas of the state economy that is adding jobs.

As a result any substantial cuts in Medicaid would mean the loss of thousands of jobs that are protected by powerful labor unions.

Rivera, a charismatic 56-year-old native of Puerto Rico who has built his health-care workers' union into one of the most potent political forces in the state, is a major reason why spending on health care has gone up, even as state tax revenues have gone down.

Wielding the huge campaign war chest that he gets in $5 monthly increments from about half of his union's members, Rivera has made his union a force by going after politicians rather than health-care facilities for money—in fact, by forging unlikely alliances with his members' bosses to get that cash.

And in a dramatic break with the history of his union, he has sometimes sided with Republicans in campaigns—Republicans who are sympathetic to his union's interests.

Using those weapons, he has not only repelled most attempts to curb Medicaid spending, he has also persuaded Pataki and lawmakers to expand health-care coverage even in lean economic times.

"He's become a national figure on the strength of what he's been able to do in Albany, largely with New York State taxpayers' money," McMahon said.

Rivera sees his role in different terms.

"We're fighting for the health care of the people of New York, and for the welfare of our members," he said.

It makes sense for Rivera, who has been the union's president since 1989, to go after politicians rather than health-care institutions because the institutions depend so heavily on government support.

In fact, the state and federal governments provide hospitals directly with 70 percent of their income, and through their influence over insurance rates, have effective control over the rest, said Kenneth Raske, president of the Greater New York Hospitals Association and a Rivera ally in the fight to get more money out of Albany.

"It's clear that most of the controlling factors in health care emanate from government—either Albany or Washington," Raske said. "Government really affects the health-care system more than any other industry."

So rather than use the traditional non-government-worker-union tools of strikes, boycotts and other job actions, Rivera's union buys TV ads, lobbies, contributes to campaigns and sends thousands of its members to the streets distributing pamphlets and running phone banks either directly for the issues they're pushing or for candidates they're supporting.

Raske said the alliance he has struck with Rivera is unique, giving them together far more power than their peers in other states.

"People all over the country are really amazed when we talk about it," Raske said.

"Basically we have an understanding that both management and workers get up in the morning and try to improve health care," Rivera said when asked to explain the alliance.

Rivera is in a unique position to influence state government, according to an analyst who follows state and city politics closely.

"Rivera has a strong hand that he plays very well," said the analyst, Fred Siegel, of the Progressive Policy Institute, a Democrat-leaning think tank. "He has what both parties need: the troops. Neither party has a ground operation any more. Dennis realized that and he stepped into the vacuum."

The TV ads are also an important weapon, Siegel said.

"When he ran the ads (in 1996, opposing Medicaid cuts)

he scared the hell out of the Pataki people and they haven't challenged him since," Siegel said.

The union has a string of successes to show for its efforts:

> ➤ In 1994, his union beat back an attempt by then-Gov. Mario Cuomo to cut Medicaid spending by $400 million, and did the same thing two years later when Pataki tried to make cuts;
> ➤ In 1999, as part of an alliance with hospital owners, he and his allies spent $10 million on TV commercials pushing a plan to raise the state cigarette tax by 55 cents a pack to pay for health insurance for those who couldn't afford it. Pataki and the Legislature approved it;
> ➤ In 2002, the union and hospital management teamed up again to persuade Pataki and the Legislature to spend an extra $3 billion on health care over four years, much of it for raises for Rivera's members, even though the state was looking at a multi-billion-dollar deficit. The deal again raised cigarette taxes as well as assessments on health-care providers.

Rivera later that year stunned Democrats by endorsing Republican Pataki, whom he calls a "close friend," in his campaign for a third term over Democrat H. Carl McCall— the first time the union had ever backed a Republican for governor.

In 2003, in a weak economy with the state facing a multi-billion-dollar deficit, Rivera and his hospital allies failed in their efforts to persuade Pataki and the Legislature to enact the new fee on businesses that didn't offer their workers group health insurance.

Rivera views the plan as a way to "stop free-loaders from passing on the cost of health care to taxpayers."

But the head of the state's leading small-business group said the plan would unfairly penalize small entrepreneurs and others already struggling with the high cost of doing business in New York.

The idea is "a well intentioned but poorly thought out plan that could only do damage to the small-business community," said Mark Alesse, head of the state Chapter of the National Federation of Independent Businesses.

But behind Rivera are the 250,000 members of his union, who pay 2 percent of their salaries in dues (the average salary is $38,000 and the maximum dues are $75 per month). That's in addition to the political-action fund that half of them pay into.

"We have $1.5 million in the bank, and more money is coming in every month," said Rivera's top political aide, Jennifer Cunningham.

That dwarfs any political muscle likely to be on the other side of the issue.

Cunningham said the union is pressing constantly to get more members to pay into the political-action fund. It is also trying to sign up new members, with 30 full-time organizers in the field, who are mostly located upstate.

There are about 600,000 health-care workers in the state, "and our goal is to represent every single one of them," Rivera said, adding that the union is adding 15,000 to 20,000 new members a year.

"He's always pushing," McMahon, of the Manhattan Institute, said of Rivera. "He won't be stopped until everybody runs out of money."

The trouble is not that Rivera and his union are so aggressive, Siegel said, but that there's no strong political weight on the other side of the issue to balance the debate.

"We're a public-sector-run state," he said. "Wall Street is our biggest industry, but it's completely detached from the rest of the New York State economy. To the extent that they are attached, they're wealthy and powerful enough to cut their own deals. So there's no counterforce (to Rivera) in Albany. That's a deep structural problem New York has."

Nor does it seem sometimes that Albany has any counterforce to the pharmaceutical industry, which has reaped tens of millions in profit from the Medicaid program, where the cost of prescription drugs is one of the fastest growing costs.

Here are the politics behind that soaring cost.

For several nights early in June of 2003, about 20 people filed into a small office under a stairwell near the Senate chambers in the state Capitol.

The mission of this group of lawmakers, legislative staffers and Pataki aides was to perform a modest trim from the enormous ($6 billion) bill New York taxpayers were paying out for prescription drugs for poor people through the Medicaid program.

The job was urgent, but also seemed eminently do-able, even in a New York Legislature that was so frequently gripped by partisan bickering and paralysis.

Even the fact that the officials were meeting behind closed doors late at night bode well for the potential success of the negotiators. One rule of thumb in Albany is the more important the issue and the more likely a bill will be passed, the more secretive the discussions and the more worn out the negotiators have to be.

The negotiators were working on a proposal, one that originated with Pataki and would limit the selection of drugs for the more than three million New Yorkers who get benefits from Medicaid, the federal program for health insurance for poor people. Washington pays about half the cost, with the state and local governments splitting the rest.

Thirty other states, some not nearly as fiscally hard-pressed as the Empire State, had already enacted something similar through what was known as a "preferred drug list."

The theory is that several brands of drugs, especially for common ailments like arthritis, high blood pressure and acidic stomachs, are all virtually equally effective. In New York, doctors could prescribe whichever brand they thought was best.

But if the state would require doctors to prescribe only one brand that Medicaid would pay for, the state Health Department could negotiate a steep discount from the pharmaceutical company that sells the drug because the state could guarantee such a big volume of business. Pataki estimated such a requirement could save taxpayers about $130 million a year.

Even advocates for those who use the drugs thought it was a good idea.

"I don't see any reason why you can't do this for cholesterol or arthritis or other common illnesses where the drugs are similar," said Michael Burgess of the Statewide Coalition for the Aging. "You have to do cost-saving somewhere and this seemed like a good plan."

"It's a terrific idea," said Senate Health Committee chairman Kemp Hannon, R-Nassau County, who was at the late-night meetings. "Most private health plans already do it."

The only losers in the plan appeared to be pharmaceutical companies that would be forced to provide the discounts if they wanted to keep the state's business, cutting into their profits.

In the end, the pharmaceutical companies prevailed in a way that illustrated why ideas that seem to have such common-sense appeal so often fail at the Capitol. Even in a time of dire fiscal crisis (the worst since the Great Depression, Pataki said) in a state already laboring under the highest tax burden in the country, a modest attempt to reign in costs died with the public mostly shut out of the process.

It is also a classic illustration of a new political phenomenon known as "astro-turf" lobbying. That's what you use when you need instant "grass-roots" support for an issue.

The blame in this case appears to falls squarely on the Assembly, since this was something both Pataki and Bruno wanted to do, although there's no way of telling if other snags would have developed later. Certainly the Republicans are willing to put all the blame on the Assembly.

"The Assembly was unwilling to legislate any meaningful program," said Robert Hinckley, then Pataki's top health advisor.

Medicaid is more important to Democrats than Republicans since not only are many of the people served by the program more likely to be Democrats, but so are the majority of health-care workers whose paychecks are provided by Medicaid.

The formal reason given for the demise of the deal was that the Assembly didn't like the idea of having cost-saving as the chief criterion for deciding what's suitable, said Assembly Health Committee chairman Richard Gottfried, D-Manhattan.

Another key objection was raised by Assembly Mental Health Committee Chairman Peter Rivera, D-Bronx. He issued a torrent of press releases that spring when the idea was under consideration, blasting what he called "prescription drug rationing" that would be "a dangerous step that will adversely impact the lives of millions of New Yorkers."

He objected to limiting the use of drugs that were used to treat mental disorders.

But when Pataki and Senate negotiators agreed to exempt such medications, he went further and said that the selection of drugs for other disabilities that mentally ill people are as likely to have as anyone else—like ulcers, high blood pressure and arthritis—shouldn't be limited either. That was unacceptable to the Republicans, and the notion that any limits should be imposed at all died.

Why was Rivera so adamantly against it? He said he didn't want poor people to have their drug choices limited.

But there may have been other factors at work as well.

Rivera was also chairman of the Legislature's Puerto Rican/Hispanic Task Force. Drug companies and their industry-lobbying association, the Pharmaceutical Research & Manufacturers of America, have given Latino community groups hundreds of thousands of dollars over the past several years.

Is there a connection between those donations and Rivera's efforts on behalf of those making them?

Of course not, Rivera said.

"Historically, pharmaceuticals have a large interest in giving out moneys to different groups—elderly, youth groups, so on and so forth," Rivera said. "The fact they may give money to the task force is not the reason I'm for or against the PDL (preferred drug list)," he said.

As an example of his objectivity, he cited his opposition to further deregulation of cable TV, which the cable industry wants in spite of the fact that those companies also give money to Hispanic community groups.

The state Mental Health Association, which lobbies for the mentally ill and their families, backed Rivera, in what could be seen as an example of astro-turf lobbying.

The group's then-executive director, Joseph Glazier, said the group opposed the drug list idea because it "protects pills and not patients."

He also acknowledged, however, that his group had received about $50,000 from the pharmaceutical industry, but said that the money hadn't influenced the association's position on limiting drug choice.

"We have a board resolution that says we will take no money intended to influence our policies," he said, adding that the drug company money amounted to only about 5 percent of the association's million-dollar annual budget.

Regardless, the association's opposition gave the pharmaceutical companies an instant grass-roots ally, which was critical since drug companies aren't popular among voters.

Despite the board of the mental-health association's resolution, could there be a connection between its stance and the donations?

"Nationally, there has been a concern that some advocacy groups are affected by drug-company funding," Gottfried said. "Whether it's true of some groups in New York I wouldn't want to comment."

Certainly the drug companies didn't see any quid-pro-quo.

The pharmaceutical trade group gave money to the organizations because "we like to work with our allies," said Jeff Trewhitt, a spokesman for the Pharmaceutical Research & Manufacturers of America.

He said his group opposes the preferred drug list idea because the decision of what medications to prescribe should be left up to doctors.

Whatever the motivation, Rivera and Glazier played important roles in defeating the attempt to knock about $130 million off the state's stratospheric Medicaid tab.

Finally a compromise was reached in 2005. Over the objections of Rivera and others, lawmakers passed and Pataki adopted a preferred drug list. But it came with one important caveat: doctors in the end would have the final say—they could prescribe whatever drug they wanted if they thought it was in the best interests of their patients.

In the summer of 2005 the state Health Department was still studying how to implement the rule, so it was not yet clear whether giving the ultimate power to the doctors will mean that much of the projected savings will evaporate, as some critics fear.

Bigger money is at stake in efforts to care for people at home rather than in institutions, but homecare has its own set of problems.

One afternoon last winter, Natalia Mhlambiso, a South African native who is a registered nurse and works for the Visiting Nurse Service of New York, traveled to East Harlem.

She went there to look after a 70-year-old woman who had lost the use of her legs and most use of her arms after a series of strokes, and a 72-year-old man suffering from emphysema.

The woman that Mhlambiso visited, Doris Hasell, a mother of seven, spent some time in a nursing home after her first stroke about five years ago, but, as Mhlambiso cleared her breathing passages in her apartment, the patient talked about how much more content she is now.

"There's no place like home," she said.

One of the major challenges for those who want to reform the state's Medicaid system is to care for more people at home, like Hasell, and fewer in institutions, like DeWitt, the centenarian living in a home near the state Capitol. It would be both cheaper and better for the patients, advocates argue.

"We need to deliver more services at home," said Daniel Sisto, head of the Healthcare Association of New York.

That's one of the directions other states are moving in as they try to cope with the same cost pressures that are choking New York.

In Arkansas, Florida and New Jersey, some people who need long-term care are given the option of taking control of the money the care costs themselves rather than having the money put in a nursing home. They can hire aides, buy equipment or spend it on whatever else they decide they need.

In Arkansas, that has meant that some people who before needed help with cooking bought a microwave and others who couldn't do laundry on their own bought washing machines. Then they found they could live on their own.

In Maine, the state hired a company to help people decide what kind of care they needed when they were faced with the prospect of entering nursing homes. Nine years later, the state is spending less on nursing homes and more people are getting care at home.

In Arizona, a company gets a fixed amount of money for caring for those with long-term illnesses. Arizona has among the smallest proportion of its elderly population living in nursing homes of any state.

These states all have taken innovative steps in the face of the twin challenges of sharply rising spending on Medicaid and the desire of people to stay in their homes as long as possible.

New York is only now starting to emulate these innovators. A task force appointed by Pataki recommended that New York set up a program to help people decide what kind of long-term care they need, called NY-ANSWERS. The state Health Department is studying the idea, which is similar to the one Maine adopted in 1995.

Politics is the reason that New York has found it hard to be as innovative as other states, said the co-chairman of a state Senate task force studying Medicaid.

"Part of it is everything we do is so political it becomes very difficult to maneuver your way through the Medicaid system," Meier said, citing the unions, health-care officials and others that have a stake in the $42 billion system. "I've been in town (Albany) for seven years and I can't figure it out."

Hinckley, the former Pataki health-care adviser, disputed the notion that the state has not tried innovative approaches to improve care and cut costs.

He said the state had a foundation grant to set up a program similar to the ones operating in Florida, New Jersey and Arkansas, but it was abandoned because the massive personal-care system in New York City didn't fit the program. He added that the state does have a small consumer-directed care program that now has about 3,500 clients.

"We have tried many approaches, such as managed long-term care, personal-directed care, etc.," he said. "But (we) believe that now, more than ever, we need a system-wide reform. That is what has led to NY-ANSWERS."

The early results are promising for states ahead of New York in terms of improved care and greater efficiencies, although those involved in them caution that a lot of money won't be saved immediately.

"The results have exceeded our fondest expectations," said Kevin Mahoney, a Boston College social-work professor who is overseeing the experiments in Arkansas, Florida and New Jersey. "There have been gigantic improvements in client satisfaction, and the health outcomes have been either as good or better than the control group."

He has the most complete results for Arkansas, where the program started in 1999. He said the first year was more expensive because more people started using services, but those extra costs were offset by a decline in nursing-home patients in the second year, and that it's likely there will be a savings in the third year and beyond.

In Maine, spending on nursing homes declined 17 percent between 1995 and 2001, according to the state Department of Human Services.

"Back in the early to mid-1990s, there was a recognition that Mainecare (the state Medicaid program) was pursuing a course that was fiscally unsustainable," said state Human Services spokesman Newell Augur. "We needed to do a better job of allocating our resources, and also wanted to provide patients with better choices."

"We think this system has worked very well," said Steve Jennings of the Maine chapter of the AARP. "The key is it's provided by an objective third party, not by providers, so you get objective information about your options."

Arizona has kept costs down by holding the number of people in nursing homes to 1.1 percent of its over-65 population—compared to 4.5 percent in New York and a national average of 3.7 percent. Why the difference?

Before 1989, Arizona counties paid the whole cost of

long-term care. "We've always had a model that was based on people's desire to stay in the community," said Leonard Kirschner, who went to medical school in Albany and who ran the Arizona Medicaid long-term care system when it was established in 1989. "You've got big institutions and we don't. We never did," he said.

And then there's California, which has almost twice as many people as New York (36 million to 19 million) but spends less on Medicaid.

One reason for his disparity is that California pays less for care. For example, the state pays nursing homes a flat $115 a day for nursing-home patients, compared to rates that vary from $192 to more than $300 a day in New York.

The $115 a day is "ridiculous," said Ann Burns Johnson, head of California's nursing-home association. She said the actual cost is about $145 a day, with patients who pay out of their own pocket picking up the slack.

Since there is no allowance for high-cost areas, there are no nursing homes that depend on Medicaid in San Francisco— the land is too expensive.

She said there are also cultural reasons for the gap in Medicaid spending. For example, people of Hispanic and Asian heritage, who together make up half of the state (37 percent Hispanic, 13 percent Asian) usually care for their elderly relatives at home. And she said the state has a far more extensive system of private assisted-living facilities than New York.

New York spends so much more than California for three major reasons, according to Tallon, the United Hospital Fund president:

> New York has more elderly and disabled Medicaid beneficiaries;
> New York makes more extensive use of the program to pay for health-care costs, like mental health and mental retardation;
> Like the rest of the Northeast, people in

New York use hospitals more frequently
than those in the rest of the country.

"New York and California are the yin and the yang of
Medicaid," Kirschner said. "New York wants to suck up all the
money it can while California doesn't want all those federal
rules and regulations."

Or another way to look at the New York health-care
program is as the Yankees of Medicaid, in the view of one
analyst.

Like the Yankees baseball team, it's the biggest, most
expensive organization in its league. And by some measures,
like the number of people served and the pay it provides its
employees, it is the best program.

But Rodat, the former state Budget Division analyst,
health-care consultant and baseball fan, thinks the Oakland
Athletics—as cited in the best-selling book "Money Ball" by
Michael Lewis—would be a better model for New York to
emulate: excellent results at a modest cost.

"The Oakland A's are a small-market team, but they
win as much as the Yanks," he said. "If we get into the playoffs
for one-third the price, we'll be doing fine."

Of course, there are no playoffs in Medicaid's league,
which complicates the task.

"In baseball, but not government, there is a clear sense
of wins and losses," he said. But there are ways to measure
success—and ways not to measure success—in delivering
health care.

"The goal of Medicaid was to allow the poor and elderly to access mainstream medicine. We succeeded," he said. "So
we say, the more services we pay for, the more successful we
are. That's silly. Money is not a uniform indicator of the quality of care."

To support that point, Rodat points to a study done by a Dartmouth College medical professor, Elliott Fisher, which showed that despite a large per-capita difference in Medicaid spending between Manhattan ($10,550) and Portland, Oregon ($4,823), there was no difference in either the quality of care or patient satisfaction.

The study suggested that as much as a third of medical spending is wasted on services that don't improve the quality of care, and that some people would be better off if they saw their doctors less frequently.

Members of a task force set up by Pataki agree.

A key recommendation of the report it presented to Pataki last year called for people who need long-term care to get information and counseling that would steer them toward options other than nursing homes.

"The system will support self-determination, promote personal responsibility, provide services that meet consumer demands, provide quality care and affordability," according to the report. A Senate task force issued a similar proposal a few weeks earlier.

The recommendations also conform to a 1999 U.S. Supreme Court decision which requires states to care for the disabled outside of institutions whenever possible.

An estimated 10 percent to 15 percent of nursing-home residents could live in the community if there were adequate services for them, said Young, the president of the nursing-home trade group.

The state took a step in the direction of providing care for disabled people more efficiently in 2004. Lawmakers passed, and Pataki signed, a bill to allow the state to ask the federal government for permission to provide care for as many as 2,500 disabled people outside nursing homes on a trial basis.

The plan could save as much as $10 million when it's adopted, Young said. "This is the right concept," he added.

"They did something right this time," said Burt Danovitz, director of the Resource Center for Independent

Living in Utica, which aids disabled people. He has been a frequent critic of what he sees as state policies that force people
who need care into nursing homes when they would be hap-
pier and healthier if cared for in cheaper community settings.

As of early 2005, however, the state Health Department
had not yet applied for the waiver, and it was unclear when the
program would start.

Even beyond nursing homes, Rodat said the state could
save money just by looking more closely at patterns of illness
and treatment.

For example, in a study he did in 1992, he noticed that
children in the southwest corner of Niagara County were five
times as likely to be admitted to hospitals with ear infections
than children elsewhere in the state.

He found out that the area didn't have enough pri-
mary-care doctors, so that a problem treated as a routine doctor visit elsewhere required an expensive trip to the hospital.

"There are huge differences in how health-care services
are used around the state—differences that generally go unno-
ticed by the state Health Department," Rodat said. "We tend to
work off aggregate numbers and averages."

He added that the state could save money if it adopted
the successful strategies used in some areas, known as "best
practices."

Hinckley acknowledged that Rodat's analysis was
valuable, and is being looked at in the changes that Pataki's
task force wants to implement.

"Part of the goal is to adopt best practices," he said.

New York vs. the Nation

Here is how New York state compares with the rest of the country in some key measures of Medicaid spending. New York ranks No. 1 in spending in all categories compared with other states.

Total New York Medicaid spending: **$31.6 billion**
Total New York nursing-home residents: **114,141**

	New York	**National average**
2001 Medicaid spending*		
Per recipient	**$7,500**	**$4,600**
Per-capita long-term care	**$708**	**$264**
Per-capita nursing-home care	**$336**	**$150**
Per-capita personal care	**$98**	**$18**
Per-capita home-health care	**$55**	**$9**

Source: Center for Governmental Research
        Federal Center for Medicaid and Medicare Services

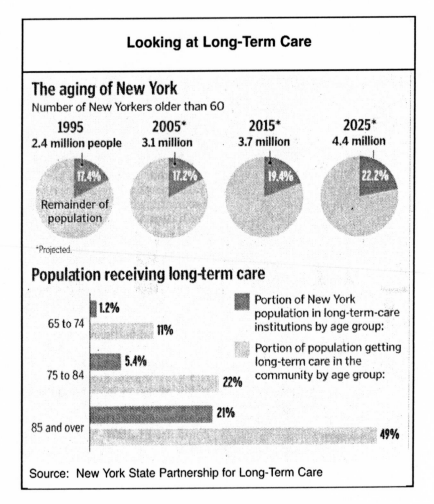

Looking at Long-Term Care

The aging of New York
Number of New Yorkers older than 60

1995	2005*	2015*	2025*
2.4 million people	3.1 million	3.7 million	4.4 million

17.4% 17.2% 19.4% 22.2%

Remainder of population

*Projected.

Population receiving long-term care

Portion of New York population in long-term-care institutions by age group:

Portion of population getting long-term care in the community by age group:

65 to 74
1.2%
11%

75 to 84
5.4%
22%

85 and over
21%
49%

Source: New York State Partnership for Long-Term Care

Medicaid Spending on Nursing Homes

Medicaid spending on nursing homes per capita, selected rates, 2001:

State	Amount	Rank
New York	$336.24	1
Pennsylvania	299.83	2
Connecticut	229.06	3
Louisiana	259.43	4
New Jersey	258.51	5
Massachusetts	223.31	8
Ohio	203.42	11
Florida	103.86	37
Texas	75.22	45
Virginia	73.51	46
California	73.31	47
Nevada	43.79	48
Utah	40.67	49
Arizona	2.31	50

Source: Federal Center for Medicaid and Medicare Services

Spending is Growing

How Medicaid spending and enrollment have grown in New York since 1995 (dollar figures are in billions):

Fiscal year	Enrollment	Total cost	Federal share	State share	Local share
1995	3.10 million	$24.1	$11.5	$8.9	$3.7
1996	3.05 million	24.4	12.0	8.8	3.6
1997	2.91 million	25.7	12.4	9.4	3.9
1998	2.83 million	27.6	13.5	9.8	4.3
1999	2.73 million	27.9	14.0	9.6	4.2
2000	2.73 million	30.1	15.0	10.4	4.7
2001	2.87 million	30.9	15.5	10.5	4.9
2002	3.40 million	33.4	16.8	11.4	5.3
2003	3.66 million	38.3	19.6	12.8	5.9
2004	3.70 million	42.1	22.5	13.0	6.6
2005*	3.70 million	42.7	21.9	13.8	7.0

* Projected
Note: Figures may not add up to total due to rounding.

Source: New York State Division of the Budget

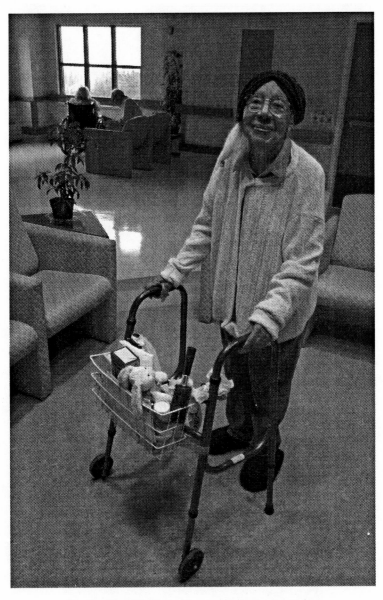

Gladys DeWitt has no complaints about her
nursing-home care
(Photo by Mark Vergari)

Lisa Sivers greets her son outside her Binghamton home

Howard Krooks worries about healthy spouses
being "pauperized"

(Photos by Mark Vergari)

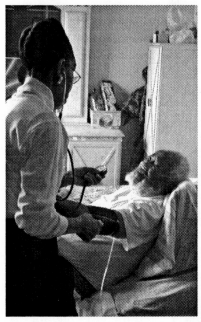

Natalia Mhlambiso
looks after a home-care patient
in the Spanish Harlem section
of Manhattan

Carol Raphael
runs the nation's largest
home-care service,
The Visiting Nurse
Association of New York City

(Photos by Mark Vergari)

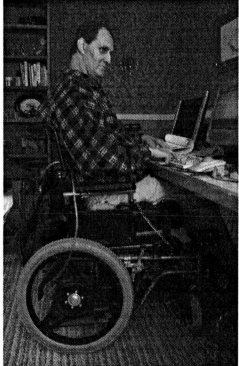

<u>Top:</u>
Burt Danovitz at the
Resource Center for
Independent Living in
Utica: "They did some-
thing right this time."

<u>Left:</u>
Kirk Marshall of
Mohawk is able to work
from home as a medical-
supply salesman because
of special equipment that
relieves the discomfort of
his wheelchair.

(Photos by Mark Vergari)

Dennis Rivera—the state's most powerful union leader—
at the headquarters near Times Square in Manhattan
(Photo by Mark Vergari)

CHAPTER 6

NEVER ENOUGH:
EDUCATION

☆ ☆ ☆

NEW YORK—PS 18 fits in with the light industrial ambience of the neighborhood in the Washington Heights section of Manhattan.

The converted candy factory sits amid a city Sanitation Department garage, a cable-TV truck depot and an MTA bus terminal a block from the Harlem River.

The playground is a small pitch of asphalt tucked next to a garage surrounded by a fence. The gym is small (about 3,000 sq. ft.) and interspersed with posts that make playing most games impossible.

There are no crossing guards to help the children, most of whom range in age from 5 to 14, cross the four lanes on Broadway just a block from the school but far from the glitter of Times Square, about eight miles to the south.

"When one of my students gets killed, then we'll get some crossing guards," the principal, Aurea Porrate-Doria, commented bitterly.

Teacher Crystal Felix readies her windowless classroom for the 28 6th graders she's expected to teach. Last year she taught first grade, but the school was shifted from an early-childhood-learning center to a K-8 school.

"I can adjust," she said.

Rosemary Salce is trying to adjust, too. The school's only guidance counselor was sitting in her office that has been converted from a bathroom. It smells when toilets are flushed elsewhere in the building, she said.

The office is so tiny that it has barely room for two chairs.

"It's frustrating," she said. "I'd love to have groups of four or five in here, or talk to parents in private."

"We never get enough money for what we need," Porrate-Doria complained. "We need literacy and math supplies. Science material is always short. We don't have enough books. Dictionaries are a luxury."

PS 18 is neither the best nor the worst of the 1,100 public schools that serve 1.1 million children in New York City. But it does embody many of the problems that the state's highest court cited when it ordered the Legislature to provide more money for the city's schools: overcrowded classrooms, paltry supplies and inexperienced teachers.

But the Legislature punted the court's mandate this year, failing to agree not only on how much extra the city schools should get but on how to raise the money to pay for it. In the wake of the failure of the Legislature to act, the court appointed a three-member panel to decide the money issue. It called for an extra $5.6 billion for city schools in four years. But that recommendation just kicked off another round of legislative proposals and, potentially, lawsuits as well.

Meanwhile, as Michael Rebell, head of the Campaign for Fiscal Equity, the group that started the lawsuit more than a decade ago, said, "kids can't wait for this to go through the Court of Appeals." He hopes to use a court order as a lever to get the Legislature to pass a bill to increase aid to needy school districts all over the state.

While education is arguably the most important service the state provides, the Legislature and Gov. George Pataki haven't come to grips with the fact that, as the Court of Appeals put it, many public-school students in New York City are not getting the "sound, basic education" the state constitution says they're entitled to.

On the other hand, many New York students are getting far more than that. Overall test scores are up. New York is among the nation's leaders in high school graduates going to college; Empire State students dominate many national awards and its teachers are among the best trained. Elite high schools in New York City are among the most rigorous and famous in the country.

But even Thomas Hobart, the retired president of New York State United Teachers, acknowledged, "excellence is not everywhere."

While the difference is narrowing, there is a significant gap between the performance of suburban and urban schools, and between white and minority students.

The problem isn't limited to New York City. Schools in other large cities, including Yonkers, Rochester, Buffalo and Syracuse, as well as in other smaller districts, also are failing many of their children, critics say.

Judgments like that can be made because education is one of the few services government provides where there is a reasonably accurate measurement of results: student test scores.

Those scores and financial records show that while New York spends more per pupil than all but one other state, the results are only middle of the pack.

A few numbers: New York spent $39 billion on education in 2003, or $11,827 per pupil, the most of any state except Connecticut and 41 percent above the national average.

But the state ranked only 27th in the scores of 4th graders on math tests, and 24th in 8th grade reading tests. It had the worst rate of graduation for black students (35 percent) and Hispanic students (32 percent) of any state in the country.

But some analysts point out that many factors outside

school, like poverty, health and family structure, affect student performance.

To try to measure the effects of outside influences on school performance, a researcher for the Manhattan Institute tried to quantify those factors. The researcher, Jay Greene, concluded that New York gets less value for education dollars spent than any other state except New Jersey and Connecticut.

The major reason for the high cost is teacher salaries and benefits, which account for about 60 percent of all school spending—an average of $56,927 a year or $43.71 per required work hour, according to figures from Rochester's Center for Governmental Research. Starting teacher salaries in New York, $36,387 last year, were ahead of all other states except Alaska and New Jersey, according to the National Education Association.

The state also has the third lowest teacher-pupil ratio, 12.6 to 1, of any state.

But teacher salaries in New York City are not among the state's highest, even though arguably they have the greatest challenges, and class sizes are far above the norm.

"I have a classroom with 34 students, which is too many," said Julia Haltiwanger, who teaches 7th grade math and science in PS 189, which is on the border between the Brownsville and Crown Heights sections of Brooklyn.

She graduated from college in 2002 and earned $39,000 last year as a first-year teacher in the city system. "We have four computers in the classroom, none of which work, and a printer that doesn't work," she said.

"We're missing some textbooks," she went on. "For 1,200 students, we have one gym teacher. . . . The classrooms aren't big enough. . . . My phone is hanging out of the wall."

"I thought it was going to be hard but I didn't know how hard," said Haltiwanger, 24, who is considering leaving teaching next year to go to graduate school.

Conditions like she described and the PS 18 officials complained about are a major reason for the relatively poor performance of the city schools, advocates for spending more money there say.

"The majority of the city's public high school students leave high school unprepared for more than low-paying work, unprepared for college and unprepared for duties placed on them by a democratic society," CFE, the group suing for more state aid said in court papers.

"Teachers in New York City are much more likely to leave than teachers upstate," said state Education Commissioner Richard Mills, long an advocate of sending more money to urban districts. "Kids going to a city school are more likely to have a brand new teacher, a brand new superintendent. They're more likely to have old books. These deficits accumulate."

There's also a reason that Haltiwanger's phone hadn't been fixed: the city Division of School Facilities management gets 30,000 work orders a year, but completes only half to two-thirds of them, according to the court papers.

The extra $5.6 billion the courts say the New York City schools ought to get would bulge to $8.5 billion if other poor districts in the state got the same level of funding. Then there is another $9 billion the advocates say is needed for capital projects in the city system.

While some critics say the city could make do if it spent the $12 billion it has now more wisely, few politicians have made that case. The sticking point instead has been where that money is to come from, especially in light of the fact that New Yorkers are already the highest taxed people in America. Beyond a proposal by Pataki to dedicate a few hundred million dollars from new gambling revenues, politicians haven't been specific about the source.

It's not hard to see why. To fund the new spending through the state income tax, which proponents see as the most "progressive" way to raise the money, the top rate would have to increase far above the current 7.5 percent.

And away from the cities and other poor districts that

would get more money under the plan being pushed by the courts, the idea of sending even more state tax money to needy schools looks very different.

"We hardly get anything back now for our schools from Albany. It's absurd," said Denise Cypher of Rye, a financial analyst who is married to a lawyer and has two children in the schools in that affluent Westchester suburb. A third child graduated from Rye High School last year. "Sending more? That's not going to happen," she said. "We should keep more of what we have."

Her district, which plans to spend about $40 million this year, is getting only about $2.2 million from Albany, or only about 5.5 percent of its budget. The statewide average is about 47 percent, while New York City gets about 51 percent.

While advocates for the low-wealth districts think that people in Rye could afford to pay more, since the average household income in the city is about $275,000 and the median value of homes is about $500,000, most residents are already paying school property taxes far into five figures and are loathe to pay more.

"Two-point-two million, whoop-de-doo, " Cypher said. "Given the income taxes we pay, how little we get back from it in the form of education aid. . . . I don't understand how we can do any more."

Like most states, New York divides the responsibility for raising money to pay for schools between the state government and local school districts. This year, the state share of education expenses is about 47 percent, localities 49 percent and the federal government about 4 percent. The state raises the bulk of its money from the income, business and sales taxes, as well as lottery receipts, while most local funds are raised through the property tax.

In an attempt to lessen the disparities between districts, the state parcels out aid based in part on the average income and the property wealth of the district. Even though that system has been distorted by a political deal that divides the state money by geography as well (13 percent for Long Island, 37 percent for New York City and 50 percent for the rest of the state) the formula does have the effect of lessening spending disparities, although not nearly as much as critics would like.

In Rye, for example, the per-pupil spending is about $16,000.

That allows the district to pay teachers as much as $107,000 a year and pay attention to individual students in a way that most urban districts can just dream about.

Cypher recalled that her older son, who likes to write, had a teacher mentor in all four years of high school who helped him develop that talent.

"Robert could go to him and talk about the structure, the development of his writing," she said. "When our kids go to college, they really know how to write," she said. "Our schools, I love 'em. I feel blessed to live here."

In Brooklyn, meanwhile, part of a school district where the average spending per student was $11,627 in 2002, Haltiwanger frets that she has so many students in her classes that she doesn't have the time to call their parents to enlist their support, or pay enough attention to children who aren't demanding it.

"It's hard to get to the ones who are silently struggling because others are loudly struggling," she said. "The biggest thing is class size."

New York City parents have long been aware of this disparity. The seeds of the lawsuit were sown in the Washington Heights section of Manhattan, where Robert Jackson, a parent and school-board member a decade ago and now a member of the City Council, was angry that the schools his three daughters attended had to cut programs because of reductions in education aid from Albany.

"As a school-board member, I was the bearer of bad news," he recalled, "and things were bad enough already."

"This was the most overcrowded district in the city," he recalled. "We had double sessions. Involuntary busing. 1,000 kids bused to a district south of here. 1,300 Spanish-speaking kids and one bilingual coordinator."

He helped to form the Campaign for Fiscal Equity (CFE) that sued to make the state provide all children with equal educations.

But in 1993 a court ruled that the state constitution didn't require the state to provide equal education to all children. But it suggested another line of attack to the parents: that there was a requirement that each child receive a "sound, basic education." The parents filed another lawsuit.

On the first day of the trial on that issue, October 12, 1999, Jackson led a group of about 40 people on a 12-mile hike from his neighborhood to the courthouse in Foley Square in Lower Manhattan.

Later he would be part of a group that walked 150 miles to Albany when the case got to the state's highest court, the Court of Appeals. That court ruled in their favor on June 26, 2003 and gave the Legislature until the end of July of 2004 to craft a solution—a deadline that the Legislature failed to meet.

Jackson has a solution to that as well: "Albany is not working. We should put 'em in jail. All 213 of 'em," he said at a recent CFE meeting in Manhattan. "Bet they'd come up with a solution real quickly."

Short of that, it's unclear what the solution will be, since, in the end, the court cannot appropriate money and seems to have no way to force the Legislature to do that, either.

CFE officials are hoping that the court order will spur the Legislature next year to pass a bill increasing aid to New York City and other needy districts.

But some lawmakers are skeptical.

"I think New York needs some big changes, but New York is not so good with big changes," said Assemblywoman Sandra Galef, D-Ossining, Westchester County.

Part of the reason is concern that the money now spent on education in New York is not always spent wisely.

While walking toward the entrance of PS 8, the Luis Beliard School on 165th Street in Washington Heights, Sarah Morgridge, a fierce advocate for more money for New York City schools, pointed out some crumbling concrete on a wall along a walkway.

Once inside the building, which opened only 10 years earlier, she also pointed out a staircase just inside the main door that is seldom used because it comes before the security-guard station, meaning the doors at the top have to be locked all the time.

In the vestibule immediately inside the door, there were two radiator covers. She said there were no radiators behind them.

"For those who say some money is wasted on New York City schools, there's some truth in that," she said.

Certainly, in terms of school construction, costs in the city dwarf those in the rest of the state: about $300 a square foot, compared to an average of about $150 elsewhere, according to the state Education Department.

That may sound like a lot, but it was worse as recently as 2003, when the average cost of new school projects in New York City was $433 per square foot.

"Since then, we have begun to streamline and reorganize," said city Education Department spokeswoman Margie Feinberg.

Still, higher land and labor costs as well as problems building in congested areas all drive up costs in the five boroughs, officials said.

But such disparities have given fuel to those who say that merely sending more money to urban schools, as the state's highest court has ordered the Legislature and Pataki to do, doesn't mean the money will be well spent, or that New York City is doing all it can to provide enough money for schools, or that more money is necessarily what's needed.

"People in Albany say sending money to New York City is like throwing it down a rathole," an advocate for more money for city schools, David Sealy, said at a recent conference. "The key to getting the money is a credible plan of accountability."

"We believe there are sufficient funds to provide high-quality education now," said Jason Brooks of the Foundation for Education Reform and Accountability, a group that promotes charter schools. "We're already near the top for spending. It's just what we're spending money on that's the problem."

But officials of the group bringing on the lawsuit, the Campaign for Fiscal Equity, said that safeguards and benchmarks will be included in any final deal to make sure that any extra money is used wisely.

"CFE is the party that argued that we need a new system of accountability," said deputy director Samira Ahmed. "We want to make sure that all of the money is spent in the best interests of the children."

Here are some other facts cited by those who oppose sending more education aid to New York and other cities without stricter oversight:

> In Buffalo, a state panel that is overseeing the city's finances found that school janitors didn't have to account for $15 million in funds earmarked for maintenance, and estimated that as much as $5 million could be saved by closer monitoring of the funds. It also found millions more could be saved if the district used just one health-insurance carrier instead of several and eliminated some benefits for school workers and their families like payments for cosmetic surgery;

> In Rochester, as much as $6.3 million a year could be saved if the schools paid the same wages as city employees doing

essentially the same job, according to a
consultant's report commissioned by the
city.

For example, the report said that while librarians hired
by the City of Rochester made $50,208 a year, the school district
was paying workers doing similar jobs $65,500; the schools
were paying clerk-typists $39,500, compared to $27,300 for city
workers doing the same job.

While the schools were paying maintenance mechanics
$48,978 a year, the city had workers doing the same job for
$26,910 a year. The schools were paying security guards
between $30,000 and $37,000 a year, while guards working for
the city made $24,400.

Barbara Jarzyniecki, a Rochester school spokeswoman,
disputed those numbers, saying that the school-district salaries
were lower than the report indicated and mostly in line with
what the city pays. She said the district hadn't seen the consultant's report.

Some also see Rochester as a case study of how spending more money doesn't necessarily lead to better results.

In 1987, the city schools signed a new contract calling
for raises of 40 percent in an effort to attract and keep better
teachers and lift student performance. But 17 years later, the
test scores of Rochester pupils were the worst of any big-city
students.

"What we've obviously learned is that money alone will
not solve all of the problems we have," said Adam Urbanski,
then and now president of the Rochester teachers' union.

He said the lives of children outside school have dete-
riorated over that period, with more than 80 percent of the district's children now categorized as poor, compared to 60 percent in 1987.

"Our efforts in education were outpaced," he said. "We
were beat to the punch by the continuing neglect of the condition of children in urban districts."

But the state's top education official rejected that notion.

"I don't accept the excuses," Education Commissioner Richard Mills said. "It's self-evident that some youngsters come to school with problems. . . . That's why for children who can't see the blackboard (you get them glasses) that's a pretty simple fix. That's why schools have breakfast programs, and lunch programs. It's hard to do well in school if you're hungry. So feed the child. We can't accept the dollars for our salary and make excuses for our failures. . . . The goal is to educate all these youngsters and do whatever it takes."

While New York City is looking for more state money for schools, Mayor Michael Bloomberg, up for re-election in 2005, in 2004 mailed out $250 million worth of property tax-rebate checks to city homeowners.

"That's seen by a lot of people as symbolic: they want the state of New York to come in and help them but they're not going to help themselves," said Galef, the Westchester assemblywoman.

"It's apples and oranges," responded Bloomberg spokesman Paul Elliott. He said the rebate, made possible by a strengthening city economy, amounts to only one-eighth of the tax increase Bloomberg imposed shortly after he took office, and that it's not related to the extra money courts have ruled the state owes the city for schools.

Overall, the city taxes at only about $13 per $1,000 assessed valuation for schools, compared to an average of more than $18 for the rest of the state—a difference that costs the city schools about $2 billion a year, according to a state Education Department study last year.

But city officials point out that city taxpayers still pay more overall than residents elsewhere, mostly because of far higher spending on police and fire protection as well as debt service.

The other large cities—Yonkers, Rochester, Buffalo and Syracuse—also have upped their contributions to local schools at a far lower rate than the rest of the state over the last decade.

Records show that they in aggregate hiked taxes for school purposes by only 15 percent in the last decade, well below the inflation rate of 25 percent, while aid from the state was rising rapidly, allowing the school budgets to almost double this year from a decade ago. In fact, this year Rochester, citing spending pressures from other areas and cuts in aid from the state, reduced local education spending by $7 million.

Meanwhile, across the state, school budgets increased about 23 percent in just the last three years, according to figures compiled by the state Business Council.

"We believe that at a minimum, the local effort from the cities should be maintained year after year," said Georgia Ascutto of the Conference of Big Five School Districts.

"Cities have been squeezed in other places," responded Edward Farrell, of the state Conference of Mayors, citing higher public protection, pension and health-insurance costs.

New York City can't cut its local spending on education—a requirement the Legislature inserted in the bill that allowed Bloomberg to take over control of the city's schools in 2002. But lawmakers have shown no interest in extending that rule to the other cities—the only municipalities in the state where residents don't get to vote on school budgets, Ascutto pointed out. Farrell said his group opposes the maintenance-of-effort idea.

Some districts in the state fare well, as measured by student test scores, spending far less money than the big cities.

"We have lots of AP (advanced-placement), college courses and most elementary classes are under 20 students," said Robert Munn, superintendent of the 2,000-student Broadalbin-Perth school district on the shores of Great Sacandaga Lake, about 40 miles northwest of Albany. "So we don't feel too disadvantaged."

Yet his district spent just $8,701 per pupil in 2002, one of the lowest figures in the state, according to the state Education Department. The average school tax bill is under

$800 a year. The tax rate is about $13 per $1,000 of full value, compared to the state average of about $18.

There are two keys to this: teachers recently signed a new contract that puts their top pay at $67,654, and the state pays about 70 percent of the district's expenses.

"We are a highly aided district," Munn said, in part because the state gives a bonus to districts (like Perth and Broadalbin) that merge. The state also gives more money to districts like this with modest incomes and property values.

So the state is paying 95 percent of the $36 million addition the district is putting onto its combination high school-elementary school building that will add classrooms, a media center and a gym.

Without the merger incentive, local taxpayers would have had to pick up almost 20 percent of the tab.

"That incentive is huge," said Munn, who added that his own school property tax bill is about $1,500 a year.

The key to helping schools—and saving money—is to give individual schools more autonomy and increase accountability, said Brooks, the education foundation official.

He said that should include many of the features of charter schools, such as longer school days and years, the elimination of teacher tenure, merit pay for teachers and flexibility in where to assign teachers.

CFE's Ahmed said that the court case doesn't deal with work rules for teachers, but that a key component of the plan for improving schools is improved accountability.

"There has to be appropriate consequences for poor performance," she said. "In schools that are persistently low performing, we would have the state Education Department send a distinguished educator to conduct a review and turn the school around."

"Then if there was no improvement," said Ahmed, "we'd have to look at how to restructure the school. Maybe fire the principal or make other personnel changes."

☆

Turning over control of schools to private organizations by means of a "charter" is another option—one that appears to be working well at a middle school in a poor neighborhood in the South Bronx.

As the 5th graders in the KIPP Academy charter school started to recite their multiplication tables one afternoon in the fall of 2004, they banged on their desks, clapped their hands and shouted out the numbers.

All were wearing T-shirts emblazoned with the slogan, "Knowledge is Power." On the classroom wall are signs with the school motto, "Work Hard! Be Nice."

"Can you count by eights?" the teacher and founder of the school, 34-year-old David Levin, asked the class.

"Yes," the 34 children in the class answer in unison.

"Duke up," Levin, a lanky, curly-haired graduate of Yale, said.

Children: "BOOM! KIPP, KIPP, good as gold, let me see your fingers roll. 8, 16, 24, 32, 40, with the forties down here and the forties up there, 48, 56, 64, 72, 80, with the eighties down here and the eighties up here, 88, 96."

Then on to the threes.

"Now you know we can count by eights, I bet you think we're really great, but if you want to see, our specialty, we'll count by threes."

"3, 6, 9, 12 . . . 15, 18, 21, 24, 27, 30, 33, uh huh, 36 uh huh, these KIPPsters got it going oh, oh yeah. We've got to keep on rolling."

"4, 8, 12, 16, 20, 24, 28, a boom bitty boom, 32, 36, we're the bomb, 40, 44, 48, a piece of cake, a piece of cake."

Interspersed with claps and banging their hands on their desks in unison, the class proceeded to go through the rest of their multiplication tables.

"Way to go 5th grade!" said Levin, a New York native

who a decade ago helped to found the first KIPP school in Houston.

Throughout the 90-minute math class, Levin used games, chants and energy to keep the children in the class focused on their lessons. When a couple of times the attention of a student strayed, he stopped the class, approached the offender and spoke softly while gazing directly into his eyes before resuming the lesson. Few eyes left him for the rest of the class.

Studies show that charter schools have had mixed results around the country—the students at some charter schools perform better on standardized tests than their public-school peers, and others worse. But there is no such ambiguity so far about the results at KIPP schools.

Without exception, student test scores in the KIPP (Knowledge Is Power Program) schools nationally are dramatically higher than in nearby public schools. For the last six years, the Bronx KIPP school has had the highest math and reading scores and attendance rate (96 percent) of any taxpayer-supported middle school in the Bronx. About 80 percent of KIPP 8th-grade graduates from 2000 are enrolled in four-year colleges this year, while only about a quarter of high-school graduates from the area even apply to college.

The success of the schools gives hope to those discouraged by the generally poor performance of students in poor, urban schools as well as ammunition to those who think that redesigned programs, rather than more money, is the key to turning around urban public schools.

"One of the important things I learned about KIPP is that the teachers are so enthusiastic," said U.S. Rep. Louise Slaughter, D-Rochester, who has been working without success to get a KIPP school in Rochester for several years. "The parents are also excited about it. This seems to be a model that works."

"They're not plucking elite kids—that doesn't explain their test results," said Dorothy Hutcheson, the head of the

Nightingale-Bamford School in Manhattan, an elite private
school where classes average 15 students and tuition is $25,000
a year. "It has a common mission that seems to energize the
school. The results are amazing."

There are now 42 KIPP academies, grades 5-8, around
the country, including six in New York—four in New York City
and one each in Buffalo and Albany—besides the Bronx school.

The academies, which spend less per pupil than public
schools in their districts, are all located in poor neighborhoods
and pick their students from a lottery.

"We're not getting above-average kids," Levin said.
"People are looking for ways out of the regular public school.
We have several hundred on the waiting list—and we don't
advertise."

Levin, an alumnus of the Teach for America program
that encourages college liberal-arts graduates to try their hands
at public-school teaching, points out that there is no mystery to
KIPP's success.

"What it is mostly is really hard work," he said.

Here are some of the things that set KIPP apart:

> The school day runs from 7:25 a.m. to 5
p.m. daily, plus four hours on three out
of four Saturdays a month and three
weeks in July. It adds up to two-thirds
more classroom time than in traditional
schools. KIPP students also do between
90 minutes and two hours of homework
a night.

  "The whole (traditional school) calendar
was set up to accommodate a farm
economy," Levin said. "Why not stay in
school and keep learning?"

> Classes are large (generally over 30) but
the teachers are exceptional: KIPP pays
between 15 percent and 20 percent more
in salary to its faculty than the average
New York City teacher gets.

"We invest heavily in personnel," Levin
said. "Good teachers is the key."
➤ Every student learns how to play an
instrument and read music. The 180-
member KIPP String and Rhythm
Orchestra has toured the country for the
past three summers.

The music is "skill-based, not talent-based," said music
teacher Jesus Concepcion, meaning that it is designed so that
children who aren't musically gifted can master it.

"It's not about the music. It's about all of us being a
team," he said.

Few students drop out after being initially accepted,
despite the long hours.

"It was hard in the beginning," 8th grader Lakiema
Alexander, 13, said later that afternoon, with more hours of
school stretching before her, even as public-school students
were getting out for the day.

"Sometimes I wish I was outside with everybody else,
but then I think this is really worth it," she said. "But it's better
to be here than to be a lot of other places."

The most striking part of visiting KIPP, which shares a
four-story building across from a high-rise housing project
with a public intermediate school, is how quiet it is. The children barely whisper while changing classes.

But that was too much noise for Levin.

"Eighth grade, let's go back to the music room," Levin
said to a group that was talking in low tones as they came into
the hallway where he happened to be passing by.

"We appreciate how quiet you were," he told them.
"But you're supposed to be silent."

"Remember the e word: empathy," he said, while
motioning to a boy to tuck in his shirt. "We don't want to dis-
turb people in classrooms. We want you to whisper all year in
the hallways, but you have to be silent first." He said they had

to be silent for three days in hallways before being allowed to whisper.

KIPP's approach to discipline is reminiscent of former Mayor Rudolph Giuliani's approach to crime: crack down on minor offenses and the big ones will take care of themselves.

"There is a 'tipping point,'" Levin said later, echoing a phrase police officials use. "You have to deal with small stuff. . . . In the suburbs, if I was this tough, you'd have parents swearing at me."

Carrots are also an important part of the philosophy. Privileges like field trips and summer excursions can be revoked for misbehaving students.

The school, which has about 240 students, couldn't afford to offer the program it does on the $8,586 per student it gets from the city, development director Mandy Gauss said— about 80 percent of what the city spends on public-school pupils. It raises about $500,000 a year to make up the difference, as well as another $800,000 for its program to support alumni in high school and help them with college preparation.

Despite the schools' success, neither Levin nor state Education Commissioner Richard Mills see KIPP as the total answer to the woes of urban schools.

"We have to stop thinking there will be one solution for all of our public schools," Levin said, adding he believed that city Education Chancellor Joel Klein is "on the right track" by emphasizing smaller schools and accountability.

Mills pointed out that since state law allows for a maximum of only 100 charter schools (there were 66 in 2004) they can never be a big part of the solution in New York.

"I've seen good charter schools and I've seen bad charter schools," he said. "The search for the one best thing (is futile). It's a package of things. It involves leadership, instruction, curriculum, extra help, resources that match the need."

The upshot could be more schools that resemble KIPP, where another favorite chant is, "With a dose of knowledge we'll be ready for college."

☆

Urban-school advocates who want more city high-school graduates to be ready for college sometimes gaze longingly at a pot of money that is connected to education but mostly off-limits to them: the $2.5 billion a year the state spends on the STAR (School TAx Relief) program.

While most of the money the state spends on schools is distributed in a way that helps to equalize how much is spent between rich and poor areas, the STAR money goes predominantly to affluent areas.

STAR, first adopted in 1997, has sent more than $11 billion to school districts to make up for tax breaks given to homeowners—but not renters or businesses. About 3 million homeowners benefited in 2003.

Because the suburbs have a far higher preponderance of homeowners than cities and because property values tend to be higher there, the money goes mostly to people in those communities. There are no income limits for the rebates, except for people over 65 who have to make $64,650 or less a year to get an additional break.

"STAR is a way to get money to New York City suburbs that you never could through the school-aid formula," said Frank Mauro of the Fiscal Policy Institute, a labor-backed think tank. "It's not based on need or ability to pay, but on the number of owner-occupied dwellings and how expensive the average home is."

The program has been effective at driving state money to those areas.

In 2003, for example, $325 million of STAR funds went to Suffolk County on Long Island, well more than twice as much as the $137 million New York City taxpayers got. Suffolk has about 1.4 million people, New York City about 8 million.

The two other large suburban counties, Nassau ($311 million in STAR aid, about 1.3 million people) and Westchester

($285 million, about 925,000 people) also got far more than the city.

Buffalo's Erie County ($131 million from STAR), the largest upstate county with about 950,000 people, got almost as much as New York City, while Rochester's Monroe County ($129 million and about 735,000 people) was not far behind.

Within those counties, affluent suburbs with expensive homes got far more per person than the central cities.

To partly make up for the small number of owner-occupied homes in New York City (about 70 percent of New York City residents rent their homes, while about 70 percent of people in the rest of the state own homes) STAR gives New York City residents a partial break on their state income taxes, but it falls far short of making up the difference.

"Distribution of STAR hurts places without a lot of owner-occupied homes," Mauro said. "New York City doesn't do well, and neither do Buffalo, Rochester and Syracuse, and they don't even get the income-tax break the city (New York) gets."

But the program wasn't designed as another aid program for schools—it was established to lower the property tax burden of those who are paying the most, said state School Boards Association spokesman David Ernst.

"The idea of STAR was not to be a supplemental-aid program for schools, but a tax-relief program. It has been effective at delivering that," he said.

But it hasn't delivered that for businesses in the state, which don't qualify for the breaks, Robert Ward of the state Business Council pointed out.

"STAR subsidizes higher education spending and thus drives up tax rates," Ward said. "School districts have taken the STAR dollars and driven them into above-inflation budget increases, in most cases twice the rate of inflation. That's why we continually see property taxes going up and up."

But the program has helped equalize what many people in the suburbs see as the unfair burden they bear: both higher income taxes that pay for state spending in other regions as well as high property taxes to fund high quality schools, one state lawmaker said.

"The STAR program has worked effectively to reduce the burden of property taxes," said Sen. Nicholas Spano, R-Yonkers. "Because of some of the peculiar ways the school-aid formula works, school districts in Westchester that are very often treated well by the education formula are getting a benefit on the flip side for the STAR program."

"STAR is one of the only benefits our residents get for putting so much of their heart and soul, as well as their resources, into our schools," said Assemblywoman Amy Paulin, D-Scarsdale, who added that the quality of the suburban schools might slip if STAR aid were removed.

Shifting STAR aid to badly pressed urban schools should be considered only if all other options fail, said an influential Manhattan lawmaker.

"That would be a point of last resort," said Assembly Education Committee chairman Steven Sanders, D-Manhattan. "We haven't reached that point. I think it (funding urban schools adequately) can be done without intruding on STAR."

Spending Across the Nation

Not all metropolitan areas in the country have higher spending on education in the suburbs than in central cities. Here is a comparison on
schools in six metro areas for the 2001-02 school year.

State	Spending per pupil	Average teacher salary
New York		
Inner city	$6,057	$42,285
Suburb	7,218	72,591
Boston		
Inner city	5,770	61,079
Suburb	4,433	38,180
Chicago		
Inner city	4,482	46,661
Suburb	3,216	39,852
Denver		
Inner city	3,852	38,044
Suburb	3,313	32,753
Fort Worth		
Inner city	3,058	41,402
Suburb	4,246	33,316
Oakland		
Inner city	4,022	53,440
Suburb	4,849	60,395
St. Louis		
Inner city	5,337	33,223
Suburb	3,467	34,304

Note: Costs exclude building and transportation expenses.

Source: Federal General Accounting Office

Education Money Gap

New York had the biggest gap of any state between the revenues available per student in its wealthiest and poorest districts in 2002.

State	Gap	Rank
New York	$2,040	1
Illinois	2,026	2
Virginia	1,105	3
Pennsylvania	882	4
National average	868	n/a
New Hampshire	795	5
Vermont	766	6
Louisiana	725	7
Arizona	681	8
Michigan	564	9
Maryland	558	10

Note: 21 states spend more on poor districts than high ones. The highest is Massachusetts, which spends $1,343 more per pupil in its poorest than in its wealthiest districts.

Source: Education Trust

Comparing Teacher Salaries

ALBANY—Here is how the salaries of teachers in New York compare to those in some other states in 2003:

State	Average salary	Rank
California	$55,693	1
Michigan	54,020	2
Connecticut	53,962	3
New Jersey	53,194	4
New York	53,017	5
Massachusetts	51,942	7
Pennsylvania	51,425	9
U.S. average	45,771	n/a
Vermont	42,038	23
Florida	40,281	28
Texas	39,972	29
South Dakota	32,414	50

Source: National Education Association

PS 18 in Washington Heights, Manhattan

Crystal Felix's classroom lacks windows

(Photos by Mark Vergari)

Top:
Guidance Counselor
Rosemary Salce in
her office, a former
bathroom in PS 18

Left:
PS 18 Principal
Aurea Porrate-Doria
in her office

(Photos by Mark Vergari)

Julia Haltiwanger, a teacher in a Brooklyn middle school,
works on a lesson plan

Denise Cypher, right, of Rye,
and her children load up the minivan
(Photos by Mark Vergari)

Kipp Academy: quiet hallways

Kipp Academy head David Levin teaching math

(Photos by Mark Vergari)

Kipp Academy mottos
(Photo by Mark Vergari)

Kipp's homework always beckons

Kipp students all play an instrument

(Photos by Mark Vergari)

CHAPTER 7

THE ULTIMATE FRINGE BENEFIT: PENSIONS

☆ ☆ ☆

Ogdensburg is about 220 miles away from the new $82.5 million limestone-and-granite-veneered, 15-story building that houses the offices of the state Retirement System in downtown Albany.

But decisions reached there and at the Capitol have affected the lives of people like Shelly Breen, a mother of eight who lives in Ogdensburg, a city of 12,000 people along the St. Lawrence River near the Canadian border.

Breen has given birth to four children and has adopted four others, while also serving as a foster parent for still more.

For the past eight years, her brood has taken part in the city's day-long recreational program, which she said kept them busy and entertained for much of the summer.

"Day camp was wonderful for my kids," she said. "It gave them structure and fun. Some of the counselors were like big brothers and sisters to them."

But the city, facing a steep increase in pension costs last year, cut the program, and Breen has to struggle daily to keep her children busy.

"Nothing has hurt us more than the crunch on the

retirement system," said city parks director Tim Irvine, who also complained that he can't buy new equipment needed to maintain the city's green space and baseball diamonds.

Ogdensburg is typical of other communities across the state that are struggling to hold down taxes, maintain services and pay skyrocketing pension bills.

"The explosion in pension costs is by far the most serious issue facing local governments," said Edward Farrell, executive director of the state Conference of Mayors. "It dwarfs everything else."

New York taxpayers may not realize it, but in terms of paying for the retirement benefits of government and education workers, for the last decade or so they never had it so good.

Although they were paying the highest taxes of any Americans, they were contributing almost nothing toward public-worker pensions. That's about to change: the bill grew by more than $2.7 billion in 2005.

The pension hikes are helping to force cuts in police, parks, health, pre-school and other services around the state, as well as raising taxes to the point where some local officials say it's scaring away potential developers who could help to revitalize their communities.

"Every department was hit," said Ogdensburg City Manager John Krol, who cut about $242,000 in spending to balance the budget to help offset pension costs that grew from about $29,000 in 2002 to $637,000 this year. "We dipped into reserve funds, cut police and fire. We're cutting back across the board." The city eliminated three of its 32 firefighter positions and two of its 20 police posts along with the recreation cuts.

The police cutbacks mean that in Lisa Sargent's neighborhood near downtown Ogdensburg, vandalism has been more of a problem than usual.

"There have been tire slashings several times a week, broken side mirrors, things like that," the 35-year-old fifth-grade teacher and mother of three said. "A couple of weeks ago, someone stole a wicker chair right off a front porch."

Krol said that in previous years the city would send out police "impact teams" to handle spikes in vandalism, but that the budget cutbacks this year made that impossible.

The pension funds support the state's 432,000 retired public workers outside New York City and 898,000 teachers, firefighters, police officers and other government workers. They guarantee that those who make public service a career will have comfortable incomes when they retire after as little as 20 years on the job. The booming stock market was paying the tab until it tanked.

The Legislature granted extra benefits six years ago when the market was flush. It also cut what workers have to pitch into their retirement accounts.

While in 2003 taxpayers had to kick in the equivalent of 4.5 cents for every dollar a government worker earned, last year it was 12 cents for most workers and 17 cents for police and firefighters. It will dip slightly this year because of the stock-market rebound, but is expected to start to go up again in later years.

The Legislature tried to ease the pain in 2004 by delaying the payments due from counties and some small cities and towns and allowing them to borrow to put off some of the extra burden as well, temporarily saving them $1.2 billion. But eventually, the costs have to be paid.

The costs are such a burden in part because almost every local government and school district in the state is part of the pension system that was established in 1920 (New York City has separate systems). So taxpayers feel the pinch in their school, town or city, village and county property taxes—in most cases a triple hit for property owners.

The funds pay out a total of about $8.5 billion annually. The benefits, while large compared to those offered by many private-sector employers, are in line with what other states pay out. All benefits are exempt from both federal payroll and state income taxes.

The most generous are to police and firefighters, who get half-pay (figured on the average of their three highest earning years) for a minimum of 20 years of service regardless of their age. The average benefit for police and firefighters who retired in 2003 was $54,330 annually. But half of pensioners, many of whom retired more than a decade ago, get less than $10,000 annually.

Workers other than police and firefighters get 40 percent of their annual pay if they retire after 20 years and are at least 62 years old (55 for the longest tenured workers). Those retiring in 2003, many of whom worked more than 20 years, are getting an average of $31,154 as an annual benefit. For teachers, the figure was $47,365 a year.

Workers with 30 years on the public payroll can retire and get 60 percent of their pay at any age.

A few people collect more than one public pension. For example, 67-year-old Comptroller Alan Hevesi, who runs the pension system, gets two: one for his years of service in the Legislature and as New York City comptroller, and another for his years as a City University teacher. His total pension benefits, $160,000, are greater than the $151,500 a year he earns as comptroller.

Until the Legislature and Pataki in 2000 instituted annual cost-of-living increases (pegged at half the inflation rate, with a maximum of 3 percent and a minimum of 1 percent) the pension benefits were hiked only sporadically by the Legislature.

Pataki and lawmakers also eliminated the 3 percent payment into the fund for employees with more than 10 years of service, saving them (and costing taxpayers) about $200 million a year.

Hevesi is the sole trustee of the employee and police-and-fire pension funds worth about $115 billion in 2004. He is the country's largest individual investor.

The $80 billion state teacher fund is administered by a 10-member unpaid board.

Both funds, like most large pension systems, are invested predominantly in a mix of stocks and bonds, with lesser amounts tied up in real estate, treasury bills and other securities. Their returns have generally followed, or slightly bettered, the performance of the overall market.

The funds have so much money because they are designed to meet all future obligations, rather than just providing money on a pay-as-you-go basis. They are in better financial shape than those funds in some other states, such as Illinois and New Jersey, where the funds have been raided to balance state budgets. That hasn't happened in New York because the governor and Legislature can't touch the funds, which Hevesi, who is independently elected, controls.

Until the stock downturn early in this decade, the system of pre-funding the pension benefits was a spectacular success for the prior 10 years.

But now, with the market lower and interest rates also low, the funds need more taxpayer cash at what local-government officials say could hardly be a worse time.

"We will experience a whopping 75 percent increase in the amount the town is required to pay as a contribution to the New York State Retirement System—that is an added expense of $575,000 or more than a 6 percent increase in our tax rate," Webster Town Supervisor Cathryn Thomas said in her budget message in 2003. Borrowing part of the money will delay some of the bite, but the bill is accumulating.

And it's not going to get better any time soon. Hevesi and teacher-system officials warn that contributions from taxpayers will stay high indefinitely, probably staying around 12 percent of payroll costs.

"It was the result of an anomaly of the last 14 years that the state and local governments paid almost nothing into the fund," Hevesi said, pointing out how high payments were before the stock-market boom: 16.4 percent of payroll for most workers and 30 percent for police and firefighters.

"I'm not minimizing the budget problems of local governments," he said. He said the mindset of local officials
should be: "this is a cost of doing business."

And local officials can control to some extent their pension costs by holding down the number of employees they
have and how much they pay them, said Hevesi spokesman
David Neustadt.

The local governments and taxpayers who support
them also didn't get much sympathy from Charles Peritorie, an
81-year-old resident of Sonyea, Livingston County, who retired
in 1980 after 38 years as a state worker, for much of the time as
an attendant at the former Craig Developmental Center. He
gets a pension of about $1,000 a month.

"All of these years they have been contributing nothing
because the investments were so outstanding," he said. "They
should have had the foresight of saying someday we're going
to have to contribute."

Pension benefits for existing workers and retirees can't
be touched without amending the state constitution. The
Legislature and governor can change them for future employees, but the idea has almost no support at the Capitol.

The guarantee of benefits goes even for convicted
felons. In fact, neither fraud, nor bribery, nor theft can stop
former public officials from collecting taxpayer-financed pensions in New York.

So when Guy Velella, the former state senator convicted on bribery-related charges in 2004, emerged from prison in
2005, the long-time lawmaker got a pension of about $80,000 a
year.

Several other lawmakers convicted of crimes, as well as
other public officials and government workers convicted of
felonies, many of them involving stealing money from the
public, are either already collecting pensions or are entitled

to once they get old enough, according to state records.

That right is enshrined in the state constitution, which says that benefits shall not be "diminished or impaired."

The rule should be changed, one prominent political leader thinks.

"Taxpayers should not have to foot the bill for a pension after a person has violated the public trust and has broken the law," said state Conservative Party chairman Michael Long. "It's certainly something the Legislature should look into."

But the Legislature at this point seems unlikely to try to change the law.

"I don't see how you do not pay the pension even if a person is convicted of a crime," said Assembly Public Employees Committee chairman Peter Abbate, D-Brooklyn. "What happens to the family?" Abbate asked. "Rather than take away the pension, add more time to the sentence."

Abbate's counterpart in the Senate, Joseph Robach, R-Greece, Monroe County, said he'd consider the idea of changing the system.

"I have concerns about taking money away from people," he said. "But . . . I do think people who extort public funds should be in jeopardy of losing pensions and as chairman of the committee will research doing a bill to rectify that."

"But the issue is not as simple as it looks," warned E. J. McMahon of the Manhattan Institute.

"The pension supposedly is something that accrues to him while he worked," he said. "Unless you're going after his back pay, you shouldn't go after the pension."

He said the more serious problem is the overall level of benefits, which he thinks taxpayers can't afford any more.

Long said he agrees that felons should be allowed to keep the money they contributed to their retirements, but that they have no call on getting taxpayer subsidies for their retirements.

"I don't think that taxpayers are obligated to contribute

to one's pensions if in fact you broke the public trust and you're guilty of a serious crime," he said.

Pataki favors the concept of taking away the pension benefits of officials convicted of crimes involving official misconduct, said spokesman Todd Alhart. But he said the governor had no immediate plans to push the issue.

Hevesi had no comment on the idea.

Practices differ around the country, but generally states are leery about limiting pension benefits of criminals, said Ron Snow of the National Conference of State Legislatures.

"Some courts have ruled that pensions are compensation for previous employment. It's property they own," he said.

But that didn't stop Pennsylvania from passing a law in 1978 that cut off pensions for government employees and workers convicted of stealing from the public, said Pennsylvania teacher-pension spokeswoman Evelyn Tatovski.

And in 2004, she said the Legislature also decided to take pensions away from school employees who commit sex crimes that victimize students.

Here are some New York elected officials and government workers charged or convicted of crimes or misconduct who are receiving pensions, according to the state comptroller's office:

> JAMES COYNE • former Albany County executive. Spent four years in prison after his 1992 conviction on corruption charges related to the construction of the Pepsi Arena in downtown Albany. Annual pension: $37,207.
>
> GORDON F. URLACHER • former Rochester police chief. Convicted in 1992 of embezzling more than $150,000, served three years in prison. Annual pension: $44,897.61.
>
> JERRY JOHNSON • former Assembly member from Livingston County first elected in 1992 who

resigned in 2000 after pleading guilty to sexually harassing one of his aides. Annual pension: $38,025.

GLORIA DAVIS • former assemblywoman from the Bronx who was forced to resign last year after taking a cash bribe to steer state contracts to a Florida firm. Served 90 days in jail. Annual pension: $61,290.

GERDI LIPSCHUTZ • former Queens assemblywoman who admitted in 1986 that she had two employees on her payroll who never showed up to work. Annual pension: $9,494.

JOHN E. GAFFNEY • former head of the state Bridge Authority, who pleaded guilty last year to using public money to finance private trips. Annual pension: $24,872.

JAMES J. MCGOWAN • former state labor commissioner who quit last year after admitting he took a bribe. Annual pension: $4,589.64.

WILLIAM CABIN • former chief of staff to then-Lt. Gov. Mario Cuomo. Sentenced to prison for misappropriating $178,000 in state funds by creating five fictitious jobs on the 39-member Cuomo staff in 1981. Annual pension: $8,345.

Taking away their pensions wouldn't make much of a dent in the system's expenses, but here's an idea that would: require newly hired workers to pay into the system for their whole careers, as government workers did before the rules were changed three years ago.

But Pataki shot that idea down.

"We don't need to do that," he said, pointing out that

such a change would save little money in the short run. He said that he expected the stock market to rebound so that the cost to taxpayers could be stabilized without benefit cuts.

He also pointed out that he and lawmakers in 2003 passed a bill setting a floor on contributions from governments at 4.5 percent of payroll no matter how much the funds earn in the stock market. He said that should help smooth out future rate shocks.

Another option that some analysts like but also has virtually no political support would have the state follow the lead of many private employers and have taxpayers give workers a set amount of money every year to set aside for their retirements, shifting the risk of volatile financial markets from taxpayers to the employees.

"The state has managed the fund literally like there was no tomorrow," said McMahon. He advocates the switch to 401K-style funds for public workers. "They managed it like the greatest stock-market boom in history would continue eternally."

New York City Mayor Michael Bloomberg proposed in 2003 that new city workers get a 401K-style pension, but the City Council blocked it. The idea is also being pushed by California Gov. Arnold Schwarzennegger.

There is a precedent for rolling back benefits. With the state and New York City both on the brink of financial collapse in the 1970s, the Legislature established the "tier" system, which for the first time required payments into the fund by workers and cut benefits for workers retiring before age 62.

"With the New York City fiscal crisis and the city staring at bankruptcy, people knew we had to do something dramatic," said former state Sen. Fred Eckert, a Republican from Greece, Monroe County, and architect of the tier plan.

He said that lawmakers could do the same thing now, and said only "cowardice" is stopping them.

"It takes guts to do something that will be harmful to

the comparatively few, because they'll remember it to their dying day," he said. "So what usually happens is the noisy few buy everyone off, and everyone else gets shafted."

Although specific proposals for cutting benefits have little support, there is some realization that with state and local taxes already the highest in the nation and other costs continuing to escalate, something has to give.

"For anybody not whistling past the graveyard, since we're not going to raise taxes, we need at some point to look at costs," said Senate Social Services Committee chairman Raymond Meier, R-Western, Oneida County.

In the meantime, school districts and local governments around the state are struggling to make ends meet:

> ➤ In the Whitney Point School District in Broome County, the district eliminated tutors for some students with special needs after voters twice rejected a pricier spending plan. The district's pension bill went from $217,169 in 2003 to $485,183 in 2004;

> ➤ In Monroe County, mental-health, anti-smoking, prenatal and foster-care programs were among the victims of more than $2 million in budget cuts. And still the county's fiscal condition was precarious enough that the Standard and Poor's ratings agency lowered the county's credit rating, which could make borrowing money more expensive. The county's pension bill went from $13 million in 2003 to $32 million in 2004;

> ➤ In Elmira, a popular pre-kindergarten program has been cut from a full day to a half day.

Despite the cuts, Elmira residents still had to pay 9 percent more in school taxes last year. The need to both cut programs and raise taxes has proven frustrating to the school district's financial chief, Robert Gosden.

"People are standing behind their schools, but there is going to be a revolt if there's another 9.35 percent tax hike," he said. A major culprit: pension bills for school employees that were less than $200,000 two years ago but will be almost $2.9 million this year.

In Amsterdam, a struggling former mill city in the Mohawk Valley about 30 miles west of Albany, Mayor Joseph Emanuele decided he wouldn't borrow any of the money needed for the pension payments. "We'd just have to pay it back with interest," he said. That means paying $1.36 million into the fund this year, compared to about $60,000 in 2003.

"The only place to cut is personnel," he said. But the City Council rejected his bid to trim the fire department. Early delivery of $350,000 in state aid will help, but otherwise the rest has to be made up through higher property taxes.

And that carries a price even beyond the extra dollars residents have to pay: scaring off potential developers who could help to revitalize the city.

"I was talking to a developer recently who was interested in putting in some houses," Emanuele said. The plan seemed to make sense, because the Target Corp. is building a distribution center in the nearby town of Florida, which is expected to generate about 1,000 new jobs.

"Then he asked me what the taxes would be and he said to me, 'You people have to be crazy. The taxes are out of control.' I had to agree with him."

And there's more bad pension news on the horizon for New York taxpayers.

While New Yorkers in 2003 absorbed a huge jump in payments to the state Employees' Retirement Fund, the state Teacher Retirement System, which depends on local school districts for some of its funding, is increasing its bite as well.

In July 2004, the system's 10-member board meeting in a posh suburban office building in Albany unanimously passed a motion that effectively raised school taxes for New Yorkers by $400 million in 2004.

In 2003, a similar vote raised taxes by $260 million.

And that could just be the beginning.

The system oversees the fund that pays close to $4 billion annually in benefits to the 121,000 retired teachers outside New York City and builds up assets to eventually pay for pensions for the 255,000 members still working.

Most teachers who are now working will be eligible to get 60 percent of their average salary for their three highest earning years after 30 years of service when they turn 55. The pensions are exempt from payroll and state income taxes, but not federal income taxes. The average annual payout for teachers retiring in 2003 was $47,365.

Because the teacher system's timing of payments from school districts is different from the state Employee Retirement Systems, the full effect of the stock-market collapse that started in 2000 hasn't been felt yet. But it will.

While the employee fund this year will require local governments to contribute 12 cents for every dollar they pay most of their employees (an average of 17 cents for police and firefighters), the school pension system will get only 5.63 cents.

Still, that totals $700 million, compared to the $300 million paid last year. That's 15 times what the districts paid in 2003. And it's going higher.

"We expect the contribution rate to stay at about 12 percent," said the system's actuary, Lawrence Johansen. A 12 percent rate for next year would mean another $750 million from taxpayers.

The pension hikes this year plus higher health-care costs accounted on average for about half of the school-tax increases last year, said state School Boards Association spokesman David Ernst.

He said the pension expenses could increase tax-rate hikes over the next few years.

"We're concerned that the contribution rate is going to go up dramatically in the future," he said.

But they have a long way to go before approaching the levels reached in the late 1970s and early 1980s. The bills peaked at 23.49 percent of payroll in the 1980-1981 school year and stayed there the following year before stating a decline that bottomed out at .36 percent in 2001-2002.

Factors in the drop included a change in state law to allow the fund to invest in more stocks, the booming stock market and the 1976 state law that mandated new teachers to start paying three percent of their salaries toward their retirements.

Before 1983, "we had a very limited ability to invest in the market," said George Philip, the system's $278,000-a-year executive director. Lawmakers worried about stock-market volatility limited the stocks to just 60 that were deemed prudent risks.

But now those factors that led to lower costs for taxpayers have turned around. Not only is the stock market (where the fund has about 60 percent of its assets) down, but four years ago the Legislature passed and Pataki signed a bill that eliminates the contributions from teachers after 10 years of service.

"Had the benefits not been enhanced to the extent they were, the hit on employers today would not be as dramatic," Ernst said. He added that school boards favored automatic cost-of-living increases for retirees that were approved four years ago, but opposed eliminating the worker payments.

The sweeteners adopted in 2000 add about $1 billion to the system's annual expenses, said spokesman Robert DeLuca. But he added that market performance is the main factor in determining contribution rates.

But more than enhanced benefits and stock-market fluctuations are at work here. So are demographics. While in

1940 there were 10 active teachers for every retiree, the figure is now two to one. And 10,000 members are turning 55 every year, with the average retirement age about 58 and a half.

"There's going to be continued upward pressure on contributions," Johansen said. "Liabilities continue to grow."

How Pension Benefits Have Increased

Here is how much new retirees and all retirees have gotten from the state pension systems for the last decade:

Police and Fire Employee Retirement System

Year	All retirees & beneficiaries	New retirees
1994	$19,372	$30,542
1995	20,337	33,670
1996	21,281	34,223
1997	22,077	35,664
1998	22,838	37,413
1999	23,889	36,266
2000	25,098	39,677
2001	27,745	47,744
2002	29,246	48,456
2003	31,154	54,330

Employee Retirement System

Year	All retirees & beneficiaries	New retirees
1994	$7,829	$13,116
1995	8,226	13,313
1996	9,183	17,735
1997	9,775	16,878
1998	10,171	15,026
1999	10,603	14,693
2000	11,086	15,795
2001	12,299	15,968
2002	12,984	19,899
2003	14,176	21,755

Source: Office of State Comptroller Alan Hevesi

Pension Fund Assets

Here is how the assets of the teachers and state employees' retirement funds have changed since 1985, in billions of dollars:

Year	Teachers	State Employees
2004	80.3	115.0 *
2003	72.4	97.3
2002	73.0	112.7
2001	81.0	114.0
2000	88.3	128.9
1999	84.8	112.7
1998	76.2	106.3
1997	64.1	83.9
1996	53.4	77.5
1995	45.7	65.4
1994	38.9	60.1
1993	38.7	58.0
1992	34.5	53.7
1991	31.0	50.5
1990	29.0	47.1
1985	14.5	27.4

* Estimate

Source: State Retirement System

Taxpayer Contributions to Pension System

Here is how much school districts have had to pay into the state Teacher Retirement System for the last 25 years, expressed as a percentage of payroll:

Year	Percentage of Payroll
1978-79	21.4
79-80	22.49
80-81	23.49
81-82	23.49
82-83	23.49
83-84	22.9
84-85	22.8
85-86	21.4
86-87	18.8
87-88	16.83
88-89	14.79
89-90	6.87
90-91	6.84
91-92	6.64
92-93	8.0
93-94	8.41
94-95	7.24
95-96	6.37
96-97	3.57
97-98	1.25
98-99	1.42
99-2000	1.43
00-01	0.43
01-02	0.36
02-03	0.6
03-04	2.52
04-05	5.63

Source: Teacher Retirement System

Taxpayer Contributions to Pension System

Here is the percentage of payroll that local governments have paid into
the state employee (ERS) and police-fire pension systems (PFRS) since
1984:

Year	ERS rate	PFRS rate
1984	14.4	27.3
1985	14.2	26.5
1986	10.4	19.8
1987	9.4	13.3
1988	9.7	14.8
1989	3.7	8.5
1990	3.6	8.3
1991	0.3	7.8
1992	0.4	11.5
1993	0.6	14.0
1994	0.7	11.3
1995	0.7	13.9
1996	2.2	13.0
1997	3.7	9.8
1998	1.7	7.0
1999	1.3	2.4
2000	0.9	1.9
2001	0.9	1.6
2002	1.2	1.6
2003	1.5	1.4
2004	12*	17*

* Payment deferred until February 2005. Local governments have to
pay at least 7 percent in cash but can borrow the rest.

Source: Office of State Comptroller Alan Hevesi

Teacher Retirement Benefits Going Up

Here is how retirement benefits for teachers have increased over the last decade:

Year	Average retirement age	Average length of service	Average benefit
1994	58 years, 10 months	27 years, 7 months	$32,151
1995	59 years, 2 months	28 years, 3 months	34,351
1996	59 years, 1 month	29 years, 5 months	37,151
1997	58 years, 5 months	29 years, 8 months	38,688
1998	58 years, 1 month	29 years, 6 months	39,254
1999	58 years, 0 month	28 years, 8 months	38,882
2000	58 years, 1 month	28 years, 3 months	39,739
2001	57 years, 11 months	30 years, 8 months	44,681
2002	57 years, 9 months	30 years, 2 months	45,426
2003	57 years, 5 months	31 years, 1 month	47,365

Source: State Teacher Retirement System

Amsterdam Mayor Joseph Emanuele thinks borrowing to pay
pension costs would make the city's problems worse
(Photo by Mark Vergari)

Left:
Shelly Breen
cares for her children
in Ogdensburg

Bottom:
Ogdensburg City
Manager John Krol:
Pension costs forced
cuts across the board

(Photos by Mark Vergari)

Top:
Charles Peritorie of
Sonyea Livingston
County: not living large
on $1,000-a-month
pension

Left:
Lisa Sargent:
less money to fight
vandalism in
Ogdensburg

(Photos by Mark Vergari)

CHAPTER 8

ONLY IN NEW YORK

☆ ☆ ☆

What's frustrating to those who think that taxes in New York are too high and are helping to depress the state's economy is that the state has some laws and rules unique to New York that seem to help only those who depend on taxpayers, either directly for a paycheck or indirectly through wasteful laws. Yet they are among the major reasons why businesses find it hard to stay or relocate here and why the state's job growth has been so anemic compared to other states.

Here is how a few of those laws and rules operate.

☆ Wicks Law ☆

The $28 million addition to the White Plains High School was finished almost two years late and cost potentially millions more to build because of a law, unique to New York, that requires breaking up control of the taxpayer-funded project among four separate contractors.

Things got off to a bad start when, not long after the project began, union construction workers, who were angry that a contractor had hired non-union laborers to do excavating work, erected a huge inflatable rat in front of the school. There were fights big (getting union and non-union workers to work together) and small (who is responsible for filling in the soil around a fuel tank?).

"There is absolutely no question in my mind that this law is clearly more expensive and causes serious delays," said Saul Yanofsky, who was district superintendent when the project started. "There is no justification for keeping it."

State, school and municipal officials have been saying for years that the 93-year-old statute, known as the Wicks Law, adds hundreds of millions of dollars to the expense of building public structures in New York.

"Part of the problem with Wicks is there is no leader on the job," said Jeffrey Zogg, managing director of the General Building Contractors of New York State. "Single financial responsibility gives the owner the best project—someone who is willing to guarantee a price."

Every year for the last two decades, abolishing the Wicks Law has been near the top of the wish lists for school and local-government officials when they come to the Capitol to lobby. And although its reach has been whittled down some, the law has remained in effect for most local governments and school districts outside New York City.

Little has changed because subcontractors and labor unions have considerable clout at the Capitol. Their power comes from political donations and their ability to provide workers for political campaigns. They fear that without Wicks general contractors would use their broader power to squeeze costs.

The most significant reduction in scope in the law occurred in 1989, when lawmakers set up a public authority to oversee school construction in New York City. Unions had to agree to that deal to guarantee an influx of state money to help pay for the new buildings, which provided thousands of new jobs.

School projects in Buffalo and Niagara Falls have also gotten Wicks exemptions, with unions accepting the same trade-off.

But Wicks remains in effect in most of the rest of the state, even as pressure is mounting from school districts, which have dramatically increased building projects in the past few years. Pataki has proposed abolishing the law, as he has in the past, and Senate Majority Leader Joseph Bruno supports doing away with it as well.

On the other hand, Assembly Speaker Sheldon Silver, D-Manhattan—the third member of Albany's ruling troika—has consistently blocked it.

Giving the reform plans a boost are the state's current fiscal woes. Although experts admit it's hard to put a number on how much money would be saved, a study done more than a decade ago by the state Budget Division estimated the annual savings at $400 million.

There's also the issue of letting local schools and governments make up their own minds on the best way to run their construction jobs, one influential Democrat said.

"There's no doubt we ought to allow school districts and others to do construction in ways they believe to be most efficient and cost-effective," said Assembly Education Committee chairman Steven Sanders, D-Manhattan, sponsor of a bill to eliminate the law.

But politics—and the Legislature's traditional inertia on controversial issues—weigh against action, he added.

"The trouble is you've got different unions on different sides of this issue," Sanders said. "If you resolve it, you are going to cause a lot of people to be unhappy. Usually when that happens . . . the Legislature tends to gravitate towards the status quo. By maintaining the status quo, you probably make the least amount of people angrier than they are now."

The cause of the anger is a law originally passed in 1912 designed to curb the power of general contractors and corruption on public jobs.

There was a flurry of action by other states to adopt similar statutes in the early part of the last century, but they were generally repealed as problems with coordinating jobs became apparent.

Now most construction projects around the country—private and public—are awarded to a single bidder, typically a general contractor. That firm then hires subcontractors, such as electrical, plumbing and other specialty firms, to do much of the work.

But under New York's Wicks Law, four separate contracts are awarded—for general contracting, plumbing, electrical work and heating/ventilation/air-conditioning.

The problem with this arrangement, its critics claim, is that nobody is in charge.

"Often I've wanted to get a striped shirt and whistle to use on the job site," said Russell Davidson, the architect of the White Plains High School addition whose job included helping to coordinate the project. He described himself as a referee among the four contractors.

"I've had to stand in the middle of a concrete slab on a job site for an hour and a half while four contractors argue over who has to clean up the garbage," he said. "They'll say, 'Those aren't my wires, pipes, drywall, etc. They belong to somebody else.' It's unproductive work and it causes delays."

Delays started early on the White Plains High School project, which added a new science wing, media center and cafeterias to the 40-year-old building.

Summer is a crucial time for school renovations, not only because the weather is favorable for construction but because the building is empty.

But shortly after the work started in the summer of 2000, it was halted by a labor dispute.

The general contractor, Trataros Construction Co. of Brooklyn, had both union and non-union workers. The other three contractors were all union shops.

When Trataros hired non-union laborers for excavation

work, the union workers put up the rat and a picket line. Work ground to a halt for about three months—the prime of the construction season.

"Trataros didn't want to use union labor, and the other three wouldn't cross picket lines," Davidson said.

"We go to the general contactor and say he's not maintaining labor peace," as required by his contract, Davidson continued. "'But mine are all peaceful,' he responds. 'It's the others who aren't working. They're demonstrating. . . .' Divide up the contracting it becomes impossible to hold anyone accountable for labor peace."

Eventually Trataros hired union excavators and the job continued. Trataros officials couldn't be reached for comment. Their telephone in Brooklyn had been disconnected.

There was also a dispute over who had to fill in the hole dug for a fuel tank.

Davidson explained that fuel tanks used for most projects now are made out of two layers of fiberglass and are so light they have to be strapped down to concrete slabs. When buried, special fill has to be used around them because they're delicate. The preferred material is a small washed stone known as pea gravel.

It was the general contractor's job to dig the hole for the tank, and the HVAC contractor's job to install the tank. But responsibility for the pea gravel was a "transitional area," Davidson said.

The argument went on for a month before Trataros agreed to do it.

"If there was a single prime contractor, there would be no dispute," Davidson said. "He would just order someone to do it."

But with a Wicks job, he said, the four contractors tend to look to shed work since that increases their profit.

And sometimes it is just cumbersome.

Michael Lynch, director of buildings for the White Plains schools, pointed to a light switch in one of the school's new corridors while leading a reporter on a tour. But instead of just a switch flush against the wall, the entire electrical box for the switch was exposed, as was a small metal conduit that carried the wire up to the ceiling, giving the hall an industrial, or unfinished, feel.

"At first, we thought we didn't want any light switches in the corridors. We'd just leave them on all the time for security," he said. "But then we changed our minds. We told the architect. He made drawings. But by the time we negotiated a price and signed a contract with the electrical guy, the general (contractor) had already put up the wall. So here are the switches on the outside. There were a billion things like that."

Another example, according to Davidson: When the general contractor pulled heating units out of a terrazzo-tile floor, the floor needed to be patched. But the general contractor said that was the heating contractor's job. The heating contractor disagreed and it still hadn't been done by the spring of 2004, Davidson said.

The project was declared substantially completed in June of 2003. But in the end, the project ended up where many Wicks projects do—in court.

The school district is trying to get $2 million from Travelers insurance company, which took over the liabilities of Trataros when the district decided Trataros wasn't performing adequately. The other contractors, meanwhile, are trying to collect a total of about $6 million from the school district because of delays in the project.

Things were at least as bad in the nearby Bronxville school district, where a construction project that was supposed to be finished almost two years earlier was still going on last year. The latest tentative completion date is almost three years late. And the cost, originally pegged at $22.3 million when voters approved it in 1999, is now slated to be almost $31 million.

"Our graduating class this year went four years without a gym or a cafeteria," said superintendent Warren Gemmill. "That's just unconscionable."

He blames the Wicks Law for much of the delay and extra cost, echoing White Plains officials about the problems of trying to coordinate the work of the four prime contractors.

Like White Plains, Bronxville had a problem with a general contractor who used non-union workers and the other contractors who did.

Gemmill said the district hired a competent firm, the Turner Construction Co., to manage the project. But the problem is that because of the Wicks Law, Turner didn't have enough authority to properly manage it.

"Rather than having that single point of accountability, they're really more in the position of advising us and convincing and cajoling contractors," Gemmill said. "They don't have the leverage they have when they have a private job."

But subcontractors and union officials say the blame is misplaced, and that jobs done under the Wicks Law can and often do come in on time and on or under budget.

Michael Misenhimer, head of the state Subcontractors' Association, is also a former member of the school board in a district in rural Albany County, Berne-Knox-Westerlo.

"When we built a $5 million addition under Wicks a few years ago, it came in six months early and $50,000 under budget," he said.

Most construction job problems are caused by incompetent general contractors—not the Wicks Law, said Martin Hopwood, vice president of Richards Conditioning of Tuckahoe, which did the heating/ventilation/air-conditioning work on the White Plains project.

He said that if insurance companies held those firms to higher standards before selling them policies, incompetent firms would be weeded out. No contractor can bid on a public job without liability insurance.

"Then Wicks would work better," he said. Otherwise he likes the current arrangement.

"I like the fact I can bid a job directly and if I have the low bid I get the job," Hopwood said. "When I work for a general contractor I'm not sure I'll get paid. There is more incentive for the general (contractor) to cut back on what I do."

"If there was not a Wicks Law I would go out of business," said Louis Coppola, whose plumbing firm, L. J. Coppola of Thornwood, did the plumbing work at White Plains High School.

"I don't like to be shopped on every price I put in," he said. With Wicks, "I can bid what I think the job is worth and if I don't get it I move on."

More important politically than the subcontractors are the union plumbers, electricians and sheet-metal workers, many of whom earn more than $60 an hour on projects like this. They also don't want the law changed.

"The main concern for union members working for subcontractors is there are places in the state where there are no union general contractors," said Denis Hughes, president of the state AFL-CIO, which opposes any change. "They purposely don't want union guys on the job. So a union contractor will never get the work without Wicks."

Labor and government leaders along with contractors agree that the wages paid to construction workers wouldn't change if Wicks were abolished. Virtually all public construction jobs in the state are covered by the prevailing-wage law, which in practice mandates that union-scale wages be paid to workers whether they're organized or not. But it may affect the craft-union members who work for the electrical, plumbing and heating contractors who now get Wicks contracts.

Despite the opposition, some lawmakers think that the law could be modified, but probably not repealed, soon.

"We keep talking about mandate relief," said state Sen. Nicholas Spano, R-Yonkers, the Senate sponsor of Sanders' bill to abolish Wicks. "This is one way of providing meaningful relief without having to provide real dollars. It would be popular to enact."

He said full repeal is unlikely, but that the threshold for

jobs covered by Wicks, which has stood at $50,000 for decades, could be raised to $1 million or more.

"There has been a lot of public attention drawn to Wicks by school districts who feel the costs have risen steadily as a result of this law," he said, and changing it could be a way to slow that rise.

A potential compromise would be to mandate that the general contractors when bidding on a job specify how much they intend to spend on subcontractors, to prevent them from being squeezed, suggested Assemblyman Joseph Morelle, D-Irondequoit in Monroe County.

"That would answer the major objections of the subcontractors and the organized opponents of reform on this issue," he said.

What strikes Lynch, head of buildings for the White Plains district, is how the law has survived this long largely intact.

"How can there be something so many people don't want and they just don't change it?" he asked, speaking of the Legislature. "I don't understand that."

In 2005, no change was made to the law.

☆ Court of Claims Awards ☆

Two hasty dives off a pier at Coney Island Beach in Brooklyn on May 23, 1992 not only made quadriplegics out of two young men from Staten Island, but also cost the City of New York $25 million.

It could have been much more. The brothers who made their fateful Memorial Day leaps sued the city and the initial verdict rendered by a Brooklyn jury called for the city to pay more than $104 million, but was reduced in later court action.

The two brothers, Virgil Brown, then 26, and John, then

27, dove off a 700-foot-long city-owned fishing pier that juts out from the boardwalk of the famous seaside resort. They had to scale a three-foot wooden-slat fence to do it, and look down at the shallow water about 10 feet below the pier.

"I was cooling off. It was very hot that day," Virgil Brown, now 39, who was a construction worker before the accident, recalled recently.

He said he couldn't tell from his perch on the pier that the water was only a few feet deep. He broke his neck when his head slammed into the sand.

His brother, John, seeing Virgil in distress, dove in to try to help, and suffered a similar injury.

New York City taxpayers had to pay because the jury decided that the city was totally responsible for the accident, despite what the city claimed was the bad judgment of the two men. The key fault of the city, the court ruled, was not posting "no diving" signs. That warning is now stenciled every few feet along the fence.

"If there had been a sign telling me not to dive, I wouldn't have done it," Virgil Brown said.

If the pier had been owned by the state government rather than the city, however, the award likely would have been far less because the state Legislature has established a separate system, known as the Court of Claims, to hear lawsuits against it. Judges appointed by the governor, not juries, decide the awards. Municipalities want to be allowed to join the system, but the Legislature has kept the door firmly shut.

Many other states have a system that limits awards against all levels of government, on the theory that all citizens and taxpayers have an interest in restraining the payouts.

But there is no protection for local governments in New York. It's another reason that combined state and local taxes in New York are the highest in the nation, local-government officials claim.

"We're not a private party. We're a branch of government," said Edward Farrell, executive director of the state

Conference of Mayors, and a leading advocate of extending the
protections the state government has to municipalities. "We
believe some coverage should be afforded to public entities.
We're not saying there shouldn't be awards, but we should
have protections, such as caps (on awards) that are available to
governments in other states."

Pataki has proposed amending the constitution to
extend the same rules that govern suits against the state to
local governments. The idea also has the support of Senate
Majority Leader Joseph Bruno. The Senate, however, won't
move on the bill until the Assembly acts—under the usual
Albany common wisdom that it makes little sense to anger
people for something that is unlikely to happen.

And the measure has virtually no chance in the
Assembly, which is dominated by Democrats from New York
City, where most of the awards—and the opposition to chang-
ing the system—come from.

"You know the real world," said Assemblyman
Anthony Seminerio, D-Queens, sponsor of the reform measure. "This isn't going anywhere."

Those who want to change the law claim that "runaway" juries in New York City vote for big awards because
they see a chance to reward injured people and have a distant
and sometimes hostile entity pay the cost.

Opponents to change say the lawsuits are so prevalent
in New York City because the jury system provides a vital layer
of defense for citizens against wrongs committed by the city
government—often its police department.

In 2003, New York City paid out about $500 million in
claims. In 1978, the total was just $21.4 million. There is no
figure for a total paid out by municipalities in the rest of the
state, but officials estimate it to be in the millions of dollars.

Meanwhile the state paid out just $32.6 million in Court
of Claims awards in 2003.

"People sue the City of New York for just about any
injury sustained on city property or incurred during involve-

ment with a City employee," according to a city proposal to limit the awards. "Because of sympathetic and generous juries and laws that do not create an even playing field, they often recover in full, even when the city is just the innocent or slightly responsible deep-pocket defendant."

The City Law Department cites other cases as examples of what it sees as unfair verdicts:

> ➢ $2.1 million to a passenger who was hurt when a taxi rammed into an abutment. The jury found that the driver was mostly at fault, but that the road design was 5 percent responsible. But under a doctrine of "joint and several liability," the city has to pay the bulk of the claim;
> ➢ $4.8 million to a 12-year-old girl who was a passenger in a car that swerved to avoid hitting a city-owned ambulance and hit a tree. She suffered a broken leg that fully healed;
> ➢ $1.2 million to a fifth-grade teacher who hurt his knee playing basketball in the school gym/cafeteria. He claimed the cafeteria floor was slippery and not level.

However, opponents of changing the law say that giving up jury trials would deprive citizens of one of their most fundamental rights, and would be unfair to many city residents, especially minorities.

"The right to a trial by jury is rooted in the New York State Constitution," said Martin Edelman, president of the state Trial Lawyers Association. "That is a most precious right. To give that up, you need a very powerful reason."

"Getting rid of jury trials would put regular folks at a disadvantage," said Assemblyman Keith Wright, D-Harlem. "If the city needs some relief, it needs to be more vigilant about making things safer."

Opponents to the move have their own case to cite to make their point. It involved a 29-year-old Florida resident named Anthony Baez, who died after being assaulted by a police officer outside his family's home in the Bronx in 1994.

Baez was asphyxiated after he and his brother got into an argument with police officers after the football they were throwing around banged off the roof of a police cruiser. Family members testified that one of the officers put him in a choke hold.

The officer was cleared of a criminal charge, but the family sued and was awarded $3 million by a jury. Some of the evidence brought forward in the civil case also led to the officer being found guilty in a later federal trial of depriving Baez of his rights.

All of that may not have happened if the Baez family hadn't been able to bring a lawsuit heard by a jury, Edelman said.

Nor do the lawyers think that the city got a raw deal in the case of the brothers injured in the dive off the Coney Island pier.

"There was more than ample evidence that the city had violated state regulations by not posting 'no-diving' signs on that pier," said Harvey Weitz, the lawyer who represented the Brown brothers (Weitz and Assembly Speaker Sheldon Silver are associated with the same law firm). "This was no runaway jury. . . . Factually I had a powerful case."

The city doesn't contend that the brothers should not have been compensated, said Thomas Merrill, deputy chief of the city law department's tort division. A court of claims judge would have certainly mandated a significant award, he said.

"You get juries who are prone to sympathy," he said. "There is a sympathy element. There's not supposed to be."

The Brown brothers are now living on their own, with around-the-clock care paid for with the award from the city, and have learned to manipulate TV remote-controls, telephones, computers and other devices with their mouths.

"Sure I'd like to be able to walk, but I still got my brain, I still got my health," Virgil Brown said. "Some people give up. I'm not in that state of mind."

He thinks the ultimate decision about awards in cases like his should be left to a jury.

"A judge, most likely is not going to feel as compassionate as a jury. The jury will have more compassion," he said.

Not all of the money, of course, went to the brothers. Weitz, following standard legal practice, got a third of it, or more than $8 million.

"Do I make a good living at it? I certainly do," Weitz said. "I make no bones about it. I try tough cases some people deem impossible, and I've been successful."

☆ Scaffold Law ☆

On a snowy Saturday morning in January in the Rochester suburb of Henrietta in 1999, a roofer named Scott Miller was laying shingles on a two-story home in a new subdivision.

When it was time for him to come down, according to lawyers involved in the case, he decided to first climb onto the lower garage roof. So he unhitched his safety line to make that switch.

But he slipped and fell to the ground about 20 feet below. He broke one ankle in two places and shattered the heel on his other foot.

Miller, who under state law was entitled to workers'-compensation benefits to pay for his medical care and a portion of his lost wages, also sued the roofing company for $5 million.

While in other states the case would be decided on how much blame would be placed on the company for any failure

to provide a safe workplace versus how big a role Miller's decisions played in his injuries. But, in New York builders say the
deck is stacked against them: Miller's role couldn't even be
brought into the case.

"Because it was absolute liability, we didn't have any
defenses," said Eileen Buholtz, the Rochester lawyer who represented the roofing company, Besroi Roofers, in the case. "We
couldn't argue bad judgment or any negligence on his part. We
were stuck."

And so, builders say, are they. Because of a unique
New York statute known as the Scaffold Law that holds
builders absolutely liable in most instances for injuries caused
by falls on work sites, they are having trouble getting liability
insurance. And when they can get it, it is so expensive that it
adds as much as $10,000 to the cost of building a home, they
say.

"I guess I'm one of the lucky ones," said Bernard
Iacovangelo, the CEO of Faber Homes, which built the house
whose roof Miller fell from. "I can still get insurance." But the
price went from $14,500 five years ago to almost $92,000 now.

Miller's case was eventually settled for less than $1 mil-
lion. But that and other awards like it, builders say, are driving their rates through the roof.

Tony Putrelo, who runs a commercial construction
company in Sequoit, a small Oneida County community south
of Utica, said he saw his liability insurance premium go from
$137,000 a year to $460,000 after a worker was awarded $75,000
for a fall that Putrelo claims was the worker's fault.

"That just about put me out of business," he said.
"When I bid a job for $35 an hour for a carpenter, the insurance
costs me almost as much."

While many builders traveled to Albany last March to
press their case to get the Legislature to change the law, Putrelo
wasn't among them.

"It's not worth it. It's like talking to a freaking wall," he
said.

The cause of their problem looks clear to people like Putrelo, Iacovagelo and other builders: the state's antiquated law gives them little or no chance to defend themselves against lawsuits resulting from injuries that are not their fault. The way to fix it is to have the Legislature pass a law that allows juries to consider whether actions of the worker—like Miller unhooking his safety line—may have contributed to the injury. (Miller couldn't be reached for comment and his lawyer, Dominic Pellegrino, didn't return phone calls.)

But to those on the other side, the situation looks far less clear.

Trial lawyers, who usually get one-third of the awards given to injured workers, blame the insurance companies, which they say have artificially inflated rates to increase profits in the wake of the decline of their investment income from Wall Street.

"This is an insurance problem," said Robert Brenna, a Rochester trial lawyer who handles scaffolding cases. "Their basic goal is: give us your premiums and we don't pay anything."

"People still have this idea that this is a runaway jury system," he said. "It's not. You know that McDonald's case that a woman spilled coffee on herself and got millions? That's not true," he said.

(The award against McDonald's to 79-year-old Stella Liebeck of Albuquerque, New Mexico, who suffered third-degree burns over 16 percent of her body in the 1992 incident, was reduced to $480,000 on appeal.)

However, losses on general-liability policies in New York are five times higher than seven comparable states, according to a study done for the American Insurance Association.

The discrepancy is highest in New York City—745 percent above the norm, according to the report. Even in the rest of the state, the losses were still 235 percent higher than the average of the other states.

The report said about one-third of the difference is due to the Scaffold Law.

A study by the St. Paul Travelers insurance company, the largest writer of liability insurance for contractors in New York, said the scaffolding law accounts for much more: about three-fourths of the losses they have paid out in New York on the claims of general contractors are because of the Scaffold Law.

"There has been a tremendous upsurge in claims since 1996," said Raul Allegre, a St. Paul Travelers spokesman— almost 150 percent.

He said he suspects that a change in the workers'-compensation law in 1996 that limited lawsuits for injured workers under that statute led to more suits being filed under the Scaffold Law.

"There has been no upsurge like this anywhere else," he said. "This is not a crisis anywhere else."

But if New York has more worker-injury-related lawsuits than other states, it is also safer than most states to do construction work, according to federal Bureau of Labor Statistics figures used in a study done by the state Trial Lawyers Association.

The state had fewer than five nonfatal injuries per 100 workers in 2001, lower than all states except Louisiana, which had fewer than four and a half, according to the study.

A year earlier, 30 of the 1,183 construction deaths in the country were in New York. That was only 2.5 percent of the total, while the state accounts for about 6.5 percent of the nation's population.

"New York State's unique Scaffold Law has been a significant factor in achieving this success," the trial lawyers claim in their report.

But builders say that other factors, like responsible contractors, might be behind the stellar safety record.

The trial lawyers' report also points to the collapse of a pedestrian bridge over a road project near Utica in 1992, when a worker died and seven others were injured, and the collapse of a 14-story scaffold in Manhattan that killed five workers as evidence of the danger of the job and the need for strict laws.

The scaffolding law has been around since 1885. "New York has had a lot of tall buildings for a long time," as well as a sense that the people working on them needed to be protected, pointed out Assembly Labor Committee Chair Susan John, D-Rochester.

But two decisions in the last dozen years—one in 1992 and the other last December—highlight the dispute over it.

The 1992 decision involved a contractor named Daniel Spano, who was hired by the Roman Catholic Diocese of Buffalo to help demolish the Corpus Christi Church school in that city.

Spano and two men working for him were on the fourth floor of the school, a floor above the gym. The workers testified that Spano ordered them to knock out trusses that were supporting the floor they were standing on. They said they warned him that if they knocked down the trusses, the floor on which they were standing would collapse.

Spano told them to do it anyway, according to court records. The floor collapsed and all three were injured. The Appellate Division of the state Supreme Court ruled nonetheless that the diocese had to pay damages. The court said that under the Scaffold Law, the owner essentially had no defense if a worker on a construction site was injured in a fall.

"Absolute liability is imposed on defendants, the owner and contractor, where, as here, plaintiff was engaged in the performance of his work at the time he fell from an elevated worksite," the Appellate Division of the state Supreme Court ruled.

The verdict in this case was part of a trend that seemed "like a violation of common sense," Michael Steinberg, a law clerk and labor-law expert, wrote in an analysis of the case.

But some lawyers say a case decided in December 2003

by the Court of Appeals, the state's highest court, turned the law back in the direction of the owners.

The court said that Rupert Blake, a New York City contractor, was not entitled to damages after he fell and broke his ankle while working on a two-family house in the Bronx because the accident was completely his fault. He apparently forgot to lock the extension clips of the ladder in place before climbing up on it. He fell when the ladder retracted.

"The point of the (Scaffold Law) is to compel contractors and owners to comply with the law, not penalize them when they have done so," Judge Albert Rosenblatt wrote in the court's unanimous decision.

But that's not the end of the builders' or insurers' problems, officials say.

"Now (the Scaffold Law) is not a complete giveaway, just a big giveaway," said Bernard Bordeau of the state Insurance Association, an industry group. "But it doesn't have insurance companies flooding back into the market. The only thing that will get them back is to repeal it."

The builders are planning to launch their own insurance company through the state Builders' Association in response to the refusal of many private companies to write policies for them.

Lawmakers in Illinois, the only other state for years to have a similar statute to the Scaffold Law, repealed their law in 1995.

"It's been a tremendous help and a definite savings. General liability rates dropped dramatically," said Todd Maisch, a lobbyist for the Illinois Chamber of Commerce. He said liability insurance rates have dropped about 20 percent.

The Illinois AFL-CIO is working to get the law reinstated, because "the more safety the better,'" said union spokeswoman Beth Spencer.

Maisch pointed to figures that show Illinois workplaces are now safer than they were when its version of the scaffold-

ing law was still on the books, but Spencer said they could still
be improved.

Maisch said "sheer political muscle" got the change
through when Republicans gained control of both branches of
the Legislature as well as the governorship for the first time in
decades.

Late in March of 2004, a group of builders met with
John, who as the Assembly Labor Committee chair is the key
New York legislator in this debate. A bill to repeal the law
sponsored by Morelle, the Monroe County Democrat, was sitting in her committee. Although she was open to talking about
the issue with the builders, she wasn't convinced the Scaffold
Law should be repealed.

Steve Spitz, who runs the Javen Construction Co. in
Penfield, Monroe County, told John that until 1996 he was paying about $35,000 for a $15 million liability policy. Now he is
paying $153,000 for $5 million of coverage.

"I used to sleep well with $15 million of coverage. I
don't sleep so well with $5 million," he said.

He blamed the steep rise in premiums in part to a claim
of a painter who was hurt on stairs his firm had installed on a
school-construction job.

"I have absolutely no defense," he said.

"For the first time I've considered, should I be in this
business?" Spitz told John. "Maybe not."

John said she sympathized with the squeeze Spitz and
the other contractors are in, but she said she's not convinced
repealing the scaffolding law is the answer.

"I know premiums are going up and some can't get any
insurance at all," she said. "This a problem we're trying to
work through."

"We're trying to get a handle on how much the increase
in insurance rates has to do with (the Scaffold Law)" she told
the builders. "Other kinds of insurance are going up fast as
well.

"Some of my colleagues would say this is a manufactured crisis. I'm not saying it's a manufactured crisis," she said.

In a later interview, she said she looking for a way to get insurance more available and premiums down without doing away with the law, which she thinks is important to keep workplaces safe. But so far there have been no discussions along those lines.

"They don't want a modification of the law," she said of the builders and other scaffold-law opponents. "They want no law. I'm not sure the Legislature is ready to have no law."

No change in the law was passed in 2004 or 2005.

☆ 207A ☆

When a Yates County deputy sheriff named Loren James slipped on a patch of ice and fell while making a routine patrol stop in Branchport, New York, on a January night in 2001, he had no idea that the legal dispute resulting from his injury would start a chain of events that local-government leaders in New York think will cost them millions of dollars.

There had been a rash of business break-ins in the rural Finger Lakes county that holiday season, so Sheriff Ronald Spike had urged his deputies to be vigorous in their nightly rounds. James, then 38 and an 11-year veteran of the force, got out of his patrol car a little before midnight on January 12th to check the Branchport Hardware building on Route 54A.

"I was checking the hardware store when I slipped on the ice," he said. "I tried to grab something to break my fall and that's when I wrenched my back."

He was out of work for almost a year.

Yates County thought that workers' compensation, the state insurance program that pays for the medical bills and a portion of the salary of injured workers, would cover the cost.

But James sued, claiming that under a 41-year-old state

law unique in the country that affects only fire and law-
enforcement workers, he should get his full regular pay of
$666.80 per week, tax-free, in addition to medical care.

The county was confident it would win the legal fight
because the Court of Appeals had issued a ruling in 1999 that
was generally interpreted to mean that a police officer or firefighter had to be performing a duty involving "heightened
risk," like fighting a fire or chasing a criminal, when injured to
get the extra benefit. Making a routine check didn't seem to fit
that category.

Yet in a ruling that surprised municipal officials and
lawyers alike, the state's highest court ruled in December 2003
that any time a public-safety worker is on the job and injured,
he or she is eligible for the benefit.

At the same time, the court ruled that a Greenburgh,
Westchester County, police dispatcher, David Wagman, was
eligible for the benefits after he hurt his back trying to move a
box of teletype paper with his foot.

The court also ruled that four Nassau County jail
guards should get the benefits. They were hurt by:

> walking into a TV hanging from the ceiling;
> opening a door;
> sitting in a chair whose leg collapsed; and
> getting hit in the shoulder by a swinging door.

The immediate financial implications of these cases
were small. Wagman, for example, was back at work in a
week. The James verdict cost Yates County $8,000.

But lawyers agree that the decision means that more
firefighters, who are covered by a similar but more lucrative
pension plan, will be eligible for the supplemental benefits.

Disabled firefighters get full pay, tax-free. When the
salaries of working firefighters go up, so do their pension payments. They also get taxpayer-financed medical benefits.

"This could vastly increase our costs because so many

more people will be eligible," said Linda Kingsley, the City of Rochester's chief lawyer.

Rochester paid about $2 million in the extra pension expenses for firefighters in 2001, out of a statewide total of almost $16 million in supplemental payments, according to the state Conference of Mayors.

The International Association of Firefighters could come up with no other examples of states that provide so generous a pension plan.

Especially in the wake of the September 11th terrorist attacks that killed 344 firefighters, few would begrudge firefighters and their families adequate pay and benefits. Still, the supplemental pension is another unique New York program that helps to make residents of the Empire State the most heavily taxed in the country.

While most of the Rochester firefighters who are getting pension supplements from the city were hurt while fighting fires or on related tasks, Rochester taxpayers are also paying to those who injured:

> A knee stepping off a fire truck;
> A back lifting a heavy object; and
> A back moving laundry in a fire house.

"If someone is fighting a fire and falls off a roof, we'd be crazy not to grant those benefits," said Michael DeLong, a Scarsdale official and former village administrator in Pelham, which fought a long, losing battle over benefits for a firefighter who twisted his knee when he slipped on a wet floor while answering a telephone. But he said those not injured in the line of duty should not be entitled to the enhanced benefits.

"We've been fighting this for years," he said. "It traditionally comes up in the Legislature, but it never goes anywhere. They're not going to fight the unions."

Nor should they, said Charles Morello, president of the state Professional Firefighters Association.

"It doesn't matter what job you're on, whether you're walking in the door of a house on fire" or waiting at the fire house. "When you punch in, you're on the clock. When a worker becomes injured, he should be eligible for any benefits that are available. It's totally ridiculous and very shortsighted to even consider changing that," he said.

James, now back at work as a Yates County deputy sheriff, agrees.

"It's good that everybody who works in law enforcement doesn't have to be questioned about how he got hurt," he said. "If he gets hurt while on the job, he should get paid."

There are about 7,200 paid firefighters in the state outside New York City (which has about 13,000 and a separate pension system), Morello said, and their salaries vary from about $45,000 a year in most of upstate to $50,000 to more than $60,000 downstate.

About 5,000 of those firefighters outside New York City work for cities and villages, with the rest employed by fire districts set up by towns that typically have departments that are a mix of paid members and volunteers.

Seven firefighters died in duty-related incidents in both 2002 and 2003, with four of them volunteers in each year. Their survivors are eligible for federal and state life-insurance benefits.

There are about 1,100 former firefighters that receive disability pensions ranging from about half to about two-thirds of their salaries, tax-free. The decision on who is eligible for these rests with state Comptroller Alan Hevesi. Generally, the disability does not have to be shown to have happened on the job.

About half of those—551—also get the special pension supplement. That extra benefit, when added to the regular pension, equals what they would make if they were still working.

These pensions are typically decided upon by a panel

appointed by the local government, and have to be for injuries that occurred on the job.

The supplemental benefits for firefighters were established by the Legislature in 1938 in recognition of the hazardous nature of the work. They were extended to police and other law-enforcement officers by the Legislature in 1961 and later years, but with the major difference that the extra benefits end when the injured party gets a pension.

Courts have gone back and forth on what injuries entitle uniformed workers to the extra benefits, lawyers say.

In 1999, in a ruling hailed by local-government officials, the Court of Appeals decided that a Nassau County corrections officer who was injured while driving home from a special assignment was not entitled to the extra benefits. The court ruling was interpreted to mean that the officer wasn't entitled to the benefits because his injuries weren't related to "heightened risks" associated with his law-enforcement duties.

Several bills were introduced in the Legislature to remove the "heightened risk" test, but none passed.

But in December 2003, in the ruling that included the James case, the high court said that its 1999 decision had been misinterpreted by lower courts, and that any injuries sustained while on duty should be covered by the extra benefits.

"The Court of Appeals did for them (police and firefighters) what the Legislature wouldn't do," DeLong said.

Municipalities had hoped to shift the cost of the extra pensions to the state pension system in the late '90s when the state fund was flush with investment earnings. Now, the state system is having troubles of its own because of sagging investment income.

The mayors' group has a bill waiting to be considered by the Legislature that would limit the extra benefits to those hurt while performing a hazardous duty, but so far no lawmaker has stepped forward to champion it, and it's not on Pataki's radar screen, either.

"When someone is running into a burning building to try to save someone, you don't want them to worry about how they're being compensated," said Sen. Joseph Robach, R-Greece, Monroe County, who sponsored a bill to remove the "heightened risk" test before last December's court decision accomplished it. He said the way to help municipalities' budgets this year is to try to bring down their pension-fund contributions.

"It's difficult to get a majority member (of the Legislature) to sponsor a bill that would reduce the scope of this benefit," said John Galligan of the mayors' association.

No change was made in 2005.

☆ Binding Arbitration ☆

With the average pay of police officers in Long Island's Suffolk County at $105,000 a year in 2004, local-government officials are blaming a state-imposed system that takes the final decision on salaries for police and firefighters out of their hands and gives it to a state-appointed arbitrator.

"How can you control property taxes if you can't control salaries?" asked Farrell, of the state Conference of Mayors. "You can't."

Steve Levy, the Suffolk County executive who was a state lawmaker before that, agreed.

"Our experience on Long Island has been that there is a leapfrogging effect between Nassau and Suffolk counties with arbitrators in one county using decisions in the other as a benchmark," he said, "ultimately leading to an uncontrollable spiral."

Levy was the only "no" vote in the Legislature against extending the binding arbitration statute in 2003. In fact, he made trying to slow the rise in police salaries one of the cen-

terpieces of his county-executive campaign, after a state arbitration panel granted the Suffolk police a 20 percent pay raise
over four years, driving the average pay over $100,000 a year
for the first time for any department in the state, and possibly
the country.

The system has led to Nassau and Suffolk having the
highest top patrolmen's salaries among the country's 200
biggest municipal departments, according to Policepay.com, a
consulting company.

But there is little chance that lawmakers will change the
law any time soon, despite the likelihood of steep rises in property taxes in many parts of the state, caused at least in part by
state requirements that localities pay for a portion of Medicaid
expenses as well as steeply rising pension expenses.

The law is one of the prime examples of what local officials call "unfunded mandates" that help push local taxes in
New York to among the highest in the country.

The mayors for years have been trying to get state lawmakers to change the law governing police and fire contracts
first passed in 1974, when local-government workers won the
right to form unions.

As part of that deal, public workers relinquished the
right to strike. But in addition, most uniformed workers got
the right for a three-member panel to decide on a contract if
they failed to reach an agreement with the local government
they work for.

The system has resulted in the average local police and
fire salary increases awarded by state arbitrators exceeding the
Consumer Price Index every year from 1994-2003, according to
the mayors' group.

While the governments think the system needs to be
changed, the unions for the most part are happy with it.

"We think for the most part they've been fair, absolutely," said Ken Long, legislative chairman of the state conference
of Police Benevolent Associations. "Once we gave up the right
to strike (without binding arbitration) the employer could

pretty much tell you what he's going to give you and you don't have any choice."

A check of police salaries from around the country helps to confirm why. While Suffolk and Nassau counties are at the top of the list of salaries for police departments national-ly, other New York departments are also among the most high-ly paid.

The glaring exception has been the nation's biggest municipal police force, the 30,000-member New York City Police Department.

Top pay for a NYPD officer was $54,048 in 2004, com-pared to $83,766 in Nassau County and $84,545 in Suffolk County (the higher average-pay figure of $105,000 for Suffolk County, determined by the Center for Governmental Research, includes longevity pay, shift differentials and other add-ons).

That's due in part to the fact that New York City was excluded from the binding-arbitration law until 1998, when the Legislature passed and Pataki signed a bill extending the statute to the city over the vehement objections of then-Mayor Rudolph Giuliani. He said the city and the police union should have the final say over how much to pay its uniformed employees.

An arbitration panel awarded the NYPD officers a 10 percent pay hike over two years in 2002.

The biggest bone of contention in the proceedings is deciding what a local government has the "ability to pay," which is one of the benchmarks laid out in the law.

That ability needs to be "something more limited than the countless authority to raise real property taxes or increase sales taxes," Levy said in a proposal to state lawmakers to change the law. He said that his county faces a budget deficit of as much as $238 million in 2005, although that has since been reduced by tax revenues coming in faster than expected as the economy has recovered.

Arbitrator John Sands, who decided the Suffolk case, referred to what he called "the country's long established conservative budgeting practices of underestimating revenues and overestimating expenditures."

"No one can doubt the importance of a well paid and well maintained police force of high morale," he wrote in his decision that granted the police officers the 20 percent raise over four years. "The state legislature has recognized the essential and distinguishing character of police and fire work by providing compulsory arbitration procedures that apply to no other classes of public employees."

"The issue really is ability to pay, and no one wants to take it head-on," said Sen. Mary Lou Rath, R-Amherst, former chair of the Senate Local Governments Committee and a former Erie County legislator who has voted against extending the statute in the past.

She recalled that Pataki several years ago proposed a commission be established to make recommendations on what "ability to pay" ought to mean. But then he did nothing to push it, she said.

The Senate doesn't want to change the law until such a group has studied the issue and made recommendations, said Senate GOP spokesman Mark Hansen.

"For years we have advocated that ability to pay should be looked at in terms of . . . the effect on other services," said Eva Hassett, a lawyer for the City of Buffalo, whose finances are in such disarray that a state control board is overseeing them. It's also the city where a state arbitrator recently ordered the government to reinstate about 20 blue-collar employees who had been laid off in a cost-cutting move.

"Police and fire wage increases have been far greater than in the other departments," she said. "While those are important departments, those raises have resulted in cuts in other departments. There needs to be some indication here who would be hurt" by granting the wage hikes to the police and fire unions.

Pataki promised again in 2005 to propose a bill "to require binding arbitration panels to give priority consideration to a municipality's ability to pay," but doesn't mention a panel to examine the issue in detail.

"We're going to continue to encourage the Legislature to support the governor's reforms," spokesman Michael Marr said.

Rath said the governor needs to step up.

"The governor needs to get the political will somehow to appoint a blue-ribbon panel and hold hearings. We need to find out what taxpayers are expecting in relation to what they want to pay," Rath said.

"As long as we have communities that are demanding high levels of service, but also demanding officials keep taxes low, until we take that on I think this issue is going to plague us," she said.

No change was made to the statue in 2005.

Gerald Holman (left) head custodian at White Plains High School, and Michael Lynch, director of facilities for the school district, show off the school's new library. The Wicks Law delayed the project for almost two years.
(Photo by Mark Vergari)

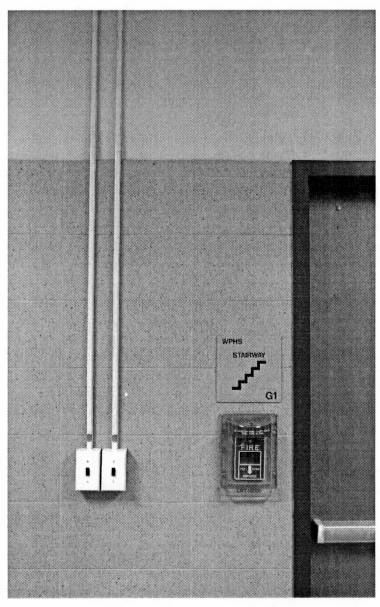

Exposed light switches and wires in
White Plains High School addition
(Photo by Mark Vergari)

Coney Island pier that the Brown brothers dove off

Ed Farrell of the state Conference of Mayors:
often on the losing side in the Legislature

(Photos by Mark Vergari)

Harvey Weitz:
"This was no runaway jury"
(Photo by Mark Vergari)

Susan John presides over an
Assembly Labor Committee meeting
(Photo by Mark Vergari)

Bernard Iacovangelo: Insurance costs up 6-fold in five years
(Photo by Will Yurman)

Tony Putrelo: talking to lawmakers
"like talking to a freaking wall"
(Photo by Marilu Lopez Fretz)

Robert Brenna: Scaffold Law "is an insurance problem"
(Photo by Will Yurman)

Top:
Assemblyman
Keith Wright: city needs
to make things safer
(Photo by Mark Vergari)

Left:
Sen. Mary Lou Rath:
"The governor needs
to get the political
will. . . ."
(Courtesy of Sen. Mary Lou Rath)

Part 4

☆ **What's Being Done** ☆

CHAPTER 9

THE ART OF THE DEAL

☆ ☆ ☆

"Team New York," a group of about 15 state and local economic-development officials from the Empire State, was ready for the big game.

The team was set to try to impress on some of the more than 3,000 corporate real-estate executives and consultants who had gathered at a convention in Chicago the advantages of doing business in New York.

They had rented a cavernous ballroom with a wall of windows overlooking the Chicago River in the convention's headquarters hotel. They had a jazz band playing softly in the background. They had tables groaning under the weight of a sumptuous breakfast buffet.

But early on a Sunday morning last May, they had the room mostly to themselves.

"This doesn't look good," said Jeffrey Janiszewski, the team leader and an official from the state agency that promotes economic growth, the Empire State Development Corp.

But two hours later, his mood had brightened considerably. About 340 people, apparently most of them late risers, were in the room, many talking to team members, who stood out in their gray-and-blue "Team New York" golf shirts.

"A lot of states do events at night, but a breakfast is more business-like," Janiszewski said. "The music isn't loud. We're insistent on an event where networking is possible."

Networking was the main activity at the convention, run by a group known as Corenet, the nation's largest and best known association of commercial real-estate and economic-development executives. The breakfast, which cost New York taxpayers about $24,000 to put on, was one of the highlights of New York's attempt to convince members of the powerful group that they should bring businesses and jobs to the Empire State.

The New York wooing at the convention also featured a lavish, $15,000 dinner on the 67th floor of the Sears Tower, overlooking the city's waterfront, put on by a Hudson Valley organization for about 70 of these catered-to influential people.

The state and localities like Rochester and the Hudson Valley made such a major effort to attract attention at the convention because the economic-development game has changed in the last decade or two, real-estate executives and government officials said.

While 10 or 20 years ago many states, cities and counties were content to accommodate whatever businesses decided on their own to move in, now most fiercely compete for them. At this convention, scores of states and localities were using tools ranging from booths to barbecues to banquets to try to attract the attention of the people who help decide where businesses will grow or relocate.

And if they can get their attention, the states break out the big weapons. New York, after what some consultants said was a late start, is in the thick of this competition, offering tax breaks, training grants and other incentives.

Yet while most of the dozens of consultants interviewed here gave the state high marks for its marketing efforts, many also said that New York is fighting with the equivalent of one hand tied behind its back: Taxes and other high costs place it at a significant disadvantage when competing with other states.

It's the problem most frequently cited in New York's dismal record of job growth, which is the lowest of any state over the last 40 years.

Overall, corporate executives rank New York's business climate as the second-worst in the country, according to a survey done in 2002 by Development Counselors International, a Manhattan-based consulting firm. California had the worst reputation—the position occupied by New York in the previous two surveys, taken in 1999 and 1996. Texas and North Carolina had the best business climates, according to the survey.

"Rightly or wrongly, New York's reputation is it is highly taxed and highly regulated," said Robert DeRocker of Development Counselors. "Its localities are viewed as being either congested or depressed."

"The business climate is improving but it still has a long way to go," said Dan Malachuk, director of business-relocation services for Richard CB Ellis, a Manhattan-based commercial real-estate firm.

"I tend to believe it has the most dysfunctional government in the western world. . . . It's the sense its got too many people on the public payroll that make too much money so the taxes are high and the costs of doing business are out of line," he said.

Others see improvement.

"In general, New York's reputation has gotten more business-friendly over the last few years," said another consultant, Michael Henderson, who works for Cushman and Wakefield in Manhattan. "It's been much more aggressive in terms of economic development. They've been able to change some laws and practices to make it more attractive to businesses."

"That said, it still is, in some companies' view, not the best place because of high costs, high taxes, strict business and labor laws, laws on workers' compensation," he said. "Things that tend to cost companies money."

Other studies put New York in a more favorable light. In a survey of new corporate facilities published last year by *Site Selection Magazine*, a trade publication, New York placed second behind Ohio. New York can be expected to score relatively high since it is the third-largest state, and the rankings aren't adjusted for population.

"It still shows that relatively we're doing better," said Brian McMahon of the state Economic Development Council, a private group of economic developers. "Seven or eight years ago we weren't even on the list. It counterbalances a lot of the losses."

New York has had some impressive "wins" in the site-selection game. The Geico Insurance Co. announced last year that it was creating 650 jobs in the Buffalo suburb of Amherst within three years, and may eventually employ 2,500 people there.

And Pfizer, the Brooklyn-based drug manufacturer, announced last year that it was consolidating its research and headquarters operation in Manhattan. The pharmaceutical giant got $98 million worth of taxpayer-financed incentives, including breaks on sales and property taxes as well as training grants and reduced utility rates. In return, it is adding 2,000 jobs to the 2,500 it already has in New York.

"We are under intense pressure to lower capital and operating costs," said Kathleen Norat, the former head of the Dutchess County Economic Development Corp., who now is a site-selection consultant and was involved in the Pfizer deal. "Without incentives, costs in New York are higher than elsewhere. Incentives are essential."

She said New Jersey and Michigan offered far larger incentives to Pfizer, but the New York breaks along with the advantages of keeping most of its operations in the Big Apple overcame the more lucrative packages.

Many states and localities have been courting potential

developers far longer than New York has been in the game, the real-estate executives said.

"The Southeast has had very aggressive incentives for years," said John Sisson of LMS Relocation Services in Greenville, South Carolina. "They had to be. Their skill set wasn't as great."

He said many states in the Northeast and Midwest figured that their new jobs would come from companies they already had, but have now come to realize they have to compete for them with the rest of the country.

"While costs (in New York) were high 40 years ago, business was good and the profits were high," said Thomas Mooney, CEO of the Rochester Business Alliance. "People were less inclined to complain about the costs then. We didn't have the competition around the world as we do today."

But now with other parts of the country and the world seeking the same jobs, "the cost structure becomes glaring," he said.

A stroll around the convention floor showed how glaring those cost differences can be. The booths resembled a candy store for businesses looking to move.

"Wyoming: where profits and mountains both reach skyward," a sign read at the booth manned by Ray Scachatti, an economic-development official for the Cowboy State.

"We're a mineral-extraction state," he said, referring to the oil and coal that are the mainstays of the economy and provide the bulk of the state's tax revenue.

"We have no income tax. No tax on gross sales. No tax on inventory. . . . We get a free ride."

That's also, essentially, the deal that the city of Burley, Idaho, has to offer developers.

The city, Robert Shepard of the local economic-development agency explained, took ownership of 276 acres that were formerly home to a potato-processing plant. The city is now offering 50-year leases for the property to potential developers with no property tax.

"The first question we hear is, 'What are our taxes going to be?'" he said. "We have a good answer for that."

New Yorkers were also busy touting their wares.

"We're promoting Empire Zones," said Mark Haggerty, who was manning the Syracuse booth. He was referring to the state program, popular with businesses, that provides deep property tax breaks, tax credits for job creation and other benefits in designated areas.

"That helps to break down the perception that New York is too expensive," he said.

When people ask about the snow (at 173 inches for the 2003-2004 season, Syracuse was the snowiest major city in the country), "We say we like snow and we're hearty," Haggerty said, "and we're good at clearing it and it doesn't impede business."

Syracuse's booth was next to one promoting two California cities—Ontario and San Juaquin—which, Haggerty noticed, also have generous incentive programs as well as snow-free weather.

But nobody was talking about snow the next evening, when a New York group—the Hudson Valley Economic Development Council—put on an extravagant private dinner for about 70 people who had the power to throw a lot of jobs New York's way.

Several other states planned similar events. Outside the convention hotel, buses lined up to take invited guests to the dinners. A waiter in white gloves, for example, passed out glasses of champagne to those heading on a trolley for a dinner sponsored by Delaware.

The Hudson Valley council is a four-year-old group headquartered in Orange County and bankrolled to the tune of $7.5 million by the Central Hudson Electric and Gas Co. Consultants said they were eager to go to the group's dinner, one of the night's hottest tickets, because of good reviews of a similar bash put on by the group at a Corenet meeting a year earlier in Atlanta.

"We look upon this as another form of advertising," said Anthony Campagiorni, the group's executive director, when asked about the thinking behind the wining and dining. "If we don't land a project from this, the event is not a success."

The Hudson Valley guests first sipped chardonnay and other wines at the Metropolitan Club, high in the Sears Tower overlooking the city waterfront and Lake Michigan.

It was a soft-sell event.

A chef imported from the Culinary Institute of America in Hyde Park, described the menu to the guests in detail: cream of asparagus soup, salad with goat cheese and vinaigrette dressing, pork medallions (from Hudson Valley farms) marinated in olive oil, sweet corn polenta with strawberry shortcake and whipped cream for dessert. Three kinds of wine would accompany the appropriate courses.

"I heard enough. Let's go," quipped one impatient diner, eager to dig into the feast.

The guests moved into the dining room, and during the meal, an influential site consultant from Los Angeles, Steven Marcussen, stood and offered a toast:

"On behalf of those of us from California, thanks for having us," he said, as executives from 3M, JP Morgan and other companies looked on.

"If you have a project in our areas, call us," Campagiorni said as the dinner broke up. "We can help you. . . . We had a wonderful time hosting you."

"So many communities would die for an audience like that," said Brian Schwagerl, a senior real-estate executive for the Hearst Corp., as the diners filed back to the bus.

"I'm confident we'll get a project out of it," Campagiorni said later.

Nothing had materialized by mid-July, but Campagiorni said that some later discussions with people at the dinner looked promising.

"We're in a good position," he said.

The pursuit didn't end when the convention did.

A week after the Corenet convention, the Hudson Valley group hosted a day-long event for about 10 consultants to show off the region.

At the end of June 2004, Greater Rochester Enterprise, a year-old group set up with $14 million in private and public money to be spent over five years to try to attract new jobs to the Finger Lakes region, hosted seven consultants and three of their spouses for a three-day tour of the area. It included golf at the Oak Hill Country Club, dinner at George Eastman House, where jazz musician Gap Mangione played, a trip on the fast ferry to Toronto and dinner at the Rochester Yacht Club.

Although no deals had materialized yet from that event, it was deemed a success by Vicki Pratt of Greater Rochester Enterprise.

"The idea with having them come here in the first place was to attract leads," she said. "We can't attract businesses if people aren't even looking at us. We want to be on their radar screens."

☆

The Chicago event also displayed a different view of taxpayer subsidies for business that appears to be far more rational and economical than the unfettered competition among American states and localities.

Wales has much to offer potential investors: a productive work force, a strategic British Isles location and spectacular countryside. But it lacks the lavish subsidies that many American locations can roll out.

"I can't believe the grand incentives being offered by some North American locations," Anne Reynish, vice president of the Welsh Development Agency, said as she sat at the country's booth at the Corenet convention.

The Wales incentives pale beside those offered by

others in part because the country is part of the European Union, the federation of 25 European states that has integrated the continent's economies to the point where most now use the same currency, the euro.

To discourage competition among states for companies, the union established a commission to regulate subsidies. The more depressed the region, the greater the incentives that can be offered.

The idea was to avoid a "subsidy race," Adinda Sinnaeve, an EU commission member, told an audience at the University of Minnesota last year. She said such a contest might just transfer problems from one country to another, waste public money and weaken companies by addicting them to government handouts.

Wales gets more subsidies than most other parts of the union because it is poorer than the EU average. Reynish displayed a map showing much of the country colored dark green, denoting the areas eligible for the deepest of the union's three levels of subsidies.

"The system is helping Wales," she said. "The region has only 2.9 million people, or about 5 percent of the United Kingdom population, but gets 8-12 percent of overseas investment in the country," she said. Foreign companies like Ford, Airbus and Sony all have major manufacturing facilities in Wales.

There are no similar subsidy controls in this country, which some think is a problem.

"The beauty of the EU system is they have a unified, multi-country, very uniform way of defining distressed areas, not 50 definitions of blight like we have," said Greg LeRoy of Good Jobs First, a non-profit group based in Washington that is critical of government subsidization of businesses. "It's a really good way to assure that (the subsidies) go to places that need them."

But even the most ardent supporters of the EU acknowledge it's unlikely to be adopted in this country.

"Detailed EU-style regulation of all types of subsidy by Washington is politically not feasible for now," said William Schweke of the Corporation for Enterprise Development in Durham, North Carolina, an advocate of more regulations for business subsidies. He said such a system runs counter to what he sees as "the strong anti-federal sentiment in this country."

That leaves New York in a position where it has to offer incentives to most firms that are thinking of making a move just to be in the game with other states, according to state economic-development officials and private real-estate executives.

"(Incentives) are overblown in their importance in many ways in the early phases of a project," said Gene Deprez of IBM Business Consulting Services in New Jersey. "The cost of labor and real estate matters far more."

But, he continued, "It becomes important in the later phases, when you're down to a short list of three or four. If any of the three or four can do it and are equally positioned, then the tiebreaker might be incentives."

Some say the tax breaks and other incentives offered to businesses by New York are already too steep and drive up the taxes of individuals.

While corporate income taxes accounted for 10.5 percent of state revenues in 1979, the figure had dropped to 6.6 percent in 2000, according to the Fiscal Policy Institute, a labor-backed think tank.

The institute and other groups called for the state to close "loopholes" that would collect about $1 billion more from corporations.

"They shake down state and local officials for more and more tax breaks, in many cases operating completely tax free," said Richard Kirsch, executive director of Citizen Action, an advocacy group. It's "a pretty good deal for them but a pretty bad deal for the people and the other businesses, which have to pick up a bigger and bigger share of the tab."

But such criticisms avoid a more basic issue, said

Matthew Maguire, a spokesman for the state Business Council, who said that small businesses, utilities and other companies pay taxes, but not corporate income taxes.

"This is just an attempt to change the subject, which should be that overall taxes are the nation's highest," he said.

For some individual firms in New York, the state economic development efforts have been important to their growth and survival. Others, however, have had less favorable experiences. Here are the stories of the interaction of four firms with the state's economic development efforts.

REFCON: Rockland County business leaders remember Herman Jakubowski weeping when he got up at a meeting last year and said he was moving his West Haverstraw-based company to New Jersey.

Jakubowski, a Rockland native, is president of a 60-employee firm called Refcon that he started almost 20 years ago. It manufactures custom food-display fixtures for supermarkets, colleges, corporate cafeterias and other clients.

He decided a few years ago to expand, and was looking to move into an existing building elsewhere in the county.

Jakubowski said he met with the Rockland County Economic Development Corp. officials more than 10 times.

"I just filled out forms. I never got a response from them," he said.

He said he also met with Empire State Development Corp. officials in their regional office in Kingston, Ulster County.

"We filled out forms that totaled 14 or 15 pages. We submitted it to them. We followed up with them," Jakubowski said. "We were told they never received it. So we Fed-Exed it again. Called them. Did you get it? Yes. But then we never heard from them," he said.

Then he called New Jersey economic-development officials. They helped ease the way for the company to move to Norwood, New Jersey, just over the border from Rockland and only five minutes from the Palisades Parkway.

"We were talked through the whole thing by the town. It was all done in one board meeting," Jakubowski recalled. The firm moved into its new building in 2004, the way smoothed by a total of about $500,000 in tax breaks and other incentives.

"If you're IBM in New York, no problem," Jakubowski said. "But if you're a small businessman, forget it.

"My only regret is that I didn't move out of New York sooner," he said.

A spokesman for the state-run Empire State Development Corp. said his records show that Refcon officials met only once with the agency in 2000 concerning a training grant that wasn't granted because authority to deliver them had been transferred to the state Labor Department. A spokeswoman for the Rockland County Economic Development Corp. said she had no information about Refcon.

The Empire State Development Corp. spokesman, Ron Jury, said that the agency has spent $864 million since 1995 trying to either retain jobs in the state or lure new ones in. He said the agency has had a hand in the retention of 205,000 jobs and the creation of 102,000 new ones. He said the agency doesn't track how much private investment its spending stimulates.

INTERCOS: But while New Jersey sometimes wins one, sometimes it loses one, as well.

In 2000, Intercos, an Italian-based cosmetics manufacturer, moved into what had been an empty 103,000 sq. ft. electronics plant in Congers, Rockland County, spending $12 million to buy it and the 27 acres is stood on. It moved 139 jobs from Ridgefield, New Jersey, and now has about 180 full-time workers.

The company was looking for land for future expansions at a location still within easy reach of its customers in Manhattan.

To help clinch the deal, the Rockland Industrial Development Agency floated $12 million in tax-free bonds, lowering the company's debt-service payments considerably.

The firm also got 35 percent knocked off its property tax bill in the first year. The discount has been reduced by 5 percent each year and will be phased out entirely in 2008 and will save the company about $300,000. The Empire State Development Corp. threw in $100,000 for the company.

"After a thorough survey of the market availability and the incentives offered in other states, we came to the conclusion that New York and more specifically Rockland County was the best choice for us," Intercos' boss Charles Gounod said when the deal was announced.

PAETEC: This Rochester-based telecommunications company wasn't looking for tax breaks or incentive payments—just a fair shake at winning a lucrative state contract.

"If you're a New York State company, it's difficult to do business with state agencies," said company president Arunas Chesonis. "It's unfortunate because there are other states, like Michigan, Massachusetts and New Jersey that give the home team an edge."

PAETEC wanted to submit a bid to the state Office of General Services to supply telecommunications services for state agencies. But he said OGS ruled the firm wasn't a qualified bidder.

Chesonis suspects that his firm just didn't have the political clout in Albany to compete with bigger companies seeking the contract.

"Companies like AT&T and Verizon can throw 30 lobbyists into Albany," he said. "Part of me says we should do that, but part of me says no."

Lobbyists weren't required until 2005 to report their activities trying to win state contracts, so there is no record of what the activity was surrounding the telecommunications contract PAETEC wanted to compete for.

A spokeswoman for the Office of General Services said

that PAETEC wasn't allowed to bid because its proposal didn't meet all of the requirements of the job.

"All contracts are awarded according to provisions of the State Finance Law and any outside factors are completely independent of the process," said the spokeswoman, Jennifer Morris. "In this case, the company's proposal failed to meet a number of substantial and material requirements listed in the RFP (request for proposals) and was subsequently disqualified from consideration."

Partly because his firm hasn't gotten state contracts, Chesonis said PAETEC has decided to build a new facility that will have about 500 workers in southern New Jersey instead of New York.

"We could have done it outside New York City or in Westchester," he said. "But the State of New Jersey is more aggressive and helpful in trying to drive business our way as well as with incentives."

FALA TECHNOLOGIES: Frank Falatyn, president of this Kingston-based precision machine shop, had never been to a trade show before state economic-development officials persuaded him to travel to "Semicon Europa" in Germany.

"It's the best thing I have ever done," he said. "We partnered with two German firms. We got some business out of it."

Before they left, the New York businesses went to meetings in Albany where they were advised how to get ready for the show.

"It looks more credible when you have a state booth and there's a dozen manufacturers around it," he said. "We all went under one umbrella and used an 'I Love NY' logo. If I went there by myself, who would have talked to Fala Technologies?"

The state also provided Fala with another key boost: job training.

When the company decided it wanted to do three-dimensional designs for precision parts on computers, Falatyn realized that his engineers didn't know how to do it. So he sent them to a state-sponsored class at Ulster Community College one day a week for 12 weeks to acquire the skill he said was vital to his company's future.

"The state has been great at providing us with training," he said.

How New York's Business Climate Measures Up

Here are the states with the best and worst business climates in 2002, 1999 and 1996. The number in parenthesis indicates the percentage of respondents who gave the state the top rating:

Most favorable climates

2002	1999	1996
Texas (25 percent)	Texas (30)	North Carolina (33)
North Carolina (20)	California (22)	Texas (28)
South Carolina (18)	North Carolina (20)	Georgia (27)
Florida (18)	Georgia (17)	South Carolina (21)
Georgia (15)	Florida (14)	Tennessee (20)

Least favorable climates

2002	1999	1996
California (57)	New York (29)	New York (55)
New York (36)	California (25)	California (47)
Massachusetts (18)	Massachusetets (19)	New Jersey (20)
New Jersey (15)	New Jersey (14)	Massachusetts (19)

Source: Development Counselors International

Business Expansion, by State

Here is the number of new business facilities or expansions that occurred in New York and other states last year:

State	Number of new faciiities
Ohio	587
New York	552
Texas	489
Illinois	451
Michigan	448
Pennsylvania	411
Indiana	401
Virginia	258
Florida	219
Kentucky	211

Source: Selection Magazine, a trade journal

The Chicago skyline viewed from the New York reception at the
Chicago Hilton Hotel
(Photo by Kenneth Dickerman)

Party favor: An "I Love NY" shirt

Consultant Kathleen Norat:
"Incentives are essential"
(Photos by Kenneth Dickerman)

CHAPTER 10

NEW YORK DREAMIN'

Just four years ago, Keith Wilson and his wife, Betsy, were living what most people would consider to be the good life in Hermosa Beach, California, a waterfront suburb of Los Angeles known for its exquisite sunsets.

Wilson, 38, had a good job with a dynamic bank, a manageable commute (about 40 minutes) by Southern California standards and, of course, warm, sunny weather 12 months a year.

But he packed up and moved to the Rochester area to become the chief financial officer of PAETEC, a fast growing telecommunications company.

"When I tell people back there that we had 10 feet of snow last year, but lost out on the "Golden Snowball Award" (for most snow in an upstate city) to Syracuse, they just shake their heads," Wilson said.

They are still no fans of upstate winters, but the Wilsons enjoy the Rochester Philharmonic Orchestra, snowshoeing as well as living in a 3,000-sq. ft. house (double the size of what they had in California and for less money) and a 10-minute commute from his Victor home to PAETEC's Fairport offices. They consider the area an ideal place to raise their two children, born in 2002 and in 2004.

Wilson's tale qualifies as a man-bites-dog story, since New York annually loses tens of thousands of people, many of them young professionals like Wilson, to Sun Belt locations and the companies, many of them refugees from upstate winters, that have relocated there.

For the year that ended October 31, 2004, the state's rate of job growth, 0.7 percent, less than half that of the nation as a whole. For upstate, jobs barely budged in that period, up just 5,500, or 0.2 percent.

Between 1990 and 2003, the figures are even more stark. New York added about 192,000 jobs in that period, a growth rate of 2.3 percent. That's only about one-eighth of the national growth rate in that period. In other words, if New York had added jobs at the same pace as the rest of the country in that period, 1.5 million more New Yorkers would be employed now.

But Wilson's experience, along with those of thousands of others, show why the economic landscape of the state is not all bleak, and that people who are optimistic about the state's economic future are not irrational.

However, officials of PAETEC, whose sales were expected to top $500 million in 2004 after only seven years of operation, and other companies that are doing well say they are thriving despite what most see as the state's difficult economic climate—chiefly, high taxes and other costs of doing business, like workers' compensation, liability insurance and energy costs.

They say that to truly thrive, the state needs to get those costs, now among the highest in the country, more in line with other states.

"We have to cut taxes and energy costs to create jobs," said Arunas Chesonis, president and founder of PAETEC.

Still, in the current climate, it is not impossible to find someone who has moved to New York for economic opportunity after working in, of all places, North Carolina, which has been luring away New York companies and workers for decades.

Tom Biggart, 48, is the manufacturing supervisor for Fala Industries, a precision machine shop in Kingston, Ulster County that does between $5 million and $10 million in annual sales.

Biggart had worked in Sanford, North Carolina for two years in a factory repairing injection molds for plastics. But his firm decided to close that operation and consolidate in another facility in the western part of the state, where costs are lower.

"The injection-mold industry is declining," he said. "I was looking to get into something more technical. There's more of a future here."

He figures it's about 12 percent more expensive to live in New York—everything from rent to fast food costs more, he said, but the salary hike more than makes up for it.

Fala, which has 48 workers, can afford to pay him more because "we have a really skilled workforce," said Fala president Frank Falatyn. "We do all precision work. We can compete on technology and small-quantity production." Production workers earn from $9 to $12 an hour, skilled workers $19-$22 an hour and engineers $60,000 to $80,000 a year.

Here's one market niche Fala has carved out.

Robots that are extensively used in semiconductor assembly typically turn on two narrow circles of metal separated by little metal balls that allow the metal circles to move in different directions with little friction. A factory may have 25 to 50 robots that use these parts, known as bearings. They cost about $10,000 each.

Falatyn said they used to last six months—but in 1998 Fala developed a way to make them (the method is a secret) that allows them to last four times longer.

"This business was created for us because IBM had a problem," he said. "Because they're a big company, they might not want to bother to figure it out. But for us it was worth it."

To some degree, the state's economic woes are self-correcting.

For example, Falatyn said markets for his products increased dramatically because engineers laid off in the early 1990s by IBM dispersed across the country. Many were familiar with Fala's products, and persuaded their new employers to do business with the small Kingston outfit. So IBM's problems had an upside for Fala.

"PAETEC has benefited from the downsizing of the corporate giants in Rochester, like Eastman Kodak and Xerox," Chesonis said. "There's a glut of highly skilled workers on the market."

"Because of downsizing, we're getting people with 5, 10, 20 years of experience at half the cost (of what they could command in salary elsewhere). And we don't have to put them through a lot of training," he said. "If it wasn't for the talent pool, we would not be here."

Then there's Con Med, a Utica-based manufacturer of medical devices that employs 1,200 people in Oneida County.

The area has been depressed for years, but that has driven down the cost of both labor and space, said CEO Joseph Corisanti.

"There's a strong work force in the Oneida County area," Corisanti said. They have been trained by GE and Lockheed Martin. Now we're getting these people."

The company also employs about 300 recent immigrants from Bosnia, Russia and Cambodia, who make between $7 and $14 an hour working mostly on assembly lines.

"We have good quality employees at good labor rates—it's cheaper than Denver, Santa Barbara or Tampa," he said—other areas where the firm has manufacturing facilities. And real estate is much cheaper.

Maybe an even more important factor in New York companies that are flourishing is home-grown leadership that has decided to accept the fact that it's expensive to do business here but stay anyway.

John Sammon is a Buffalo native, but came to love the Adirondacks while stationed at Rome Labs in Oneida County during his tour of duty in the Air Force in the 1960s. Now he is an avid kayaker and downhill skier, as well as president of Par Technology, a $140-million-a-year business that employs about 550 people in Oneida County that he helped launch more than 35 years ago.

"I get phone calls and letters all the time" from recruiters from other states, he said, but he has not been tempted to move.

"We could squeeze out a few more bucks elsewhere, but it's not worth it," he said, as an early-season snow squall whitened cars in the company parking lot last fall. "At the end of the day it was a family thing."

Among Par's products are the cash-register-type terminals on which orders are placed at McDonald's, Pizza Hut, Taco Bell and other fast-food outlets.

"The company's big selling point is the reliability of its machines, which are guaranteed not to break down for eight years," said spokesman Chris Byrnes. "They're easy to operate as well. The training course is about two hours—an important consideration in an industry where the average worker stays only 90 days," he said.

"The quality work force is the key to making reliable machines," Sammon said, "and that helps to offset New York's handicaps."

"We put up with the taxes and other high costs," he said. "We don't enjoy it. We endure it."

"We do business in spite of the economic climate, not because of it," echoed Richard Kaplan, president of Pictometry, an 87-employee firm in the Rochester suburb of Henrietta that provides three-dimensional aerial photographs to governments, fire departments, real-estate brokers and other clients. He predicted it will grow to 1,000 workers in five years.

Kaplan said he has also frequently been approached by three or four states in the last two years to move his business to a place where costs are lower.

"The reason we don't is this is home," he said. "I love

Rochester and New York State. To me it's the quality of life."

Such home-grown loyalty is less important in New York City's northern suburbs, where the continued dominance of New York City in the securities, media and fashion industries as well as the dispersal of some businesses out of Manhattan after the 9-11-01 terrorist attacks have kept the economy strong.

For example, Intercos, a Milan, Italy-based cosmetics manufacturer, moved into a vacant Sony factory in Congers, Rockland County, in 2001, mostly to be close to its customers in Manhattan.

"We decided about five years ago that the only way to increase our penetration in the New York market was to be here," said company spokesman Ann Hayden.

She said the location is close enough to Manhattan so customers, who work with Intercos to develop new cosmetics, can easily get to the plant.

Still, the company required a batch of tax breaks, including reductions on property taxes, to cinch the deal.

She said there have also been "challenges," including finding manufacturing workers (whose salaries she wouldn't disclose) who can afford to live close to the plant. She said the firm has leaned heavily on temporary-labor agencies.

That's not a concern in most of upstate, where rents and real estate are often a small fraction of what they are in the metropolitan area while jobs are far more scarce.

The charm of upstate can prove irresistible, even to those who earn a living elsewhere.

Martin Babinec, a native of the small Herkimer County city of Little Falls, started a business in California, TriNet, in 1988 that provides payroll, personnel and other services to high-tech companies, many of them in the Silicon Valley. It has since grown to a $40 million business with 200 employees.

"There's a huge cultural difference between the East and the West," he said. "In the West, there are more immigrants and an ethic of 'we're in the promised land now.' There's a pervasive entrepreneurial ethic. People are not afraid to fail. If you fail here, there is a kind of shroud put on you."

Yet even as his business was prospering, he felt a tug to move back home. He now lives with his wife and three children in a restored Victorian home overlooking a park in downtown Little Falls, and does much of his work long-distance, traveling between nine and 11 days a month to tend to his business in person.

He has also seen the downsides of living in a booming region.

"There's just not much sense of community in the Bay Area of California," he said. "More people are transients, most families have two full-time wage earners and commutes as long as two hours that give many people little time for interaction with others outside of work," he said.

He'd probably like to have a life more like that of Keith Wilson, the PAETEC official who used to live and work in California but now lives and works upstate.

"Would I like to do business in upstate New York? Absolutely," Babinec said.

But in Babinec's situation, he knows that's not likely to happen any time soon, and that government policies have to change to make the state more business-friendly.

"The transition to a knowledge-based economy has not taken place in New York," he said. "We need to make that happen faster."

Otherwise, he said, children will continue to grow up, go to school—and then leave New York.

"No parent wants to see that happen," he said.

If New York State is going to make the transition Babinec is talking about, it is likely to start in the Albany region.

The state is betting $300 million that a research center

on the SUNY Albany campus focused on nanotechnology—the study of components one-one-thousandth the width of a human hair—will become a world leader in the field, eventually drawing tens of thousands of well-paying jobs into the area.

The payoff has been modest so far, but still promising: semiconductor firms, IBM and a leading Japanese company have invested a total of $1.6 billion in related projects. And in January 2005, state leaders announced that another $2.7 billion in private investment is on the way, with taxpayers kicking in an additional $225 million. That could mean another 1,000 jobs in the Albany region.

Leaders of the effort say that Albany is well positioned to beat rivals from Japan, Europe and other parts of the United States to become the preeminent center in this promising field, but the issue is far from settled.

"Who is going to be the first to attract a critical mass of r and d (research and development) to attract companies?" asked Alain Kaloyeros, head of the Albany nanotech project. "This is our future. We're betting our name on this."

Meanwhile, the state has also helped to fund similar "centers of excellence" studying other promising disciplines, like biotech and super computing, in Buffalo, Rochester, Syracuse and Long Island. But the Albany center is the largest and farthest along toward a potential payoff.

Kaloyeros' legacy as a scientist and academic leader is still up in the air, but he has already proven himself to be an adept politician: Republican Gov. George Pataki and Democratic Assembly Speaker Sheldon Silver, adversaries on many issues, are among the center's biggest supporters.

Kaloyeros likens the center to a retail-shopping project.

"First you need anchor tenants," he said. "Then you can attract small and medium-sized spinoffs."

"We need a chip manufacturer to serve as the 'Macy's'— that's IBM," he said, referring to Big Blue's chip-making plant in East Fishkill, Dutchess County.

"Then you needed a global r and d consortium—that's Sematech," a group through which major chip manufacturers have pooled their resources to invent ways to create smaller and faster computer chips.

Tokyo Electron, a Japanese company that makes equipment used in the process, is another anchor, as is SUNY, which has created a new school—the College of Nanoscale Science and Engineering—that provides faculty and graduate students to help in research. The school has 81 students seeking graduate degrees in the discipline.

In the summer of 2005, Albany lost out on the chance to pick up two "anchor" tenants when Texas Instruments and Intel opted to build new chip plants in Texas and Arizona, respectively.

"So far the investment has yielded about 500 jobs at the center, a figure that is slated to go up to 1700 by early 2007," Kaloyeros said.

The computer-chip-manufacturing companies are attracted to nanotech because in order to keep making chips that are smaller, they have to get down to devices so small that they qualify as nanostructures—sometimes just a few molecules thick.

The industry has been making smaller and smaller chips for more than three decades, actually doubling the power of the chips every 18 months.

A small fabrication facility that has been built at the nanotech center for research purposes is designed to make chips on 12-inch wafers, considered to be the next generation after the eight-inch wafers now widely in use. The new IBM chip-making plant in East Fishkill produces 12-inch wafers.

Although the wafer is bigger, the system is far more efficient: 45 computer chips can be made on each eight-inch disc, compared to 125 on a 12-inch disc.

Each chip contains between 40 million and 50 million transistors—the switches that are the heart of the computing process.

But how to make them even smaller? That's the thresh-old problem researchers are working on.

As the size of the chips have shrunk, it has gotten more and more expensive to figure out how to make them even smaller. That's why the chip makers pooled some of their r and d resources into Sematech, and why they also sought partnerships with taxpayers and universities.

When Intel created the 386 chip that was introduced in 1986, the development cost was about $15 million, Kaloyeros said. The cost of developing the most recent chip: $16 billion.

One of the reasons that the field has attracted so much attention is that it has potential spinoffs that extend beyond the chip-making industry.

"This is not like the dot-com bubble, because this has potential applications in a number of fields," said Michael Fancher, the center's director of economic outreach, as he led a tour of the clean rooms, research labs and other parts of the center. Life sciences, drug delivery, aerospace, automotive and sensing devices are among the fields where the technology could develop significant new products.

For example, he mentioned research that is trying to figure out a way to test for blood sugar without breaking the skin, a process that could end the need for diabetes patients to endlessly prick themselves to measure how much insulin they need.

"That's the nirvana," Fancher said.

Is this a good investment for the state?

Some had hoped that the center would have already attracted another chip maker—in fact, land in Malta, a nearby community, has already been set aside for a plant. But the industry has been in a slump for the last few years and few new plants have been built. And those that have been built are near already existing plants—presenting Albany with a "chick-en-and-egg" problem.

"It does have the potential to be the next big thing in the high-tech industry," said Cary Snyder, one of the founders of Semiview, a California company that tracks technology companies.

"Commercial successes might be five or 10 years out, " he said. "Nanotech requires a heavy educational investment to commercialize it. We're in the early stages of that particular process."

He was cautious when asked if Albany has a shot at being the industry leader.

"That depends on what breakthroughs happen and where," he said. "You guys are lucky you have IBM. You certainly have the potential to do well in the New York region."

New York, with its heavy taxpayer investment in the field, is taking a different approach than Massachusetts, said Matthew Laudon, executive director of the Nanoscience and Technical Institute, a consulting firm based in Cambridge, Mass.

"It has great support from the state," he said of the Albany project. In developing its high-tech industry, Massachusetts has instead depended on university and corporate researchers to make discoveries that have spawned new firms he said.

But other states and countries have gotten into the nanotech game, Kaloyeros pointed out.

The European Community recently invested 300 million euros (about $400 million) in a 12-inch chip-making facility in Belgium. The German state of Saxony reached an agreement with two tenants to build a $450 million facility. The Japanese government has spent $1 billion to bring companies together.

Georgia has launched a nanotech initiative at Georgia Tech University and California recently approved a $1.2 billion bond issue for high-tech initiatives, $300 million of which is to be spent on a nanotech facility at the University of California at Berkeley. Texas has approved spending $395 million for a similar initiative at the state university's Dallas campus—a key to Texas Instruments building its new plant near there.

"The United States cannot compete in low-end manu-facturing," Kaloyeros said. "The future has to be in high end industry."

It remains to be seen whether nanotech is a major part of that future in New York.

Keith Wilson kisses his son, Garrett, as he returns home
from his job at PAETEC outside of Rochester
(Photo by Jamie Germano)

Richard Kaplan of Pictometry: "To me it's the quality of life"
(Photo by Will Yurman)

Frank Falatyn of Fala Industries:
Finding a high-tech niche
(Photo by Kathy McLaughlin)

SUNY Albany's Nanotech Center
(Photo by Mark Vergari)

Albany Nanotech boss Alain Kaloyeros:
"There is our future. . . ."

Roger Jakubowski moved from Rockland to New Jersey
(Photos by Mark Vergari)

John Sammon of Par Technology:
"We could squeeze out a few more bucks elsewhere,
but it's not worth it"
(Photo by Michael Doherty)

CHAPTER 11

TALKING TURKEY:
SOLUTIONS

☆   ☆   ☆

There is a New York where budgets are prepared in the open, terms of lawmakers are limited and candidates without deep pockets don't have to fawn in front of special interests to raise campaign cash.

That New York, though, is New York City, not New York State.

"If the argument is states are policy laboratories for the feds, it's not unreasonable for states to look at municipalities to see if what they are doing would work at the state level," said Blair Horner of the New York Public Interest Research Group.

The city system is hardly without warts. For example, Mayor Michael Bloomberg was expected to spend $75 million or more in 2005 to essentially buy a second term. As he did in 2001, he exploited a loophole in the campaign-finance law that allows unlimited campaign spending when it's the candidates' own money.

Still, New York City has instituted political reforms over the last 15 years that those who would like to shake up the Albany status quo can only drool over.

Here's what New York City has that the state doesn't:

> ➤ Campaign spending limits and a four-to-
> one match of public money to private;
> ➤ An independent budget office that is
> widely seen as a non-partisan dispenser
> of key information about city spending
> and tax collections;
> ➤ Term limits that make members of the
> City Council, the mayor and other elect-
> ed officials leave office generally after
> two four-year terms.

Why the city and not the state? History is an important reason.

"We wouldn't have such an open budget process if we didn't have the fiscal crisis," said Elizabeth Lynam of the Citizens' Budget Commission, a watchdog group.

She was referring to the city's near-bankruptcy in the 1970s when banks threatened to stop loaning the city money after years of the city borrowing money to pay for the salaries of cops and teachers and for operating expenses. That's the equivalent, in terms of the famous metaphor, of taking out a mortgage to buy groceries. The state had to step in and guar-antee the city's credit, and also take control of the city's spend-ing decisions.

"Ironically part of the reason the system improved so much was because of the state oversight and the threat that the state could always come back to take control," Lynam said. "That's even though the state doesn't always do a good job with its own budget."

The city also had political scandals so severe in the 1980s that a borough president, Donald Manes of Queens, committed suicide after facing corruption charges related to the city's Parking Violations Bureau.

"You need some scandal to get reforms like this," said NYPIRG's Gene Russianoff, who has been following city poli-tics for decades. "The when (Edward) Koch ran in 1989, he felt like he had to be a champion of reforms—that's where term limits came from."

In other words, things have to get so bad that they finally attract the attention of the public, which demands change. City voters felt outraged enough about the way their municipal government was operating to force change, but not so about their state government, which controls so much of their lives.

Not that Albany was scandal-free in the same period. In 1986, some lawmakers were indicted, but not convicted, of using workers on the public payroll for political duties. The Legislature responded by passing a measure requiring for the first time that legislative employees submit time cards to account for their activities while being paid by taxpayers. A state Ethics Commission and a Legislative Ethics Committee were also established.

But those panels have proven largely toothless.

Albany scandals never seem to have the same wattage as those in the city, and thus the public uproar has never been as great.

"Part of it is whatever happens in New York is on the 11 o'clock news," Russianoff said. "That's not true of what's going on in Albany."

It's not on the 11 o'clock news, of course, because no New York City network affiliate TV station regularly covers the state Capitol. Only the Time-Warner cable news station NY1, along with the public-television shows Inside Albany and New York Week in Review, regularly provide televised news about the state government for New York City area residents.

Lack of TV coverage not only from the city media but most of the rest of the state makes it harder to build the kind of outrage needed to force change, activists say.

"There has to be a lot of pressure, a lot of grass-roots activity—a lot of angst among the populace to move things," said Lynam of the budget commission. But that is much harder in the state than the city, she said, because the state is "far more diffuse."

But that doesn't mean it can't happen—this year's changes are Exhibit A. And there are some indications that state voters aren't done demanding change.

Take Mark Bitz, a 46-year-old Onondaga County turkey farmer. He sounds like a lot of other disaffected New York businessmen when talking about the problems of making a living in the Empire State.

"Property taxes, workers' comp, health insurance, electrical costs—they're all killing me," he said. "That's why I'm taking my investments elsewhere."

But unlike most business owners, he's investing time and energy into trying to force change. He has even set up a Web site (www.freenys.org) to push his reform agenda.

His goal: to persuade "the Republican and Democratic party committees . . . to nominate common, plain-speaking candidates with win-win philosophies, who are committed to restoring the democratic process."

Bitz is not alone. Other individuals and community groups all over the state have taken up the call this year for change, and dozens of lawmakers have presented different plans for how to shake up the status quo.

The ideas range from abolishing public authorities to allowing Election Day voter registration to having a one-house Legislature.

And the ideas are growing at what could be a fortuitous time: the early stages of the 2006 campaign for governor. All 212 seats in the Legislature are also up for grabs in 2006, as they are every two years.

The reform ideas are diverse, but many share one key assumption: that the state's economic woes flow at least in part from the flawed process by which laws are made in Albany.

The reasoning goes like this: If the process is fixed, the clout of pressure groups would diminish and the chances increased that problems that Bitz and other business leaders have been citing for years can be addressed. The bedrock democratic principle of the greatest good for the greatest number could reassert itself.

A key question, of course, is whether the improvements made this year signal the start of a reform era or just token moves designed to get the public, at least temporarily, off politicians' backs.

The danger, one student of state government said, is that the minor tweaks made in the system will take the steam out of the reform movement and nothing significant will happen.

"There could be just superficial changes made, and that could be passed off as reform," said Gerald Benjamin, a SUNY New Paltz dean and longtime observer of state government. He cited proposed changes in the state-budget-adoption system, where some power would shift from the governor to the Legislature, as an example of a sham reform. (The issue was to be decided by voters in the 2005 elections.)

The time for reform is now in part because "the chronic lateness (of adopting a state budget) became a symbol of legislative dysfunction, and that starting to scare people," Benjamin said. "Debt service is growing and the resources are not matching it—serious people are scared by that."

(By 2010, the state debt will have increased by 52 percent over a decade, to $55 billion, and taxpayers will be paying nearly $6 billion a year in debt service, Comptroller Alan Hevesi reported in September 2005.)

Others point to ever-higher state and local taxes, bribery, theft and sex scandals involving lawmakers and staff members and the continued economic struggles of parts of the state as creating the "perfect storm" for reform.

And the "perfect storm" produced some results in 2005.

The Assembly ended the practice of allowing members to vote while not being in their seats. The Senate still allows it, but only for routine measures. The Senate also still allows members to vote in committees even when they're not there (by written proxies) while the Assembly members actually have to show up.

The Assembly Rules Committee, formerly a phantom body that Silver uses to control the flow of legislation, now actually meets, although he still controls the agenda. Conference committees consisting of rank-and-file lawmakers were convened and did discuss budget issues, although obviously on very short leashes held by the legislative leaders.

Most significantly, the changes adopted leave the power of the leaders almost totally intact. Nothing was done to give minority members a more equitable share of power and money.

☆

What is the connection between empowering individual lawmakers and the economic health of the state? The key word is accountability.

"We need to hold these people accountable, and that's the first step towards competition," said E. J. McMahon of the Manhattan Institute. And competition means lawmakers would be more likely to make decisions that benefit the state as a whole rather than a pressure group, he said.

"They would be put on the spot on things," he said. "They would no longer be able to tell everyone they were with them and then say they're powerless because the leaders are against them."

Assemblyman Joseph Morelle, a Rochester-area Democrat who spends more time thinking about the state's economy than most lawmakers, looks upon a model for the state's economic resurgence as a pyramid, with the base of that structure a reduction in the cost of doing business.

But another way to look at it is as McMahon does—that before that can happen, the political system has to be aligned so that the overall good of the state drives government decisions. In Morelle's terms, that might be seen as making sure that we don't try to set up the base of a pyramid on quicksand.

Making the leap of faith that those foundations can be laid, Morelle, who represents an area that has been on the economic skids for years, can be forgiven for a little dreaming.

"Imagine New York State alive with entrepreneurial zeal," he said in a report on the state's economy issued in the summer of 2005. "Imagine homegrown inventors using their creativity to conceive of product and service innovations that expand our economy."

Of course, as he pointed out, he was describing his hometown of Rochester—but the Rochester of more than a century ago, when George Eastman was starting Kodak and the fruits of John Jacob Bausch's genius were sprouting into the optics company Bausch and Lomb.

Morelle's "Back to the Future" scenario doesn't involve a flex capacitor and DeLorean sedan as the Michael J. Fox movie did. Instead, after cutting costs, he wants the state to scrap tax breaks given to businesses in some geographical areas and do more to make the state friendly to entrepreneurs—the next-generation of Eastmans, Joseph Wilsons (Xerox) and Thomas Watsons (IBM).

He wants the state to concentrate on improving worker skills, attracting "creative-class" workers, making venture capital more readily available and expanding broadband technology, among other steps.

In an address to an audience of business leaders in the fall of 2005, Attorney General Eliot Spitzer, the likely Democratic candidate for governor in 2006, said much that probably resonated with Morelle.

Spitzer pointed out that government has been a key player in New York's economic success—the Erie Canal, state Thruway and building of the SUNY system were to him the prime examples of smart taxpayer investments that added immeasurably to the state's wealth.

But now, he said, government seems incapable of pulling off the projects needed for renewed economic success—like a new Tappan Zee Bridge across the Hudson River between Westchester and Rockland counties, or a new Peace Bridge from Buffalo to Canada or urban school systems that provide the skills that businesses need.

In the crowd for Spitzer's address was John Faso, the former Assembly Republican leader who narrowly lost the race for state comptroller in 2002 and wants to run for governor in 2006.

When asked for his reaction to Spitzer's speech, Faso said the attorney general seems to have lost sight of what Faso sees as the first job of the new governor: to get costs in line with other states. That's a point Spitzer mentioned but did not stress, and is also the bedrock of Morelle's plan.

Could a policy debate on reviving the state's economy actually break out in—of all places—a gubernatorial campaign?

Although history warns against such hopes, there is some reason for optimism that things are changing.

"We've gotten used to this pathology under this misapprehension that it's normal," Benjamin, the SUNY New Paltz dean, said of the way Albany operates. "First, we had to convince the state it's not normal. I think that's happened. There's a consensus that the current situation is bad and something has to be done about it."

Bitz, the turkey farmer, started paying attention a few years ago when he first considered selling his farm because of government mandates and taxes that he thought were unfairly cutting into his profit. He says the cost of doing business in New York adds about $600,000 annually to the expenses incurred by his $20-million-a-year business compared to what it would cost in most other states. He recently decided to expand his business in Canada rather than closer to home.

Besides, as Bitz pointed out, New York retains some powerful advantages over the rest of the country, which account for why he still does the bulk of his business here.

"It's a great place to live," he says of his home state. "We have the Finger Lakes and ideal climate for six to eight months of the year. We have no hurricanes. No monsoons. An abundance of water, great parks, great roads, great workers. There are a lot of reasons to be here."

So what's missing?

"We only lack a functioning democracy, fiscal integrity and discipline and leadership that is accountable to standards of performance," he said.

That also sounds like a description of New York City's government before its crises, scandals and reforms.

Will the state first have to sink to a comparable depth before changes are made? Maybe, but another route seems clear.

The public keeps up the pressure. The media pays attention. The Legislature and governor do more of their business in public. Then the politics of Albany become more closely aligned with the public interest. That would set the stage for the resurgence of the Empire State.

Bitz Turkey Farm: New York adds $600,000 to its operating costs

Mark Bitz on his farm:
talking turkey about government reform
(Photos by Kayte Martens)

Part 5

☆　Appendices　☆

Interview with Gov. George Pataki

Transcript of an interview with Gov. George Pataki and a group of his aides held in the governor's conference room on November 4, 2003. The aides present were secretary John Cahill, budget director Carol Stone, health secretary Robert Hinckley, education secretary Jeffrey Lovell, press secretary Joseph Conway and budget press officer Kevin Quinn.

GALLAGHER: The economy is the big issue to our papers and our readers, and we'll be writing a series of stories about it over the next year. There are three parts to the critique of not only your administration but also the Legislature. We're also taking a historical look at this thing back to Rockefeller, when spending and taxes in New York started to diverge from the rest of the country. There's a connection between our high spending, our high taxes and our relatively poor performance economically compared to the rest of the country.

PATAKI: I couldn't agree with you more. That's what I've been saying since before I was governor, since my first day in the Legislature.

GALLAGHER: The critique has three parts. The first is fiscal. That is, in the first two or three years of your first term, you

did a good job of holding down spending and taxes and
keeping them in line with the rest of the country. Since
then, you've gone back to the old ways. . . .

PATAKI: That's something easy to say, but the facts don't support it. Just look at the actual facts. If you look at us, New
York relative to other states in the country, we are third in
general-fund spending containment. . . . At a time when
New York has had an aging population and an influx of
immigrants, still in the top three in controlling general-
fund spending. If you go to all funds . . . we're seventh in
the country.

   That's an extraordinary record, particularly, as you say
if you want to put in historical context. Go back to the
Cuomo years, go back to the Carey years, go back to the
Rockefeller years, go back before then and tell me the last
time New York achieved those fiscal numbers.

   And I might say that's not withstanding the fact in
every single one of those budgets we've had a tooth-and-
nail fight with the Legislature that wanted to increase
spending . . . I don't think there's a governor in America
who looks at what's been done. I don't see you're going to
see a fiscal record like that. Where am I wrong?

GALLAGHER: If you take out the first three years. . . .

PATAKI: (laughs) Sure, and if you take out the last three years,
we're probably first in the country. You can't do it in a vacuum, Jay. When you cut something in year 1, 2 and 3
you're going to have to have more spending in year four
than if it hadn't happened in year 1, 2 and 3. That's just
ridiculous. . . . That was the foundation we worked hard to
achieve that we could build a firm foundation to build on.
What other state got four investment upgrades?

CAROL STONE: None that I know of.

PATAKI: As of September 11, 2001 we were sitting on massive surpluses, four credit-rating upgrades and 3rd or 7th in spending restraint in America. Ignore the first three years? That was the whole basis.

I remember sitting here with (Education) Commissioner (Richard) Mills . . . and he said, we need much more money for education. I told him that education is a priority, but we can't do it until we straighten out the fiscal condition situation of the state, and we did. When you look at the spending, Jay, we also include STAR, which is a tax cut, which is what, $2.8 billion?

The star program results in dramatically lower taxes for people across the state.

GALLAGHER: It doesn't help businesses.

PATAKI: No, it doesn't help businesses, but it certainly helps their workforce, and it helps the communities they want to locate in. I would ask you to take a look over those last eight years and say look at what they did, and look what New York did.

GALLAGHER: But the fact that we were still out of line after three years, why not continue those strict fiscal policies?

PATAKI: We have. We haven't reverted. Look at the cumulative record. Third in the country. I know people come in with preconceived notions, ahah, this is what happened, but it's just not true. Look at the facts. I am extraordinarily proud of this record. . . .

GALLAGHER: After September 11th, we had $3 billion in accumulated surplus but that was mostly used up in the 2002-2003 budget year.

PATAKI: Of course. We had an absolute catastrophe.

GALLAGHER: But spending went up that year.

PATAKI: If you remember Jay, we didn't have a budget. I refused to go along with the Legislature's spending demands. They passed a so-called baseline budget in hopes they would shame me into coming back and spending more. I refused. After the September 11th tragedy, we were able to enact a reasonable budget.

But Jay, it galls me.. Forget the first three years. Look at my fourth year. An election year. I was running for re-election. The Legislature went off on their own and passed a ridiculously bloated budget knowing since I had to run for re-election as a Republican in a Democratic state, there was no way I was going to veto these very attractive items. I line-item-vetoed I think 1,300-plus items, well over $1 billion in spending in my re-election year because I believe in fiscal discipline. I believe you build a sound foundation for the future. That was not one of the first three years. That was the fourth year.

Look at the 7th or 8th year when they passed their so-called baseline budget and we held the line and fought tooth and nail.

GALLAGHER: But then in October, you agreed on spending worth $500 million more.

STONE: If I could just interject, in October we went into special session and got some substantial reductions in spending and authorized revenues.

GALLAGHER: Wasn't it $500 million more than the baseline budget?

STONE: There were some pluses and minuses but on balance we achieved savings in the October session.

CONWAY: And we accessed more federal funds.

PATAKI: One of the things we've been working very hard on is accessing federal funds. As Sen. (the late Sen. Daniel Patrick) Moynihan used to point out, tens of billions a year we send down we don't get back. Jay, that should be part of the calculation is how much when you look at the burden how much we spend to Washington we don't get back. It's an enormous drain on the state's economy. Moynihan estimated 15, 16, 18 billion. Other analyses estimated it to be much higher. It all comes right out of New Yorkers and out of our economy.

CONWAY: That shows up in the growth of our all-funds growth.

PATAKI: Yeah, our maximization of federal funds to try to lessen that horrible imbalance.

STONE: Including the World Trade Center aid.

GALLAGHER: It's not like we don't get anything back for that money. We pay for the Armed Services out of that money.

PATAKI: The bottom line is we have a gross imbalance for Washington and it has a very real impact on the state of New York. Whether it's the Medicaid rate, where we get 50 percent where other states get 70 percent. We're now getting 52 (percent) for 15 months. Or the tax structure itself because New York and the entire Northeast are high income, high cost states, we pay proportionately much more in income taxes than other states. Whenever federal income taxes are cut, the largest beneficiary proportionately by far is New York.

GALLAGHER: Don't you believe in the progressive income-tax system? Shouldn't people who make more should pay more?

PATAKI: Of course. But I also think New York should get far better treatment out of Washington than we have.

STONE: In August (of 2001) we're still fighting with the Legislature that the national economy had turned down. In October, when they came back, we did some (school) building-aid reform, we did some revenue initiatives. We also simultaneously imposed the hiring freeze. That has saved us nearly 10,000 jobs. So there were a lot of administrative actions.

PATAKI: We also ordered all agencies to cut their spending by 5 percent.

STONE: Starting in 2001-2002 fiscal year, the governor recognized what was happening.

PATAKI: The reason we had the baseline budget in 2001-2002 is because we saw the national economic trends, and the Legislature either didn't see it or refused to acknowledge it.

GALLAGHER: In retrospect, would you have been better off saving some of that $3 billion in surplus money and using it for this year when obviously. . . .

PATAKI: No. We had an unimaginable catastrophe befall New York and it cost us enormously. It cost us most gravely in human terms. Overnight we lost 100,000 jobs. We had 30 million sq. ft. of office space destroyed.

Certainly the human consequences, but the economic consequences. We were dealing with an unimaginable crisis and we dealt with it extraordinarily well. And I'm incredibly proud of how this administration and all New Yorkers responded to the challenge.

GALLAGHER: Moving on to the economic issues, certainly during the first part of your tenure, the gap between job creation in New York and the rest of the country narrowed. I think there were two years, 1999 and 2000 when we surpassed the nation in job-creation rate.

PATAKI: When was the last time that happened?

GALLAGHER: Once under Cuomo? Maybe back to Rocky.

PATAKI: I don't know we had back-to-back years of surpassing the national rate of growth for the last 20 years. We're proud of what we did and what we're still doing to bringing back the economy in the face of very great challenges.

GALLAGHER: Since then we've slipped back. In the two years that ended in August (2003), we lost 3 percent of our jobs, compared to 2 percent for the nation.

PATAKI: I don't have the statistics, but if you look at our performance relative to the other industrial states near us, it's been virtually identical. But you have to understand Jay, those other states didn't lose 30 million sq. ft. of office space. The other states don't have a cluster of financial industry so when the stock market plummets and when the financial-services industry is reeling from scandals like Enron and others, it impacts New York State enormously. When the corporate-governing scandals hit, it impacts New York enormously. So we had extraordinary events. Maybe you could have predicted Enron. I didn't. Maybe someone could have predicted the economic consequences of 9-11. I certainly couldn't have.

Yes, New York has been harder hit than any other states by outside circumstances. California was hit by the dot-com boom collapse. But that was something Alan Greenspan was talking about year in and year out. I forget the term, maybe it was a bubble or something. Greenspan was warning about that. No one was warning about the financial-services industry the stock market and September 11th and losing 30 million sq. ft. of office space and the corporate-governance scandals.

That really hurt the New York economy. For all that, we can still look at tomorrow and next week and next year and the next decade with enormous optimism because we have provided the leadership to get through these incredible challenges. Whatever challenges are out there we will do it again. And we'll continue to build for a better future in this state. We're going to do it.

CONWAY: Back out New York City, and the rest of the state has been doing as well as the rest of the country.

PATAKI: That's the first time that's been the case in a very long time. The last recession in the Cuomo years, our recession was 5 or 6 times as strong. We went into it earlier and came out of it later. Particularly upstate, where durable-goods manufacturing is so important. That's what gets hardest hit in a recession. That didn't happen this time relative to the rest of the country. Obviously we went down as a nation. We didn't go down more. We didn't go down 5 or six times as much as was the case the last time because people do have much better confidence in the economic climate, the social climate, the quality of life and the future of this state.

GALLAGHER: I understand we're part of an international, national and regional economy. There are forces beyond New York State that caused manufacturing to virtually collapse, not only in New York but around the country. What do you see as the economic future of upstate? Obviously when employment at Eastman Kodak goes from more than 60,000 to 18,000 . . . it has an enormous impact. And Carrier and other well-paying industries are moving out. Do you think the Centers of Excellence will eventually create as many jobs?

PATAKI: Many more.

GALLAGHER: Many more?

PATAKI: Absolutely.

GALLAGHER: Are you counting on the centers to provide the catalyst that will revive upstate?

PATAKI: You don't put all your eggs in one basket. We've got to fight for every job. We're not giving up on any of the industrial and manufacturing companies that are here or that we want to bring here.

We got a new steel mill because of the Empire Zone in the Southern Tier. It's not simply high tech. We've got to fight for every job. We're fighting now to see if we can reverse Carrier's determination. But we're facing enormous challenges. I'll just tell you, when I talked about the chairman of Carrier.

In the container-compressor industry, where Carrier is one of the major components of what they produce in Central New York, ninety percent of their market is in Asia. They can produce those compressors for 30 percent of the cost in Asia as in Central New York. It is enormously difficult to compete in these times, but we are. And we're going to succeed in the competition.

We're going to succeed on a number of factors. One, we have to continue to lower the cost of doing business in New York State, which is why I'm going to continue to fight for tax cuts, workers'-comp reform, regulatory reform and energy-cost reductions. And by the way, if you look at all those things, whether it's gross-receipts tax on energy or power for jobs for energy or workers'-comp reforms, where it thinks rates are still 30 percent lower than they were despite the most recent difficult experience than they were before, we were able to get those reforms. We're going to fight for every manufacturing job and every job we can bring or attract.

At the same time, we're fighting on other fronts as well. Quality of life, having safe streets. Having clean air and more open space. In the 21st Century with personal mobility and corporate mobility you have to have the quality-of-life issues.

And then there's quality of the work force. I can't tell you what a success story SUNY and CUNY are. Having higher standards and more students and creating a great workforce that meets the educational requirements of the 21st Century. You have to do all of that. And that's apart from the Centers of Excellence.

But to me the most exciting element is the Centers of Excellence because we have the potential to create collaborate clusters not just for research and product development, but ultimately to commercialize those products across what we now call the Empire State high-tech corridor.

In 1988 Sematech made the case. When the 12 computer-chip companies from around the globe were looking for a place for Sematech, New York went all out. We lost. Sematech went to Austin, Texas. Look what has happened in Austin alone because of what Sematech and the semiconductor industry has done there. Well now, when Sematech was looking for a nanoelectronics center, they chose Albany. We won.

It wasn't just this time a competition among other states. There were other countries. The federal Republic of Germany offered a $100 million package to put the research center in Germany. There is every good reason to be very excited. I announced this initiative in the State of the State in 2001. We got authorization in the fall of 2001. It didn't start until 2002 and here we are not two years into the program and shovels are in the ground, equipment is there, the jobs are beginning to come.

Last week I was out in Hauptman-Woodward in Buffalo. We are going to have the finest center of bioinfomatics anywhere in the world. A $200 million center. The shovels are in the ground. A $300 million center. $150 million from us and $150 million from the private sector and not-for-profits. Here are capital facilities that are going to be the best in the world.

We attracted a Southern California research leader—Jeffrey Skolnick. At the time we got Skolnick, I went out to Buffalo and I said, mark my words, Skolnick coming here is going to be more important than Drew Bledsoe (former Buffalo Bills quarterback) coming here.

GALLAGHER: Drew's having a bad year.

PATAKI: Skolnick's having a good year. And we will. We just got us a new president of UB (University of Buffalo) from Santa Clara, California who was very involved in high tech. This is real. The rest of the country is taking notice. The rest of the world is taking notice.

Let me tell you one story as to how we've changed things in this state.

Before I took office in 1994, I went around and met with some of the top private-sector leaders across the state to talk to them and ask them, what do you think? Virtually to a person, they said, we're going to give up on New York. It's not going to work.

I remember sitting down with IBM. Lou Gerstner wasn't there at the time, to his number two guy, to talk about IBM and what they were doing.

GALLAGHER: Who was that?

PATAKI: I don't remember his name. But they pulled out a map . . . and said here's the IBM world headquarters. Here's the land that IBM owns. They showed me a blue line down the middle of the map of their property. They said, "do you know what that blue line is?" I said, "no."

It's a survey, maybe it's a stone wall or something. They said it's the Connecticut border. I'll never forget this. They said why should we be on this side of the border with our new world headquarters, as opposed to that side of the border, when Lou Gerstner and all our top officers live in Connecticut, and when we can be anywhere on the globe?

I was also told by Lou Gerstner at a subsequent meeting that he had made a conscious decision to pull every single IBM job out of New York State whenever there was a decision to be made about where you were going to close something, or where you were going to relocate something.

He had made a conscious decision every chance, he was going to pull jobs from New York and put jobs elsewhere.

To make a long story short, their new world headquarters is in New York State—the most advanced chip facility in the world again we had global competition, a $2.6 billion plant, is in New York. They are a key element of our Center of Excellence in nanoelectronics in Albany because they again have confidence in New York.

I remember talking to George Fisher of Kodak. George Fisher was telling me the same thing. He said, "We have a great plant," I forget what it was for, "in Colorado." And he said, "Do you know why it's in Colorado?" I said, "No, tell me." "Yes, it's the economic structure of the state, and it's also regulatory. Colorado has very high environmental standards, as does New York. But we can get the plant done in six months in Colorado, and here it would have taken, if we were lucky, two and a half years (in New York). And in the market, we couldn't wait that long."

Obviously Kodak is struggling in the global marketplace and scaling back. But we no longer have companies doing that . . . it was one of the inspirations for our shovel-ready program where we have sites where you can go in a month.

We've listened, we've responded. These are the toughest economic times we've faced as a state since I don't know when. . . . Our state, our policies, for all the difficulties we're in now, are successful.

GALLAGHER: Were you discouraged that during the last legislative session that virtually every initiative business was asking for—reforming workers comp, doing something about tort reform, scaffolding law, Wicks, all of the things we hear local governments talk about year after year as things that discourage business and drive up their costs? Despite the unprecedented crisis, the $12 billion potential hole, despite the economic downturn, despite 9-11, none of that stuff got done. What is it about Albany (that tops such common-sense reforms from happening)?

PATAKI: I think it's disappointing but it's not discouraging. You never get discouraged. You always have to live up to the fight. . . . There are enormous entrenched interests in the Legislature that just don't want change. And we saw that when we battle for the workers comp change and when we fought for some of the minimal success we've had with the tort issues. We proposed a number of tort changes that would have helped New York City Mayor Mike Bloomberg. At a time when it wasn't just the state but also the city that was facing real economic pain. None of it was passed. It's clearly disappointing but not discouraging. You have to move forward. I can't tell you the times we've talked with contractors and others about everything from vicarious liability in the automobile industry, which we should abolish.

GALLAGHER: It seems like a no-brainer.

PATAKI: It is a no-brainer. But unfortunately, it requires the Legislature to act on it. That's just one example of the unwillingness on the part of some of those in the Legislature who have the ability to prevent this type of change from occurring. You don't get discouraged. You keep fighting the fight.

GALLAGHER: Let me ask you about the process. It seems like if you're not Dennis Rivera (head of Local 1199 of the SEIU) or the Trial Lawyers or you don't hire Pat Lynch (a lobby-ist who is a former aide to Assembly Speaker Sheldon Silver) or Al D'Amato (former U.S. senator-turned-lobby-ist), it's hard to get your voice heard. You have a very closed process. In the first few years you made some attempts I thought to open it up. But we're kind of back to where we used to be—three men in a room.

PATAKI: Are you talking about the legislative process?

GALLAGHER: Yes.

PATAKI: The legislative process is something where all we can do is propose reforms and it's up to the Legislature.

GALLAGHER: I don't mean just the legislative process. I mean the entire process. We hear all the time about the HCRA (Health Care Reform Act) deal that was struck at the last minute. Voted on that night. No public hearings, without an actual written proposal.

PATAKI: I would love to explain that because I'm very proud of that HCRA deal. It wasn't the product of a one-night meeting. It's something we worked on for months. We worked on it with the hospitals, we worked on it with the nursing homes, we worked on it with 1199, and we worked on it with our budget and health experts. We were facing, as is not uncommon in New York State, a serious crisis in our health-care system. We wanted to provide stability.

What we achieved was an incredible accomplishment. We were able to give raises to our health-care workers who were at the lowest end of the pay spectrum and provide them with career ladders so they could upgrade their skills so that technicians could become nurses and fill that shortage. We did it in a way that didn't hurt the hospitals or the nursing homes who were financially worried about their status. And we did it simultaneously with getting reforms to Medicaid that in those first three years and saved $1.2 billion. In fact it was a net cost saving to the state of New York.

Now I negotiated very hard with all of those elements, the hospitals, the downstate hospitals, the upstate hospitals, the nursing homes, 1199, everybody involved coming to a consensus. Then I presented it to the Legislature. Now I can't tell the Legislature what their procedures and policies are. They could have gone out and held hearings on it.

They could have done it a month later or two months later. If they request a message of necessity from me on any bill, by and large, I'm going to give it to them because I respect their request. . . . It has helped the hospitals. It has helped the workers. It has helped stabilize the system. It has helped the state's finances because of the $1.2 billion in Medicaid reforms. And this was not an easy thing to accomplish.

CONWAY: Before Monica (Pataki secretary) has my head, we are going to have to wrap up here. I don't know if you want to give some kind of an overarching view, given where Jay is going with this story.

PATAKI: I fear (laughter). I hope it's not pre-written. I really do.

GALLAGHER: If I might just say one thing about that. Obviously this is going to be a hard look at this problem.

PATAKI: Good.

GALLAGHER: But it's not just focused on you and this administration. It's focused on the whole Albany process, and also we're looking historically as well. Obviously it was not something that was perfect when you came in.

PATAKI: Big picture. The national economy for the last 50 years has been in a transition, it has been in a transition both in a component element, where manufacturing has become less important nationally or less successful nationally, to where geographically parts of the country that hadn't been opened up in the past have been opened up, like the entire South. Where there was segregation and other walls. So they weren't a successful part of the national economy. Now they are.

GALLAGHER: Carrier air conditioners helped.

PATAKI: There is truth to that. So there has been a dramatic change. New York for the longest time, I don't believe, prior to our involvement, had any sense what to do about that change.

Let me first give Gov. Rockefeller some credit. The Thruway system and the university system were ahead of their time and are important elements of the 21st Century economy. Thank God we had them early on (we had these).

GALLAGHER: It was Tom Dewey (who built the Thruway).

PATAKI: Tom Dewey, that's true. We had that, and it was a positive. But then as things changed and New York couldn't afford the level of spending, the state did not respond in an appropriate way.

So when we took office there was no question in my mind that we needed to make dramatic changes. And I think we have. And I'm very proud of what we've done in the short term, straightening out the state's finances in specific cases working with companies to convince them to stay and generically with programs like the Empire Zones to allow manufacturers to have the opportunity to compete successfully here.

I'm extremely proud we're not just looking at Carrier here, or IBM there or Tokyo Electron here. We're saying where are things going to be in the 21st Century? New York hasn't done that before.

The answer is going to be cluster and collaboration. High tech and innovation: when I think how the United States, as opposed to New York, is going to compete successfully, there are basically two options: you can build a wall around the country and say to a company, you can't go overseas because we're going to have tariffs and barriers. Or you can innovate and compete in a global economy.

The first thing is not going to work. It's impossible to build walls in a global economy. . . . So you have to innovate. That's what we're doing with our Centers of

Excellence. That's what we're doing with our high-tech corridor. That's what we're doing with the synergies from the university sector and the private and non-profit sector involved with state government.

That's what we're doing—not just with the Centers of Excellence but with the Genesis program where you go over to RPI and see what's going on there, the strategically targeted academic-research programs and it's not just the Centers of Excellence. We came very close to landing in Rome the bioterrorism laboratory because of these types of investments we're making.

I just called for the program in 2001. . . . What we've accomplished in a short period of time is really important. But what we're going to accomplish over the course of the next years is going to be historic.

I think we have the ability just as the Silicon Valley came out of nowhere, just as South San Francisco bioengineering came out of nowhere, just as the Research Triangle of North Carolina. People never would have thought of that 20 years ago. They're not going to be talking about the Research Triangle in North Carolina in 2020. They're going to be talking about the high-tech corridor in the Empire State. I only believe we're doing everything in our power to make that happen.

Tax cuts are a critical component. I know you have a tendency to pooh-pooh the tax cuts. But in fact no state in America has done more. Twenty percent of all tax cuts in America over the last eight years have been in New York State.

GALLAGHER: But we're still paying higher taxes than anybody.

PATAKI: Of course. That's why I want to continue to lower taxes. Jay, you're sounding like a Republican. You want to control spending, reduce taxes, reform the Wicks law and torts. So do I.

GALLAGHER: They seem like no-brainers to me.

PATAKI: They seem like no-brainers to me. Whenever the Legislature wants to raise taxes and spending as they did this year, I expect you and Gannett to be out there saying, how dare they?

GALLAGHER: One more specific thing, if you don't mind. I'm also doing a story about the rivalry between Fuji and Kodak. The governor of South Carolina is part of a group of Southeast governors. Every year they meet with a bunch of Asian business people. One year in Asia and one year somewhere in the Southeast U.S. They just got back from Asia, and the governor of South Carolina announced three or four new companies from Asia are going to invest in South Carolina. What do we have to do to attract investment like that?

PATAKI: If you take a look at manufacturing jobs in South Carolina over the last eight years, we have virtually an identical record. More recently. Over the last 2-3 years. We have virtually the same record.

That's not to pooh-pooh anyone else's success. We are out there aggressively competing in the global marketplace. We are getting the word out there.

Look at Tokyo Electron. For the first time in the history of that company they are investing outside Japan. 300 million for R and D, and they're doing it in Albany, New York.

When I think of the future, a computer toolmaker putting 300 million into R and D. I'd love to have Fuji here. But given the choice, there's no reason to have a choice. We'll keep fighting to get Fuji and everybody else to come as well.

I am very proud of the fact that Tokyo Electron are coming here. We're going to do more.

INTERVIEW WITH
EDUCATION COMMISSIONER RICHARD MILLS

☆ ☆ ☆

Here is the transcript of a 50-minute interview with state
Education Commissioner Richard Mills in his office in the state
Education Department headquarters in Albany on October 7,
2004.

GALLAGHER: A report out yesterday (by the Education Trust)
said that New York has the biggest funding gap between
rich and poor districts of any state in the country. What do
we need to do about that?

MILLS: What we need to do is scrap the state-aid formula. . . .
It's been three years since they've used the formula. The
formula as it exists has so many different adjustments to it.
It doesn't really equalize at all.

There is tremendous pressure on the political system to
increase everyone. If you have to increase everyone, you
can't send scarce resources to those with the highest needs.
If you want to close the gap in achievement, you have to
close other kinds of gaps.

Teachers in New York City are much more likely to
leave than teachers upstate. Kids going to a city school are
more likely to have a brand new teacher, a brand new

superintendent. They're more likely to have old books. These deficits accumulate.

The political process requires that everyone come home and say, "we don't have much money, but I've been able to get you 3 percent or 4 percent more."

What we need to do is provide increases where they're needed most. More than 40 percent of the kids are in just five school districts. And they are poor. And in the poor districts we're spending a couple of thousand less (per pupil) than in the well-off districts.

GALLAGHER: But there is some equalization going on, isn't there? I was talking to people in Rye this week. Their budget is about $42 million and they get $2 million from the state. I was up in Broadalbin-Perth a few weeks ago. They're building a $36 million addition to their school. The state is paying 95 percent of the cost. I think they get something like two-thirds of their operating budget from the state. So isn't there some equalization going on?

MILLS: There is some but it is not sufficient to close the gap the report talked about.... The Education Trust report did not surprise anyone who has been following this. The courts have been talking about it for decades. I'm sure you're familiar with the Regents state aid-to-education proposal. In all the analysis that goes into it, there is information about income and poverty and all the problems they encounter. Why would anyone expect a gap to not exist?

GALLAGHER: So we need even more money for poor districts, you're saying.

MILLS: Yes. The whole idea behind education is a level playing field.

GALLAGHER: But if a local district wants to spend extravagantly, which I think a lot of them do, that's OK, isn't it?

MILLS: I think they can.

GALLAGHER: If they want to have an Ultimate Frisbee team or a writing tutor for every high school student they can, but you can't expect everyone to have that.

MILLS: No, but everyone should have the resources sufficient to educate all children to the standards. Standards are not some aspirational level. They are what everyone should learn in math, science, history and the rest.

GALLAGHER: In Rochester in 1987, there was an attempt made to level the playing field. The teachers got a 40 percent raise over the life of the contract, with the idea being to improve the students' performance to the level of the sub-urbs. It didn't work. Rochester is now worse off than any of the other of the big five (city school districts). Critics say just throwing money at the problem is not the answer. . . . Adam Urbanski (president of the Rochester teachers' union) thinks that kids come to school with such severe problems outside school, like their family situation, pover-ty, even health issues, that you can't really expect them to perform to the same level as suburban kids.

MILLS: I'm not going to debate Adam. He's not here. Let me take the personality out of it. I don't accept the excuses. It's self-evident that some youngsters come to school with problems. . . . That's why, for children who can't see the blackboard, you get them glasses. That's a pretty simple fix. That's why schools have breakfast programs, and lunch programs. It's hard to do well in school if you're hungry. So feed the child. We can't accept the dollars for our salary and make excuses for our failures. If there are health issues we can provide clinics and health care and find ways to get that barrier out of the way.

I remember last spring the regents and I visited schools in the South Bronx. There was one high school (The Health Opportunity High School) where the kids were just like everybody else in the South Bronx. They came from a poverty background.

The school administration decided that all of the kids would set foot on a college campus so they could visualize what they look like. They hired a young guy, set up a very elaborate extra-help program. The principal set up a system so he knew exactly where everybody was in terms of their performance on mid-term exams. . . .

When you were in difficulty, you were expected to show up for extra help. If you didn't show up, you got a call, and then your parents got a call. Or if you didn't have a parent, then your grandparent or the caregiver or whoever it was. They had a full-court press to make sure these kids got the extra help.

I talked to kids there who had taken the exams five or six times. Youngsters who did abysmally the first time, getting a 14 or 15. The attitude could have been, "What do you expect? This is the South Bronx. Poor family."

But this school is organized differently. They got him extra help. . . . He still had to go on his college visit like everyone else. And four or five attempts later, he passed. I later learned he graduated, and is now attending a SUNY school.

The goal is to educate all these youngsters and do whatever it takes. In New York City they've always had large numbers of uncertified teachers and those teachers were always in the poorest schools. They weren't at Stuyvesant. They were in schools nobody ever visits.

So the regents said you can't do that any more. We will no longer permit uncertified teachers.

We got all kinds of resistance. We adjusted the rules. We allowed them to have alternative-certification programs. They still wouldn't guarantee it. So I sued them and we won. This chancellor, Chancellor (Joel) Klein, has been very aggressive about it and we've made significant progress.

GALLAGHER: What do you feel about changing the governance of the other Big 4 (Buffalo, Rochester, Yonkers and Syracuse)? Do you think putting the mayor in charge is a good idea?

MILLS: It's too new for me to generalize. In New York City, 1.1 million children. Albany is very different. I'm very skeptical about identifying the one best thing we can do. There's not a good record for that kind of approach. . . .

But generally, there are some things we have to do to have strong leadership. Focus on performance. We need principals and superintendents and commissioners and chancellors losing sleep about poor student performance.

We have to have very strong teachers. We have to find a way to keep and support able teachers. Not geniuses, but good teachers.

GALLAGHER: Is paying them more the way to do that?

MILLS: It's part of it. Just paying teachers a lot of money isn't going to be any more successful than just paying physicians a lot of money. You've got to have a system that supports them. You have to have a strong curriculum. All the teachers have to be pretty much on the same page as far as the curriculum is concerned. . . . You can't have professional development unless every teacher is on the same page. It's like a team without a playbook.

There has to be a system of extra help because some kids get it the first time, and it takes others three or four tries. And the money has to match. It doesn't have to be super-abundant but it has to be sufficient.

GALLAGHER: In Yonkers, Rochester, Syracuse and Buffalo, the responsibility for educational policy is put with the school board but the responsibility for raising the money is with the mayor and city council—unlike the suburbs where the school board proposes a budget and voters get to decide whether to approve it. The structure in the cities seems to lead to constant conflicts because the school boards think they could always make good use of more money while the city governments see the schools getting big increases from the state every year while they have to pinch pennies. Wouldn't it be better to align the decisions on how the money is spent with decisions on how it is raised?

MILLS: That doesn't necessarily imply mayoral control.

GALLAGHER: That's right. Either mayoral control or fiscally independent districts.

MILLS: I think there is great value in having a degree of separation between the education and the political arenas. In New York, you have a board of regents that is appointed by the political process, and have to be responsive, but they are independent and therefore I don't have to check with people when I talk about what kids need and that's very useful.

I try to be very respectful of the political leaders. I try to steer a middle course. But when I testify about the regents' budget proposal I just begin by talking about what the youngsters of this state need. People accept that. They know I'm not a political figure.

GALLAGHER: Isn't that frustrating to you because as you pointed out you have a very strong opinion about what needs to be done about distributing state aid to education differently, but you don't have the political power to get that implemented.

MILLS: I don't have vote one. I'm not an elected official. But there is tremendous power in the data. What the regents and I can do is say after a long process of consultation with everyone, "Here's what everybody needs to know and here's what we need to do."

I can go to the business community and say is this what

they want and they say yes . . . I can go to the higher education community and say, hey, yes, standards are going up. . . . I can go back to the Legislature and say, here are the results. They're getting better and better and better. We can say you bought this. You own this. So keep going. . . .

In the middle-school situation, nothing was happening. People were saying the tests are too hard, they're not fair, but the regents didn't blink. They just kept going. So now in the 6th year, the results show a three-year upward trend. They still have far to go. That's a powerful argument.

GALLAGHER: Couldn't that lesson be taken a different way? We haven't changed the funding formula, we haven't implemented CFE (the court decision ordering more money for New York City schools), and yet scores are going up and the achievement gap is narrowing. Isn't that in a way an argument for the status quo?

MILLS: I don't think so because the gap is still great, while it is closing in the elementary grades, the Big 5 cities are still far below the affluent communities.

At the middle level, everyone has gone up. I would say these gains point to the fact that this spending is a good investment. It worked. Don't pull the rug out now.

GALLAGHER: No, don't pull the rug out, but don't the results lessen the urgency of the redistribution argument?

MILLS: I think the argument is even more urgent from the economic point of view. The generation now in school is smaller than the baby-boom generation. Workforce planners point out that the baby-boom generation is getting ready to retire. When they leave there are literally going to be fewer Americans of working age. So you need everyone of working age to be skilled.

The problem is at the same time this is happening the

skill content of jobs is going up rapidly. So even from a cold-eyed economic point of view, every single person needs to have a good education. And right now, New York has a large number of people not well enough prepared for these responsibilities.

It's also not just. One of the goals is to educate everyone enough to work, but we also are about building a just society here. It is not right to allow some people to emerge from schools looking at a bright future, and others to lack the knowledge and skill they need for a good job and all of the others things that are good in life.

GALLAGHER: Are charter schools part of the solution? Do they have a role in closing the achievement gap among schools or do you see them as a drain on public schools?

MILLS: I've seen strong charter schools and I've seen weak ones. The strong ones are very impressive. . . .

The principles are similar to the ones in strong public schools: focus on leadership; focus on high expectations; focus on extra time for the youngsters who need it; concentration on the data. I've seen these at successful public schools.

GALLAGHER: What do you mean by concentrating on the data?

MILLS: I was thinking of a charter school I visited just over the line from Buffalo. I talked to a second-year teacher. She had a laptop on her desk that had the weekly or bi-weekly test scores for her students. She could point to parts of the curriculum that were not working. She didn't assume there was something wrong with the child. She looked for patterns and recognized in some places changes needed to be made. She had the data that allowed her to adjust the course. She was getting continuous professional development to help her deal with the problems.

It's like going to a physician who has all of your cholesterol data going back five years.

A low performing school is usually a school that doesn't have any of that. . . .

GALLAGHER: You've seen good and bad charter schools. So in general are they part of the solution or not?

MILLS: They're clearly part of the solution in New York. It's the law. My sense is it's very hard to start a new school. The law doesn't provide startup money. And most of these charter schools were created in places where the overall performance in public schools is very low. They in many ways have the same problems as the public schools.

There are a small number of charter schools in New York State. Unless something dramatic changes, they won't be a major part of the solution.

GALLAGHER: If it were up to you, would you abolish charter schools, expand them or leave them as they are?

MILLS: I certainly wouldn't abolish them. There's no evidence that as a concept they're a bad idea. But I also don't get the evidence to expand them. The regents do an annual report on charter schools. Very rich in data. There are positives and negatives.

The search for the one best thing (is futile). It's a package of things. It involves leadership, instruction, curriculum, extra help, resources that match the need. . . .

GALLAGHER: What about STAR (the school-tax rebate problem that mostly benefits suburban homeowners)? Do you think it exacerbates the problem of misallocation of resources? Would we be better off by taking that money and plugging it into the education-aid formula or using it to help implement CFE?

MILLS: I don't get into that. It's a revenue question. I'm much better off staying out of that.

GALLAGHER: Doesn't it have the effect of sending more money to districts that don't need it and therefore starving the areas that do need it?

MILLS: It's a political judgment. I don't make political judgments. Evidently it's in response to widespread public concern about the cost of education. I don't make those judgments and I don't comment on them.

GALLAGHER: Let me ask you some philosophical questions. Kids come to school not only from different backgrounds but also with different capacities. Is it realistic to think that they can all perform the same, or be educated to meet the same standards? Or should we accept that some kids are just not going to make it? Or can you design programs so that they bring out everyone's potential?

MILLS: If anyone argues that side of the question and goes too far, they can find themselves saying some very distasteful things—very foreign to our values.

We have to have the approach that all of them can learn. We're not asking that they all perform at the same level. We're insisting that they all reach the standards. I hope they go beyond that. But they at least have to graduate knowing the math and the science and the rest, history and so on. ... When someone says, "This kid just can't read ..." we have listened to reading experts who study the way children develop, the way the brain develops and they have said virtually every child can be taught to read.

But if the teacher is prepared to teach only those who could read to begin with, who come from families where reading is done constantly, then it is not a problem of the child, it is a problem of the instructional program.

New York (City), for example, won a very large amount of money from the federal government for reading programs. And you can't get into these programs unless you agree to do it the right way. The funds go to high-need

schools. They are competitive. A lot of people that wanted the money, feeling they should get the fair share for their
cities, failed to get the money.

What you have to do is to agree to have all the teachers
participate in a very rigorous training program. The reading program has to include phonics—phonetic aware-
ness—the idea that groups of letters have sounds and that's
the way the written language works. You have to work on
fluency and vocabulary and all of this.

You can't make it up as you go along. Some people
believe you can. That's not professional.

GALLAGHER: New York spends more on education per pupil
than any other state. Yet test results are about in the middle of the pack. Why is that?

MILLS: I don't make any excuses for the results. The results are
going up. They have to go up. They have gone up but not
yet enough. If you look at a spending map of the whole
nation, the Northeastern states—New York, Connecticut,
Massachusetts—tend to be higher spenders. Salaries in
general are higher there than they are in the rest of the
country—higher than the South or West.

When we've had money to invest, we didn't invest it in
the schools' highest needs. The money went up for everybody. That's the judgment local officials made. The court
ruled the system is not providing a sound basic education
for all children. I had hoped that wouldn't have to happen,
but it did. Now the courts are going to determine (how
much more money is needed for high-needs schools).

GALLAGHER: Are you saying we don't have the best results
because we're not spending the money in the most efficient
way?

MILLS: We haven't resolved the inequities in the state-aid system. That's self evident. That's what the court said. As
long as I've been here, the regents have proposed the

increases go to the highest need school districts. If it's going to increase everyone, you're going to end up with an expensive system.

GALLAGHER: I understand your position about not talking about political things. And yet the key to your success is being able to redirect the money to where you think it's needed, which is essentially a political question. How do you get more money for places that you think need it if you try to remain above the fray?

MILLS: I'm certainly not above the fray.

GALLAGHER: Are you apart from the fray?

MILLS: I'm not elected, so I have no right to say how taxes work. The elected officials do. They make those decisions. My obligation as commissioner is to speak as plainly as I can about what the children need. I am across the street (at the state Capitol) at the Legislature virtually every day during the session. I testify to the joint finance committees. I talk to individual committees. I talk to the leadership. I talk to member after member after member. I talk to the people who disagree with my views and disagree with the regents' positions. I try to spend more time talking and listening to them than to people who are already in agreement.

It's not just me. It's all of my colleagues. The regents, all of the deputy commissioners are constantly presenting the facts as we see them. Every time there is data, we make a big deal out of it. We talk to people at the schools and urge them to talk about it. During the court process, CFE, we provided thousands of pages of documents to both sides. I spent a whole day on the stand. So did the chancellor. So did the vice chancellor. So did (deputy commissioner) Jim Kadamas. We were all giving information on what was needed and what has been provided.

The people's representatives make the judgments. But I certainly do everything possible to inform the debate.

GALLAGHER: So you're essentially lobbying for what you think needs to be done.

MILLS: I'm not a lobbyist. I'm advocating. I'm providing information. Look at these loafers. They're not Guccis. . . .

GALLAGHER: Do you expect the CFE court case to eventually get the state to where it needs to be in terms of school finances?

MILLS: It's going to take more than one jump probably because the CFE case is about New York City. It's not about the rest of the state. (Chief) Judge (Judith) Kaye and the Court of Appeals pointed to the opportunity the Legislature had to have a solution that's statewide. It's evident from the way CFE group has conducted itself that they tried to bring in other groups.

GALLAGHER: They have broad support upstate. The upstate groups see this as their chance to get more money as well. Mike Rebell, the head of CFE, said a couple of weeks ago he hopes the expected court order to provide more money to New York City, expected some time in January, will spur a statewide bill. There's no way they're going to increase aid just to New York City. That's politically not feasible. Eventually it will mean more money for every high-needs district, don't you think?

MILLS: I think that's probably right. The Legislature was unable to break this pattern. The courts have intervened. It's possible the court will break the pattern by simply directing adequate funding for part of the state. It's hard to imagine that kind of solution could not long endure without the rest of the system changing.

GALLAGHER: Doesn't New York City already score better on standardized tests than the rest of the Big 5?

MILLS: At the middle level, New York City scores have surged past all of the Big 4. In the elementary grades, Yonkers is the top performer.

GALLAGHER: Do you talk to the governor much?

MILLS: From time to time. Not a lot.

GALLAGHER: Do you try to advocate with him, the way you do the Legislature?

MILLS: I have in the past, but most of the interaction is with the Legislature. There are conversations at all levels. I talk to DOB (Division of the Budget), I talk to the executive branch. With the Legislature, I'll talk to the (Assembly) Speaker (Sheldon Silver) the (Senate) Majority Leader (Joseph Bruno). I'll talk to (Assembly Education Committee Chairman Steven) Sanders, (Senate Education Committee Chairman Steven) Saland and all of the other committee chairpeople. Then my colleagues talk to them as well and also the legislative staff. We try to keep adding things to the soup of information to keep them apprised of what we're doing.

GALLAGHER: But the governor is the most important guy. Would it be helpful if you had a closer relationship with him?

MILLS: On a personal basis, the relationship has never been a problem that I know of.

When I first came here and was discussing the position with the Board of Regents—I had had experience with strong, effective governors in other states—I asked, what is the governor's view of education?

So Carl Hayden, the chancellor at that time, said "OK, sit here." He put me in a room and I sat down. About 10 minutes later the phone rang. I picked it up and it was Gov. Pataki. I was impressed the board had that relationship with the governor.

I asked him, "What is your hope and expectation for this state?"

He said to me what he has subsequently said many times: he wants a world-class education system. He wants to get spending under control and he wants a strong economy. I think that's a position the governor has to take. He's certainly been consistent in all of my dealings with him over the years. . . .

There's room for disagreement. Every time I begin my testimony I talk about the kids. I talk about the data. Express appreciation for what they've done in the past and then point out areas where I think we need to do more. It's never personal.

In fact, in the budget process I talk about the executive. I don't personalize it. It just doesn't help.

GALLAGHER: In the other states you worked in, did the top education official report to the governor?

MILLS: In Vermont, where I was commissioner for seven and a half years, no. I was appointed by a board of seven people. The board was appointed by the governor.

They are very different kinds of states.

GALLAGHER: Was Howard Dean governor then?

MILLS: Howard Dean later became governor. Madeline Kunin was the governor.

GALLAGHER: Do you have an opinion about which is the better system?

MILLS: The states are so radically different. In New York I'm responsible for 3 million children. In Vermont, when I was there, it was 106,000. The legislators had no offices. They were either in session or in their committees. They had no staff so everyone knew everything. The commissioner was expected to know the entire budget cold.

I'd go to a community meeting, and a fourth grader

might look you in the eye and deliver a speech. It helped me immensely.

In the other place I served, New Jersey for 13 years, not as commissioner but as a staff person, the governor appoints the commissioner. In fact, the governor appointed almost everybody.

Tom Kean (co-chairman if the 9-11 commission) was governor then and it worked splendidly because of his character and tremendous ability.

NEW YORK TIMELINE:
ECONOMY, POLITICS, DEMOGRAPHY

☆ ☆ ☆

April 20, 1777: State Constitution adopted.

1811: New York becomes first state to allow companies to incorporate without an act of the Legislature.

1825: Erie Canal opens, cutting the cost of shipping freight from Buffalo to Albany from $100 per ton to $10; within 15 years, New York is the pre-eminent commercial city in the country.

1919: State adopts 3 percent tax on annual incomes above $50,000.

1948: Gov. Thomas Dewey loses race for president to Harry S. Truman. Dewey is the 14th—and last—New Yorker to get a major party's presidential nomination.

1950: New York at its economic peak: One in every 12 private-sector jobs in the United States is in New York City. The state has 43 members in the House of Representatives and 45 electoral votes.

1953: Manufacturing jobs hit postwar peak of 2.1 million.

1954: State Thruway opens.

1956: Nelson A. Rockefeller is elected governor.

1959: St. Lawrence Seaway opens, allowing Great Lakes ships to bypass Buffalo.

1965: Two percent state sales tax adopted. It was raised to 4 percent in 1971.
- New York City adopts income tax.
- Judge orders "one-man, one-vote" reapportionment. Democrats control the state Senate for the first time since the 1930s.
- Metropolitan Transportation Authority formed, combining bridge, tunnel, transit and railroad systems. New corporate and sales taxes adopted in the metropolitan area to help pay for it.

1966: Special elections ordered to comply with Supreme Court's one-man, one-vote ruling, and Republicans recapture Senate.
- Federal government approves health insurance for the poor known as Medicaid, whose cost will be split with states. New York adopts the most expansive version in the country.

1967: State adopts the Taylor Law, which gives employees the right to form labor unions but prohibits them from striking.

1969: State income tax rate raised to 15 percent, its peak.

1969-1976: National recession rocks New York. State loses 666,000 jobs as nation gains 10 million.

1969: Xerox Corp. moves headquarters from Rochester to Stamford, Connecticut, in part so its executives can avoid the New York income tax.

1970: California passes New York to become most populous state—a title New York had held since 1910.

1974: Democrats take control of Assembly in the first post-Watergate election. They have maintained a majority ever since.

1975: "The days of wine and roses are over," declares new Gov. Hugh Carey in announcing cuts in government spending.
- Banks say they will stop lending New York City money, triggering fears of bankruptcy. State takes control of city finances, creating the Municipal Assistance Corp. to borrow money to tide the city over.

1978: Top state income tax rate is reduced to 12 percent, starting a trend that will see it drop to 6.85 percent before going up to 7.7 percent for the wealthiest New Yorkers in 2003.

1980: State loses 684,000 people in the 1970s, even as the country was growing, Census Bureau reports. The number of House of Representatives seats is cut from 39 to 34. The figure will dwindle to 29 by 2002.

1981: Eastman Kodak employment in New York peaks at 61,000. Recently announced cuts will trim that to 18,000.

1982: Mario Cuomo elected governor.

1985: State budget not adopted until April 5th, five days after the start of the fiscal year. That starts a string of 20 late budgets.

1986: With Wall Street booming, Legislature votes to cut the top income tax rate from 8.75 percent to 7 percent over five years. But the third phase of the cut is delayed until 1996.

1987: Stock market crashes. Tax revenues start to drop.

1989-1992: In national recession, New York loses 500,000 jobs, or one in six lost nationally.
- 2,606 New Yorkers are murdered, the all-time high. Figure drops below 900 by 2004.

October 11, 1990: The longest bull market in Wall Street history begins. Stock values will rise by an average of more than 400 percent in the next 10 and a half years.

1991:   The state "sells" Attica prison to one of its subsidiaries, the Urban Development Corp., to raise $200 million in cash. It agrees to lease it back at a cost of $490 million over 30 years.

1993:   Manufacturing jobs in the state fall below 1 million for the first time since the 1920s.

1994:   Sheldon Silver, a Manhattan trial lawyer, becomes Assembly speaker after the death of Saul Weprin of Queens.
  - Republican state Sen. George Pataki of Peekskill defeats Democratic Gov. Mario Cuomo, who was seeking a fourth term. Pataki is the first Republican to hold the post in 20 years.

March 1995: 1.66 million New Yorkers, one in every 11, are on welfare. The figure declines from this point to about 611,000 in 2003.
  - Joseph Bruno, 66, a Rensselaer County lawmaker, becomes state Senate majority leader in a coup engineered by Pataki and U.S. Sen. Alfonse D'Amato that ousts Ralph Marino of Oyster Bay.
  - State budget shows actual drop in spending for the first time since the Great Depression.

1996:   Texas passes New York to become the second-most populous state.

1997:   Budget passed on August 4th, 126 days after the deadline—the latest ever.

1998:   Pataki and lawmakers vote themselves 38 percent pay raises. Pataki is the nation's highest-paid governor at $179,000 a year, and lawmakers, whose base salary is $79,500, are second behind Pennsylvania.
  - State budget goes up 7 percent, three times the rate of inflation.
  - Pataki crushes Peter Vallone for a second term as governor.

- Charles Schumer defeats incumbent Alfonse D'Amato in the Senate race.

2000: Hilary Clinton easily defeats Long Island Congressman Rick Lazio and replaces retiring Daniel P. Moynihan as U.S. Senator.

March 2001: Stock market reaches peak. Longest bear market since 1939-1941 begins.
- Census shows New York with 18.9 million people, finally surpassing the previous peak of 18.2 million in 1970. The state's growth rate for the previous 40 years was about the same as the country's for the past decade.

September 11, 2001: Terrorists destroy the World Trade Center, killing about 2,800 people; 100,000 jobs and 10 million square feet of office space lost.

2002: Medicaid expenses top $40 billion.
- Democrats win 103 of the 150 Assembly seats, getting a veto-proof majority. Republicans win 38 of the 62 Senate seats, giving them their largest majority in decades.
- **August:** Bruno says state faces $10 billion deficit; Pataki says there is no deficit.
- **November:** Pataki wins a third term over Democrat H. Carl McCall, admits that the deficit is actually $11.5 billion.

2003: Legislature raises sales and income taxes over Pataki vetoes. Sales tax goes to 4.25 percent and the top income tax rate to 7.7.
- New York raises taxes more this year than all but two states, the National Conference of State Legislatures reports.
- More New Yorkers, about 860,000, leave for other parts of the country between 1995 and 2000 than fled any other state, Census Bureau reports.

2004:   **April:** Lawmakers fail for the 20th straight year to pass a budget by the start of the fiscal year on April 1st. $101 billion spending plan finally passed in August.

July: Report published calling New York Legislature nation's "most dysfunctional."

November: Charles Schumer easily wins a second U.S. Senate term. Democrats increase their majority in the Assembly to 104-96. Republicans lose three seats in the Senate, narrowing their margin to 35-27.

November: Court-appointed panel orders the state to come up with $5.6 billion more in annual aid for New York City schools over four years.

December: Senate fails to override Pataki veto of a bill that would have shifted some budget powers from the governor to the Legislature.

2005:   Legislature adopts rules to make most lawmakers be in the chamber when they vote and make it easier for bills to be brought to the floor for a vote.

March 31: Budget passes by legal deadline for first time since 1984.

July 27: Gov. Pataki announces he will not seek re-election in 2006.

Top New York Employers in 2003

(Source: Economy.com)

☆ ☆ ☆

1. North Shore-Long Island Jewish Health System, 42,792
2. Verizon Communications, Inc., 33,297
3. J. P. Morgan Chase & Company, 31,318
4. New York Presbyterian Healthcare Network, 30,020
5. IBM Corporation, 24,025
6. CitiGroup, Inc., 23,596
7. Eastman Kodak Company, 18,000
8. Diocese of Rockville Centre, 17,500
9. Continuum Health Partners, Inc., 16,807
10. SUNY at Stony Brook, 14,000
11. Federated Department Stores, Inc., 13,220
12. University of Rochester/Strong Health, 13,000
13. New York University, 12,960
14. AOL Time Warner, Inc., 12,500
15. Saint Vincent Catholic Medical Centers, 12,283
16. Consolidated Edison, Inc., 11,700
17. Columbia University, 11,690
18. Montefiore Medical Center, 10,563
19. Xerox Corporation, 10,050
20. Medisys Health Network, 9,913
21. Morgan Stanley Dean Witter & Company, 9,900
22. AMR Corporation, 9,755

23. Goldman Sachs & Company, 9,673
24. General Electric Company, 9,261
25. Bank of New York, Inc., 9,016

INDEX

Printed in the United States
43324LVS00005B/85-219

9 780878 755523